The Elvis Catalog

The Elvis Catalog

Memorabilia, Icons, and Collectibles
Celebrating the King of Rock 'n' Roll

by
Lee Cotten

AUTHORIZED BY ELVIS PRESLEY ENTERPRISES

A DOLPHIN BOOK
Doubleday & Company, Inc.
Garden City, New York
1987

PHOTO AND COLLECTOR'S CREDITS

Collectibles photographed by and from the collection of Barbara and Craig Canady appear on the following pages:
15, 17-19, 23-24, 27-30, 32-34, 36-41, 44-47, 50-55, 57, 59-74, 84, 86, 89-95, 98-99, 101, 103-104, 109-110, 112-114, 122, 128, 130-134, 139, 141, 144-147, 162, 168-169, 171, 173, 175, 179-181, 183-185, 192, 194-195, 198-199, 210-211, 213, 248

Collectibles from the Elvis Presley Museum in Nashville, Tennessee and photographed by Bill Wilson appear on the following pages:
21, 29-30, 89, 105, 130, 145, 202-204, 209, 213

Collectibles from the Elvis Presley Museum in Orlando, Florida and photographed by Bruce Borich appear on the following pages:
28, 35, 37, 39, 70, 112, 117, 121, 163, 181, 185, 188, 203-204

Photographs from the following collections were taken by the author and appear on the pages indicated:
Graceland: 17, 85
Craig and Ramona Saben: 20, 24-26, 33, 35, 47-48, 58-59, 96, 104-105, 110-111, 114, 118-120, 124, 127, 129-131, 135-137, 142-143, 161-162, 166, 190
Barry Dallas: 49, 58, 88, 89, 111, 114, 116, 118-119, 121, 124, 126, 129, 135-139, 162, 165-168, 172, 186-187, 208, 212, 214, 218, 220-223, 227, 231-232, 237-238, 240, 243, 245
Eddie Fadal: 16

Photographs taken by Ken Robbins appear on the following pages:
13, 15, 54, 55, 75, 140, 219, 230, 235, 237-240, 247, 249, 251

The photograph on page 6 courtesy of *Look* magazine/The Library of Congress.

Photographs on pages 12 and 15 (top left) used by permission of Dye/MICHAEL OCHS ARCHIVES/ Venice, CA.

The photograph on page 35 (bottom left) reprinted by permission from The Memphis Press-Scimitar.

The photograph on page 66 (bottom) used by permission of Eddie Fadal.

The photograph on page 86 (top) used by permission of Richard Lightman.

The photograph on page 112 (top) used by permission of the Country Music Hall of Fame.

The photographs on page 174 used by permission of Paul Rose and The King's Hideaway, Inc.

Photographs provided by the manufacturers appear on the following pages:
140, 219, 230, 239, 242, 244-248, 251

All other photographs were taken by the author and are from his personal collection.

Copyright © 1987 by James Charlton Associates
All Rights Reserved
Printed in the United States
First Edition

LIBRARY OF CONGRESS CATALOGING-IN-PUBLICATION DATA

Cotten, Lee.
  The Elvis catalog.

  "A Dolphin book."
  1. Presley, Elvis, 1935–1977—Collectibles—
Catalogs. I. Title
ML420.P96C673   1987   784.5'4'00924   87-9133
ISBN 0-385-23705-7
ISBN 0-385-23704-9 (pbk.)

THE ELVIS CATALOG
was designed by Hudson Studio
Ossining, New York
and produced by James Charlton Associates,
New York, New York

Acknowledgments

My special thanks to the following people and institutions for their invaluable assistance as I researched this book:

In California:
Barry Dallas and Darrell Theobald in Sacramento
Craig and Ramona Saben in Modesto
Howard DeWitt in Hayward
Paul Rose, developer of the Kings Hideaway in Palm Springs
The staff of the California State Library and the Sacramento
    Public Libraries in Sacramento
The staff of the library at the University of California at
    Berkeley

In Memphis, Tennessee:
Jack Soden, Executive Director of Graceland
Todd Morgan, Manager/Communications for Graceland
Monnie Speed, Director of Tour Operations at Graceland
Patsy Anderson, Assistant to Todd Morgan
Johnny Black
Frank Taylor
The staff of the Memphis Public Library

In Nashville, Tenessee:
Jimmie Velvet, for allowing us to photograph at his Elvis
    Presley Museums in Nashville and Orlando, Florida

In Hampton, Virginia:
Craig and Barbara Canady, for access to their enormous
    private collection of Presleyana

In Tupelo, Mississippi:
Mrs. Janelle McComb
The staff of the Elvis Presley Memorial
Georgia Webb and Gloria Lucas, Community Development
    Foundation
The staff of the Tupelo Public Library

In Texas:
Eddie Fadal in Waco
The staff of the Barker History Center, University of Texas in
    Austin

In Shreveport, Louisiana:
The staff of the Shreveport Public Library

In Birmingham, Alabama:
The staff of the Birmingham Public Library

In Indianapolis, Indiana:
Mark Roesler, of Curtis Licensing Company

In Atlanta, Georgia:
The staff of the Atlanta Public Library

In Ann Arbor, Michigan:
Tom Schultheiss of Pierian Press, for believing in me in the
    beginning

In New York City:
Joseph Rascoff, Joseph F. Rascoff & Company
Jim Charlton and Barbara Binswanger, whose dedication and
    hard work made this project a reality
John Milward, editor, *USA Today* for his assistance with the
    manuscript
Jim Fitzgerald, my editor at Doubleday, and Casey Fuetsch,
    his assistant, for their enthusiasm and tremendous support

And, saving the best for last,
Special thanks to my wife, Patty, and my children, Nicole and
    Sean, for their patience

Contents

Elvis and Hank Saperstein of Elvis Presley Enterprises inspect some of the merchandise licensed in 1956.

Introduction

Elvis was unique in the world of popular entertainment, idolized by millions without the approval of either the music or the film industry. He was an outsider from the beginning. He upset the sensibilities of the news media. He was criticized by the judicial system. He was the subject of sermons by the clergy. In fact, he was denigrated by every faction of society who saw themselves as guardians of teenage morality. He was perceived to have an outlaw personality, and he was deemed to be dangerous to the nation's youth. All this outrage was directed at the image of Elvis Presley.

Not seen by his critics was the wholesome side of the man. Elvis the individual was deeply spiritual, family oriented, overly generous, fun loving, and simple in his tastes. It is this duality, first perceived by his teenaged audience, then gradually by even his most vociferous critics, that made him the most beloved entertainer of his generation. At the root of the idolization of Elvis is the fact that his popularity was kept alive in the face of all the criticism. Keeping Elvis' fame fresh and alive became a cause for the faithful.

Before Elvis came on the scene, teenagers had virtually no marketing identity, but the year that Elvis hit the big time, 1956, all that changed. By the end of 1956, teens were big business on Madison Avenue.

In the summer of 1956, Elvis' manager, Colonel Tom Parker, realizing that he was sitting on a potential gold mine well beyond the realm of popular music, had Elvis incorporated and copyrighted, turning Elvis into Elvis Presley Enterprises, Inc. The Colonel then contacted Hank Saperstein, the New York promoter who had handled accounts for TV's Wyatt Earp and Lassie as well as the Kellogg's "free prize in every box" promotions. Just a year earlier, the nation had been in the middle of the biggest fad of the century when Walt Disney brought Davy Crockett to the nation's TV screens. The result was a marketing bonanza in coon skin caps, jackets with fringe on the sleeve, and toy muskets.

Saperstein took the same approach with Elvis. The first "Elvis" item, other than his records, to be marketed was the Elvis Presley charm bracelet. On August 28,

1956, RCA Victor Records secured exclusive rights to distribute the bracelets through the same outlets as Elvis' records. The demand for the bracelets was so great (4 million were sold in a month) that it completely overwhelmed the costume jewelry industry of Providence, Rhode Island. The Colonel and Saperstein knew they had a winner. By the end of the year, almost any imaginable item a teenager might desire was available with Elvis' name and likeness embossed on it. Teens could dress from head to toe in "Elvis" sneakers or pumps, socks, black jeans with green stitching, felt skirts, belts, tee shirts and blouses, pajamas, kerchiefs, bolo ties, and such accessories as hats and mittens, purses, billfolds, and necklaces. There was even an overnight case to hold it all. For school there were bookends, notebooks, scrapbooks, pencils, and pencil sharpeners. By the end of September, sales figures show that 120,000 pairs of jeans and 240,000 Tee shirts had been sold. It is estimated that by the end of 1956, the merchandise licensed by Elvis Presley Enterprises (EPE) grossed $20 million, of which the corporation made anywhere from 4 to 11 percent profit.

Fans who collected the memorabilia and records from early in Elvis' career—and stored it carefully through the years—have made a tremendous investment. An "I Love Elvis" button from 1956 can bring $20 today, an increase in value of 40,000 percent over the nickel that it cost! An Elvis doll costing $3.98 in 1956 is today worth $1,500. Magazines featuring Elvis that cost a quarter in 1956 can be worth $50 today. Each of Elvis' first five singles released by Sun Records of Memphis in 1954 and 1955 are worth hundreds of dollars more than their $.89 list price. Even his biggest hit singles, the ones that sold millions of copies such as "Hound Dog," "Love Me Tender," and "A Fool Such As I," have picture sleeves worth $20, $50, $100 today.

The prices listed in this book are those currently being paid by Elvis fans for records and merchandise in "near mint" condition. In the vernacular of the collector, "near mint" means a record or piece of memorabilia that shows virtually no wear, no discernible flaws, and with all its various components intact. Items that do not meet these criteria are of less, sometimes *much* less, value. On the other hand, this book shows several early records still sealed in their factory-fresh wrap. These "mint" records are worth significantly more than the same record in near mint condition.

It should also be noted that the collector's price for *certain* pieces will continue to escalate with time, while the value of other items will decline. Prices for collectibles are, first and foremost, determined by *supply and demand.* When the supply is limited and the demand is high, then the price goes up. But the reverse is also true.

Items that are *limited* in their production usually are instantly collectible. For example, promotional copies of Elvis' records are usually worth twice their commercial counterpart; but if the promo record is significantly different from the store copy, the price may be even higher. Several of the promo 45s from the past few years were issued in limited quantities on colored vinyl. These were worth $50 the day they were sent to radio stations and double that price within weeks. Again, supply and demand determine the price.

Merchandise that bears Elvis' likeness, but is also of general interest to collectors, might also increase in value in a short time. Such items as whiskey decanters, plates, dolls, bubble gum cards, and movie-related advertising material have built-in buyers outside the world of Elvis Presley. These products are more collectible than others simply because of their general value to collectors in those areas. But if these items are manufactured endlessly, their future value to any collector will be nil.

When it comes to the subject of what to collect, my advice to fans is to collect the things that please them the most. Collecting, as with any hobby, should first of all be fun, not with an eye toward increasing the original investment. With the continued popularity of Elvis, picking up a bargain-priced early collectible would be rare—but not impossible. On the other hand, many recent items marketed as "collector's items" may not ever be of interest to collectors. Again, my suggestion is to buy what pleases you. Then, if an item fails to escalate in value, you still have something of personal interest.

But whether you are a serious collector of Presleyana, or simply a fan of Elvis, there should be much in this book to read about and enjoy.

Lee Cotten

For My Mother and Father

All the loud records when I was a teenager,
The rock 'n' roll bands, the music store;
Somehow, it worked itself out;
I wish you could have seen it . . .

"To measure a man by his smallest deed or weakest link is like
measuring the power of the ocean by a single wave."
—*Kathy Westmoreland,*
soprano with the Elvis Presley Show, 1971–1977

the Early Years

Tupelo lies in the northeastern corner of Mississippi, in the broad, rolling valley of the Tombigbee River. The town grew up midway between Nashville and Natchez on the ancient Indian trail called the Natchez Trace, a major artery connecting southern Mississippi with the mainstream of America. Travelers from the other direction find that Tupelo is also the midpoint of the migratory road linking Birmingham and Memphis, another well-traveled path.

On a small hill overlooking downtown Tupelo, the house where Elvis Aaron Presley was born still stands. The house is now painted with strong exterior latex house paint, not the whitewash of the 1930s. There is a neatly trimmed lawn surrounding the house, and a brick walkway where fifty years ago there was only dirt. The more recently planted shrubs surrounding the home have been trimmed into appealing hedgerows. The nice ladies of the East Tupelo Garden Club have done a marvelous job of converting the area into a shrine. No other home remains on the knoll. Those that had crumbled from years of harsh weather and erosion were torn down twenty-five years ago to make way for the Elvis Presley Center with its swimming pool, recreational building, and parking lot. And long before the neighboring houses were razed, their outbuildings, wells, and water pumps had been removed as progress caught up with East Tupelo. The house where Elvis was born still stands, but so much else has changed.

Vernon Elvis Presley was a strapping lad, barely seventeen when he eloped with his sweetheart and neighbor, Gladys Love Smith, almost exactly four years older than he, on June 17, 1933. They were married in the neighboring town of Verona. On the marriage certificate Vernon, in order to escape detection of his youth, variously claimed to be both twenty-one and twenty-two, while Gladys said she was only nineteen. (Vernon, never the educated man, also repeatedly misspelled his own name as "Virnon," and at least one early city record lists it as "Virion.") The newlyweds at first lived with Vernon's parents, J. D. and Minnie Mae, and then moved in with Gladys' relatives. In the fall of 1934, as Gladys was

An early look at what was to become the famous sneer. This photograph was taken backstage at Memphis' Ellis Auditorium in February 1956.

Elvis' birthplace

The house built by Vernon and his father where Elvis was born, as seen today.

Exterior

Tupelo souvenirs

An Elvis pilgrimage is not complete without a visit to his birthplace in Tupelo.

Tupelo coffee mug value: $5
Tupelo bumper sticker value:$1.50

Elvis Presley Birthplace
Tupelo, Miss.

Front room/bedroom

Back room/kitchen

I HAVE VISITED — **THE BIRTHPLACE OF ELVIS PRESLEY** TUPELO, MISSISSIPPI

coming to term with their first child, Vernon borrowed $180 from his employer so that he could purchase the lumber to build his own home. The small house was finished by Christmas, built by Vernon and his father, whose own home fifteen feet away was close enough so that the two families shared the same well.

The two-room frame shoebox of a home faced the old Saltillo Road (named after the town that was its destination). It has been colorfully referred as a "shotgun"-style house because the front door, the back door, and the door separating the two rooms are in a direct line that would allow a shotgun blast to pass straight through. These two rooms included a back kitchen, which served as a cooking, eating, and socializing area, and a front bedroom, used primarily for sleeping. In good weather, the neighbors visited daily on the front porch. In the South, every home, no matter how small, had a front porch. The houses in East Tupelo were all handmade and smallish, functional but uninspired. Tupelo was the first REA town, and the Presleys' neighborhood may have been wired for electricity in the fall of 1936 as part of the national REA electrification project, but the family could ill afford to have it turned on. Oil lamps, wood stoves, well water, and outdoor toilets were an everyday part of their life. Gladys kept her home neat as a pin, which included sweeping the bare dirt front yard daily.

It was in this house that Elvis Presley was born shortly after four in the morning on January 8, 1935. The birth was complicated by the death of his first-born twin brother, Jesse Garon. The doctor in attendance could save only one of the babies. Elvis' mother was left possibly barren, which had a profound impact on Elvis all his life. From the beginning, mother and child were inseparable. Even though the Presleys remained on the verge of poverty for nineteen years to come, Elvis was given as many material pleasures as the family could afford. And along with the strict southern upbringing there were mountains of love.

"Ail-vis." "Ail-vis." Gladys' soft voice carried across the front yard, searching out her toddling son. The sound seems to linger to this day. Elvis was constantly in and out of the house, visiting his cousins, his aunts and uncles and grandparents, almost all of whom lived in the little settlement of fifty-two homes fronting the other streets (Reese, Adams, Berry, and Kelly) nearby. Within view of their small home on old Saltillo Road lived six Presley families (Goebel on Berry Street; Gordon, Jack, Sales, and Tennice on Kelly Street; and J. D. on old Saltillo). Elvis would later recall, "My mama never let me out of her sight. I couldn't even go down to the creek with the other kids." That was Mud Creek, a small river that effectively cut off most of East Tupelo from the township of Tupelo proper.

The families of East Tupelo were close-knit. Years later, Elvis would reflect, "It was the way I was brought

Gate

Arena

Mississippi-Alabama Fair and Dairy Show

The Mississippi-Alabama Fair and Dairy Show grounds still looks as it did in October 1945 when Elvis sang "Old Shep" to win second place at the Children's Day talent show. He returned to play the arena twice, in 1956 and 1957, to sold-out audiences.

Elvis signs autographs for dancers at the Mid-South Fair in Memphis in September 1956. Notice that he is wearing the EPE canvas sneakers that were just coming on the market.

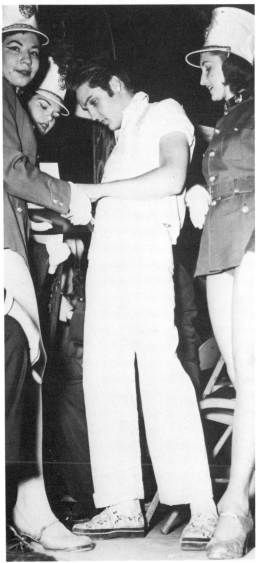

up. We were always considerate of other people's feelings. I'm proud of the way that I was brought up to believe and to treat people and have respect for people." Everyone was hard-working, but it was the middle of the Great Depression and a steady job was hard to find. Still, even in the bleakest of times no one went hungry. Flocks of chickens were kept in every yard, where they could scratch for feed. And each fall at least one hog was butchered, with the "streak-o-lean" bacon and salt-cured hams shared among the relatives.

All day Sunday and every Wednesday night, the Presleys joined their neighbors at the Assembly of God Church a block away on Adams Street for preaching and joyful praise of God. The church singing was normally accompanied by a guitarist, not an organist or pianist, and the congregation's fervor shook more than souls. "During the singing," Elvis would later remember, "the preachers would cut up all over the place, jumping and moving every which way. The audience liked them. And I guess I learned a lot from them." Spirited revivals were frequently held during the week. Vernon, it was noted, sang in a fine, strong baritone, and the Presleys were remembered for their harmonizing as a trio. Elvis sang from the depths of his heart during these church services. "Since I was two years old, all I knew was gospel music. That music became such a part of my life, it was as natural as dancing."

Days in East Tupelo passed slowly. Vernon worked at a laborer's day job at Orville Bean's dairy, less than a mile north on the road to Saltillo from the Presleys' home. It was later reported that Vernon was a sharecropper, but he was never a farmer, at least by choice, nor did the family ever live on a farm working shares for the owner. After Elvis' birth, Gladys became a full-time mother and never returned to her job as a sewing machine operator at the Tupelo Garment Company. In the fall every year she earned a little extra money by picking cotton on nearby farms, slowly dragging Elvis from row to row on the sack. Most Saturdays Vernon's uncle, Noah Presley, would load everyone into his old yellow school bus for an

Sneakers and pumps

Though EPE never licensed any blue suede shoes, they did license several other styles. The sneakers, which Elvis actually wore from time to time, were available with either a white design on black canvas or with a black design on white canvas. The leather pumps came in a variety of colors and sold for $4.99. A fabric version of the pumps sold for $3.99. In both cases, the original box in which they were sold adds $50 to the value.

Value of canvas sneakers: $200
Value of leather pumps: $200

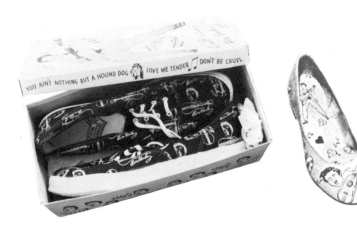

excursion to some attraction within a few hours' drive. Historic Civil War battlefields, neighboring towns (including Memphis), and riverbanks ripe for fishing and picnics were each part of the weekly itinerary.

The biggest thing to happen in Tupelo before it became known as Elvis' hometown occurred just over a year after Elvis was born. Shortly after sundown on the evening of Sunday, April 5, 1936, a monstrous tornado touched down in LaCrosse, Arkansas, before moving on to Coffeville and Booneville, Mississippi, killing a total of 17 and leaving $8 million in destruction. But the killer storm had saved its most awesome fury for the Tupelo valley. At 8:17 P.M., the Presleys had probably joined their neighbors at the Assembly of God Church for evening services when the eastbound funnel touched down in the heart of the city, destroying an area four miles long and a mile wide. Harrisburg Heights and Willis Heights received the brunt of the whipping wind. The black area near Park Lane was twisted ruins, and bodies floated to the surface of the bog alongside Commerce Street for days. On the west side of Church Street, few homes remained standing. Minutes after it first struck, the storm, now finished with Tupelo, moved on across the South, killing people in a number of towns, including a hundred in Gainesville, Georgia, before finally dying out over the Atlantic Ocean. In Tupelo, 213 died and nearly a thousand were injured. The city hospital was a shambles, and no large building in town escaped damage. It was

Lauderdale Recreational Hall

Elvis got his start singing with other kids in this building that now houses the Lauderdale Development Office and a woodshop. In the early 1950s, teenagers used it as a gathering place on evenings and weekends.

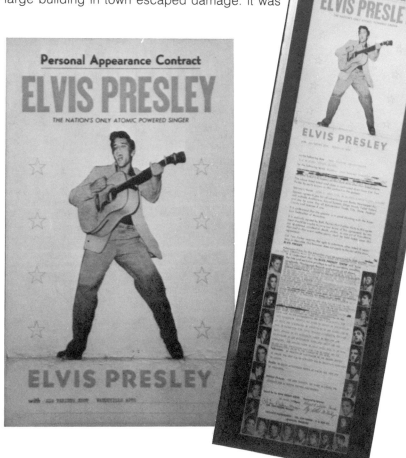

Elvis Presley personal appearance contract

The contract drawn up by Colonel Parker for Elvis' 1956 personal appearances is legendary. It is nearly 3 feet in length and covers every aspect of the show. The one shown here is for the October 12, 1956, show in Waco, Texas.

Value of contract, signed by Colonel Parker: $1,500

ELVIS PRESLEY
Exclusive RCA VICTOR Recording Artist

Early promo photo card

As soon as Elvis signed a recording contract with RCA Victor, Colonel Parker started the marketing machine, and the first item out was this wallet-sized photo card bearing the famous black-and-white picture of Elvis. It's one of those elusive items which, because of its size, doesn't command the collector's price that its rarity should demand.

Value: $15

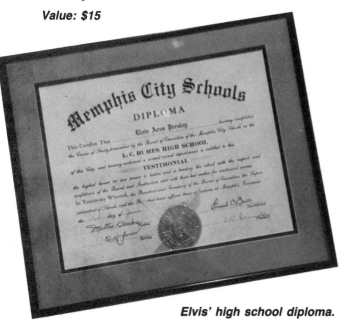

Elvis' high school diploma.

one of the most destructive storms in the history of the country, and one of the most powerful tornadoes ever. For weeks thereafter, canceled checks from the flattened Bank of Tupelo were being picked off the ground near Nashville.

The Presleys escaped the big tornado only to have tragedy of another sort strike in November 1937. Having suffered through the depths of the national Depression, Vernon and his brother Vester, along with a third man, were arrested for attempting to cheat Orville Bean on the sale of either a cow or a pig. No one recalls exactly, and the documents have long since been lost, but some say they changed a $4 check to read $40. Maybe it was $3 to $8. Everyone agrees that the money was spent to buy much-needed groceries for their families. After Vernon had spent seven months in the Lee County jail for lack of bail, the men were each sentenced to three years at the dreaded prison in Parchman, over a hundred miles away. Parchman was a work farm, and the inmates were required to toil from sunrise to dusk growing the cotton, corn, and sugar cane that were used to support the facility. When Vernon was shipped off to prison, Gladys was devastated. The family lost their precious home, which had been financed by Bean, and mother and child moved in once again with already overcrowded relatives. Brief conjugal visits with Vernon every few weeks helped to relieve the pain of separation. Vernon's incarceration left deep emotional scars, and Gladys took firm control of the family and of Elvis.

After a year, when he was released for good behavior, Vernon, who many local townspeople felt had been too severely dealt with on what would now be considered a minor charge, found work in downtown Tupelo at the Leake and Goodlet Lumber Company, with two-story stucco offices and an expanse of loading docks leading back from Main Street a full block. Over the next few years, Vernon would also obtain work with the Works Progress Administration, building public outhouses in Tupelo. With the coming of World War II, he landed a better-paying job at a war materiels plant in Memphis. Again, while he was away, the family was divided for weeks at a time.

Elvis enrolled in the East Tupelo Consolidated School on Lake Street in September 1941; the family continued to move from one home to the next, sometimes sharing rooms with relatives, sometimes renting a house. Still, they remained "on the hill," within sight of their first home. Gladys, always fearful for Elvis' safety, joined several of the other mothers in walking their children to and from school each day, making certain that they safely crossed the busy highway that separated their neighborhood from the small educational complex. It was a ritual that she would continue into Elvis' first year of high school.

The months following the end of World War II were not kind to the Presleys. Soldiers returning from Europe

Hank Snow Souvenir Photo Album

Elvis got one of his first big breaks by touring with the Hank Snow caravans in 1955. Elvis became so popular in such a short period of time that not only did he garner the prime spot just before intermission, but he was made a permanent part of Snow's tour book.

Value: $75

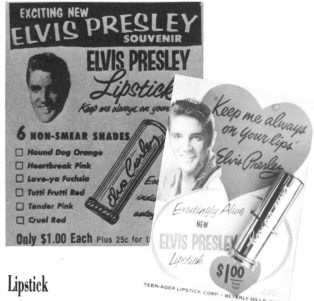

Lipstick

How can any lipstick shade compare with "Hound Dog Orange"? Girls could purchase "autographed" tubes in variety stores or by mail for only $1. Finding an unused lipstick today is nearly impossible, but one still attached to the display card is a treasure.

Value: $150
Value of lipstick attached to card: $250

North Green Street Home

The final home of the Presleys in Tupelo, Mississippi, was this four-room house on North Green Street.

and the Pacific theater were offered first choice of the better jobs, and Vernon was hard pressed to find any sort of steady work. The family, for the first time, was forced to move into the main part of town, a mile away, on the other side of the Gulf, Mobile and Ohio Railroad tracks. In 1945 Tupelo was very much an agricultural town, with wide, paved streets lined with sturdy buildings of red brick, fieldstone, and granite block. While the population of East Tupelo hovered around a thousand, its larger neighbor was home to nearly seven thousand. The Presleys first lived in a shanty on Commerce Street next to the swampy flood plain that was an area of very low income housing for blacks, and then they moved to Mobile Alley, a squalid collection of shacks and lean-tos on King Creek, in the shadow of the tall chimney of the Carnation dairy plant.

"The first time I sang in public was at an amateur program at a fair." On October 3, 1945, at the age of ten, Elvis made what is generally regarded as his first public appearance, as part of the "children's day" activities at the Mississippi-Alabama Fair and Dairy Show in Tupelo. The fairgrounds, with its beckoning neon sign atop two brick ticket booths, was a mixture of permanent livestock sheds, temporary carnival rides, and an arena just a block off the main drag in downtown Tupelo. For his part in the children's talent contest, Elvis chose to sing "Old Shep," a popular dirge originally written and recorded by Clyde "Red" Foley, which told the sad story of a boy's devotion to his dog. Elvis' efforts earned him second place: a five-dollar savings bond and an all-day free pass on the carnival rides. John Grower, manager of Tupelo's Lyric Theater on the northwest corner of Broadway and Court, also remembered that Elvis made several appearances during the theater's Saturday-morning talent shows. Already, in school as well as in church, Elvis was being noticed for his willingness to perform without hesitation. It was at this time that the family scraped together twelve hard-earned dollars to purchase the pasteboard guitar that had caught Elvis' eye in the window of the Tupelo Hardware Company.

In the fall of 1946, Elvis enrolled in Milam Junior High in downtown Tupelo, within sight of the lumberyard. Early the following year, the family moved into a more comfortable four-room home on North Green Street, in the black section of Tupelo commonly known as "Shakerag." The Presleys were befriended by black grocer John Allen Cook, whose small store stood a hundred yards from their new house. Through Cook, Vernon found work with L. P. McCarty, a vegetable wholesaler. Eleven-year-old Elvis immediately fell in love with his daddy's truck, and with truck driving as well. "When he used to bring the truck home from the wholesale grocery, I used to sit in it for hours," he would later remember. Gladys found a job with the Mid-South Laundry, and Elvis mowed lawns in the spring and summer and also shined shoes at the skating rink; but even so, there was never enough money at the end of the month.

By September 1948, Vernon had lost his truck-driving job, and the family had sunk to the very bottom of Tupelo's economic and social ladder. With mixed emotions, they packed their few belongings on the top of their nine-year-old Plymouth and drove north up Highway 78. Destination: Memphis.

The move from the small, sleepy town of Tupelo to the hubbub of postwar Memphis spelled culture shock for Elvis, which was compounded when the family moved into its new home, a single room in a dilapidated, over-crowded boardinghouse on busy Poplar Avenue, near the heart of the city. This was a gigantic step backward from their home on North Green Street. But jobs were more plentiful in Memphis, and Vernon took a loading-dock position with a paint wholesaler. Gladys was soon working part time as a nurse's aide at nearby St. Joseph's Hospital. Ever fearful for Elvis' safety, she continued to keep Elvis on a tight rein. Elvis enrolled in the eighth grade at Humes High School, and Gladys continued to walk him to and from school daily. Elvis, always shy outside of the close-knit circle of his relatives and friends, became reclusive and withdrawn. He found his only solace in his inexpensive guitar.

Within six months of arriving in Memphis, and after staying in several different apartments best categorized as slums, the Presleys moved into Lauderdale Courts, a federally subsidized housing project. As soon as they were settled, they found themselves sharing their four-room apartment with Grandma Minnie Presley, recently divorced from J. D., Vernon's father. "Dodger," as she was affectionately known, was a permanent fixture in Elvis' home from that point on.

Lauderdale Courts, despite previous descriptions, has a spacious design, not at all like the four-walled

Cowboy Songs magazine

The first article on Elvis to appear in a national publication was in the June 1955 issue of Cowboy Songs. Titled "Sun's Newest Star," the article is a mixture of fantasy and misinformation.

Value of Cowboy Songs magazine, no. 41, June 1955: $125

Poplar Avenue house

In September 1948, when the Presleys arrived in Memphis, Tennessee, the only housing they could afford was a first-floor, one-room apartment costing $35 a month. The house as it looks today.

Sun Recording Studios

Today, the home of Sun Records and the Memphis Recording Service at 706 Union Avenue, which is owned by the Elvis Presley Estate, is a Historical Monument. Because of the distance between Graceland and Sun Records, no convenient method of connecting the two for tourists has been devised, so it is currently not open to the public.

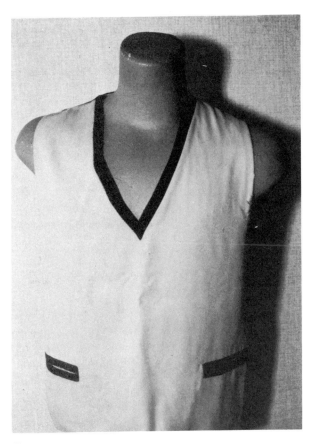

Vest

Elvis wore this vest in 1953 and 1954. Notice the mustard stain, the result of an encounter with a hot dog at a party. The vest was on display at American Sound Studios for many years.

Value: $7,500

prison usually mentioned. The red brick buildings are of one- and two-story construction, designed to hold four to eight families in relative comfort. In the late 1940s the "courts" took up several complete city blocks near the center of Memphis and were occupied primarily by women, single through widowhood or divorce, and flocks of children, who used the inner court areas as playgrounds.

The Presleys made friends with widow Ruby Black, and Elvis became close with one of her younger sons, Johnny, even though he was three years older than Elvis. Johnny recalls seeing Elvis for the first time: "He was sitting on the steps [of the courts] playing his guitar. The first time I ever heard Elvis sing 'That's All Right Mama,' he told me he wrote it and I didn't know the difference." The Black family had several musical members, including Johnny's older brother, Bill, who had quit school at sixteen to play bass in Pappy Polk's country band at night while working on the loading dock at the Railway Express Agency during the day. Johnny had also taken up the stand-up bass, and during his years in high school he shared with Elvis a desire to entertain. Together with other neighborhood friends, including the Burnette brothers, Johnny and Dorsey, both slightly older than Elvis, they practiced their music after school into the early evening in and around the inner court. On Saturdays several of the boys would gather to entertain at either the Lauderdale recreational hall, the fire station next to the Suzore Theater, or one of the many corner gas stations. Johnny Black again: "The places where we played were limited only by our imagination. Firemen would listen to most anything because they weren't doing nothing anyway. We'd pull into a service station and start unloading and in a minute set right up. We played a lot of freebies, but we liked to play." Their music was almost always welcomed, especially by the local merchants,

Five Sun singles

Don't be fooled. These five mint Sun Records singles aren't real. In 1973, an enterprising Californian acquired the best copies of Elvis' original Sun Records that money could buy. Then he duplicated the labels and mastered the music using a combination of modern technology and savvy. The sound quality on the original Sun singles is considered poor today because we attempt to play them on modern equipment, The records were designed with wide grooves to be played on the first generation of 45 rpm record players. So when transferring the music, this bootlegger used a needle made specifically for playing 45 rpm records. The result is the finest available "pure" sound of Elvis' Sun singles. RCA Victor, in the early 1960s, took the same songs and ran them through an electronic stereo mixer, with poor results. Unfortunately, the RCA "stereo" mix is the most commonly available today.

Value of five 1973 counterfeit Sun singles: $30 each
Value of "Baby Let's Play House," original Sun single: $250

Lauderdale Courts

As soon as possible, the Presleys moved into a two-bedroom, ground-floor apartment at 185 Winchester Street in the housing project known as "Lauderdale Courts." Much of the area has been torn down as part of an urban renewal project that included a new freeway system.

Sheet Music

In November 1955, a large portion of the $40,000 paid by RCA Victor for Elvis' Sun Records' contract came from Hill and Range, a major sheet music publisher specializing in country and western. It was a canny investment that ultimately earned millions for the publisher. Separate publishing companies were set up especially for the Presley material: Elvis Presley Music (under the auspices of BMI) and Gladys Music (under ASCAP). While this meant that Elvis would receive royalties from the sheet music sales, in the 1960s this arrangement restricted the quality of songs he was offered. Only the writers connected with Hill and Range were able to get their songs through to Elvis, and he was effectively cut off from the mainstream of rock 'n' roll. Weeks after the record contract was switched from Sun, Hill and Range issued the first Elvis song folio, The Elvis Presley Album of Juke Box Favorites, No. 1. The original pink-bordered folio, with the famous pigeon-toed photo of Elvis, contained several of the Sun Record releases, as well as four Hill and Range songs not yet recorded. These were "Rag Mop," "I Almost Lost My Mind," "Cryin' Heart Blues," and "I Need You So." With the success of "Heartbreak Hotel," this folio was reissued in early 1956 and the four songs replaced with "Heartbreak Hotel," "I Was the One," "Blue Suede Shoes," and "Mystery Train." Several photos were replaced and the cover price was raised from $1 to $1.50.

Elvis Presley Album of Juke Box Favorites, No. 1. *Value of 1955 version: $150 Value of 1956 version: $30*
"Heartbreak Hotel" value: $25
"Hound Dog" value: $25
"Don't Be Cruel" value: $25
"My Baby Left Me" value: $20
"That's When Your Heartaches Begin" value: $20
"Too Much" value: $25

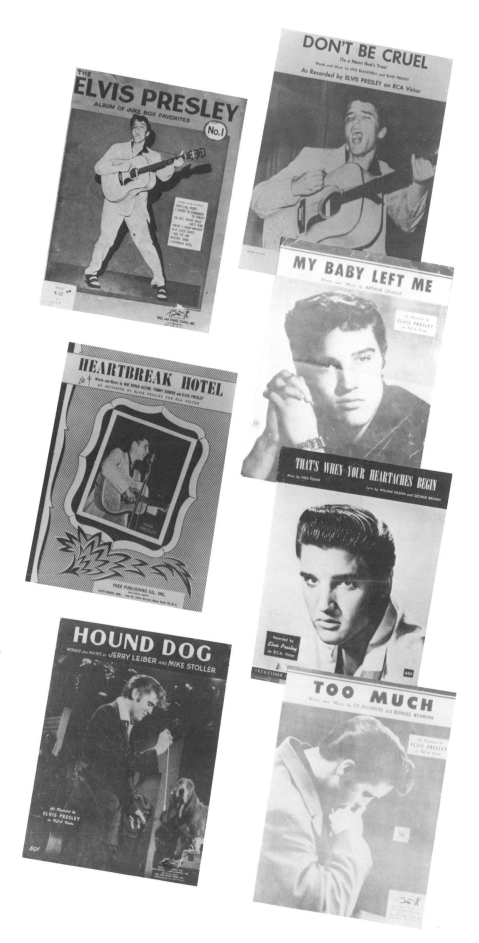

"All Shook Up"
value: $25

"Jailhouse Rock"
value: $25

"(Let Me Be Your)
Teddy Bear"
value: $25

"One Night"
value: $20

Getwell Road House

In the summer of 1955, the Presleys moved into this brick home at 1414 Getwell Road.

Love Me Tender song folio

This four-song folio from Love Me Tender *also features five full-sized photos of Elvis traveling on a train and backstage at the September 26 Tupelo concert.*

Value: $25

because when they started singing people just naturally gathered around.

Nights, they would venture farther downtown to Beale Street, the center of the black entertainment district. Johnny Black remembers: "In the older days it was a place to hang out. Not in the sense that the term is meant today. I like blues . . . rhythm and blues. On Beale Street they had blues, jazz, whatever you wanted. I was about sixteen at the time, and we walked into Beale from the 'courts.' If you were lucky, from time to time you'd get a ride. We'd wash the old man's car just to get to use it on Saturday night. We went down for the music. We wasn't hassled at all. In different areas of town they would have a restaurant or beer joint or combination of both, with one side for the whites and one side for the blacks. Well, lots of times, if I wanted to dance, I'd go over and dance with the girls on the black side, because they knew how to dance the way I wanted to dance. Of course, now, you didn't do that on a late Friday or a late Saturday night. It was a little tougher." A few clubs like the Green Beetle, only a block from Beale Street, were strictly white then, and the teenagers from Lauderdale were frequent customers when they had live entertainment.

Otherwise, Elvis' high school years were uneventful. As his confidence grew, Elvis was able to persuade Gladys to discontinue her duty as his daily chaperone as he walked to and from high school. Johnny Black put it this way: "She wouldn't have walked him to Humes, no way! I don't think even at that age and being as protected as he was by his mother—and I can appreciate that—he would've let her. It would have embarrassed him." His grades were mediocre, and the only subjects that caught his interest were woodworking shop and Army ROTC. At the end of the eleventh grade, after completing the two-year ROTC course, Elvis took his certificate home and hung it on the wall. It was his first educational honor. The only other highlight in four years of high school came during one of the annual Christmas talent shows, when he was allowed the show's single, coveted encore, based on the student body's positive reaction to his first song. "They liked me! They really liked me!" he shouted joyously as he ran offstage to the applause of his classmates.

"I Don't Care If the Sun Don't Shine" sheet music

This collector's item sheet music, although for a song released by Sun Records in September 1954, was not issued until February 1956.

Value: $50

Elvis did make a few friends in high school who would follow him all through his life: George Klein, a born leader and the president of Elvis' senior class; Marty Lacker, a New York refugee who moved to Memphis in 1952 and who shared with Elvis a fondness for "outlandish" clothes; and Bobby "Red" West. Red was a year younger than Elvis, and he lived with his mother in Hurt Village, another housing project near Lauderdale Courts. Red was an excellent high school football player (something he shared with Lacker), and he saved Elvis from the school toughs on at least two occasions when it appeared that Elvis' longish hair might be shorn as a practical joke. Elvis also tried out for the football team, but whether it was out of respect for Gladys' fear for his safety or the coach's ultimatum that his long hair had to be cut, he didn't stay with the sport long enough to make the team.

Elvis worked at a variety of odd jobs after school, including a stint as an usher at the Loew's State Theater, where he was able to spend hours watching the matinee idols. A special favorite of his was the young Tony Curtis. Elvis dated infrequently, finally settling on a steady, Dixie Locke, whom he met at the local Assembly of God Church. Other times, he and his pals caught the rhythm and blues shows at the Handy Theater on Park Street featuring B. B. King, Johnny Ace, Bobby "Blue" Bland, and Rosco Gordon, all Memphis musicians. Or they would hop into one of their parents' cars and cruise between the drive-in burger joints and Charley's Record Shop, searching for other friends. Elvis, like most teenag-

"Perfect for Parties" promo EP

RCA Victor devised a novel promotion for their line of Fall 1956 albums. The "Perfect for Parties" extended-play 45 rpm record opens with Elvis' spoken introduction to a cut from his second LP, Elvis, and follows with his introduction to five other numbers by other artists. "Perfect for Parties" was either given away in record stores or sold for as little as a quarter by direct mail.

Value of EP and cover: $200

Elvis Presley felt skirt

This is said to be the rarest of all original 1956 Elvis Presley collectibles. At this time only two are known to be in collections around the country. The skirt is made of heavy dark blue felt, and the drawing is printed directly on each piece of fabric.

Value: $1,500+

"Love Me Tender" necklace

Though issued to coincide with the release of Elvis' first motion picture, the "Love Me Tender" necklace had nothing to do with the movie. Available in both "gold" and "silver," the "gold" finish is slightly more valuable today. If it is still with the original display card, the value is increased by another $50.

Value of "gold" finish necklace on card: $130
Value of "silver" finish necklace alone: $75

ers, was struggling to find a personal identity. In his case, the most obvious signs were his wardrobe and his hair. He was fond of wearing bright pink shirts with ruffled fronts, green pants with a black satin stripe down the outside seams, and Italian-style two-tone shoes with pointed toes. And then there was his hair: long beyond faddishness, and primped and teased into a monument to Rose Oil Hair Tonic. The hair was often the first thing people noticed about Elvis, and the only thing about him that they remembered.

When he wasn't hanging out with the guys, Elvis spent many afternoons in the audience at one of the local radio stations that featured a mixture of live country-and-western entertainers and gospel quartets. It was no secret that Elvis loved the spiritual singers. He always had and he always would. He was especially fond of the Blackwood Brothers and of Jake Hess, lead tenor with the Statesmen Quartet. Elvis became such a fixture at the all-night gospel sings at Ellis Auditorium that he was allowed to visit backstage on a regular basis. His face, if not his name, became familiar to many of the gospel singers, including J. D. Sumner, bass with the Blackwoods, and later leader of the Stamps, the vocal group who sang backing vocals for Elvis in the 1970s. The building superintendent at the auditorium later recalled that Elvis worked selling soft drinks to the crowd so that he could get into the auditorium for free. After the shows Elvis would go up onstage and sing to the empty theater.

After four years, in January 1953, the family was forced to leave Lauderdale Courts when their combined incomes edged above the government's accepted level. They didn't go far, finally settling across from the "courts" on Alabama Street, where the family could maintain their friendships. Elvis was usually found hard at work on his twelve-year-old green Lincoln Zephyr, which, Johnny Black recalls, "set a lot more than it ran."

Elvis gladly graduated from Humes High in June 1953. He was the first member of his family to receive a high school diploma, and it was the personal achievement of which he remained the most proud. In later years, after achieving more fame and fortune than anyone could possibly have imagined, he would point with a sense of self-respect to that diploma hanging amid dozens of gold-record awards.

The summer after graduation, Elvis was immediately hired to work at Precision Tool on the company's tool-and-die assembly line. He remained at Precision for about six months, and left to drive a delivery truck for a local contractor, Crown Electric Company. Elvis was overjoyed. One of his secret ambitions ever since he had sat in Vernon's grocery truck had been fulfilled. He was finally a truck driver. His rig was a Dodge pickup truck, and his gig hauling electrical supplies to job sites. Elvis continued to turn over most of his salary to Gladys. Johnny Black recalls how it was: "When you got out of school,

you gave your check to Mama." It was expected of any young man who still lived at home.

It was on a Saturday morning in the summer of 1953 when Elvis finally worked up enough nerve to approach the small, single-story building that housed the Memphis Recording Service and its fledgling Sun Records to make a personal demonstration record. He'd been told often enough that he was a natural singer; now he wanted to hear for himself. In later years, he would nonchalantly say, "My career started by accident. I went into a record shop to make a record for my mother, just to surprise her." Elvis coughed up four dollars and was given ten minutes to run through two songs. His name was duly noted by secretary Marion Keisker, who was impressed enough to record a portion of Elvis' short session on a scrap of audio tape for Sam Phillips, the company's owner, who was out of the office at the time. With his acetate disk in hand, Elvis hurried home to listen. Phillips did not call; and next Monday, Elvis was back driving the truck. When weeks passed without word from the recording studio, Elvis looked to his immediate future and started taking night classes so that he might advance into the ranks of the electricians.

Throughout the winter of 1953–54, Elvis continued to promote himself as a singer, playing local house parties with a variety of other hopeful teenagers and auditioning for the Songfellows, a junior group associated with the

Elvis Presley doll

One would think that a whole series of Elvis dolls would have been a natural, but EPE licensed only one, which was manufactured in 1956. It is one of the rarest of all the Elvis collectibles ever produced. The reason is that the "magic skin" that covered the upper torso of the doll was made of a lightweight rubber and deteriorated with age if not cared for properly. The likeness and general appearance of the doll is not really like that of Elvis; it more closely resembles a lumberjack. This is still the only official doll from the 1950s to bear Elvis' name.

Value: $1,000+

The Elvis Presley Game

This board game gave girls the opportunity to play out their fantasies about falling in love with Elvis. Players were required to move through various stages of love from "getting to know you" to "send for the preacher!" The complete package sold for $3.49 and included the game board, a spinner, direction booklet, penalty cards, and an 8" × 10" photo of Elvis.

Value: $150

Cake decoration

If you ordered a birthday cake in 1956, chances are the bakery could adorn it with this Elvis overlay. The decoration was licensed by EPE and sold to bakeries; the charge to the customer was an extra quarter. The example pictured here is the only one known to exist, and it still sits on the original icing.

Value: $3,000

Blackwood Brothers. Elvis was equally admired by both groups of musicians. The Songfellows even offered him a place in their lineup in the summer of 1954, but, by then he had a contract to "sing the blues."

Finally giving up on any hope of being contacted by the Memphis Recording Service, Elvis returned to their studios for a second time on January 4, 1954. Again he paid his money to make a two-song demonstration disk, and although he lacked any professional training or experience, this time he caught the ear of Sam Phillips. He put Elvis' name "on file just in case something came up." Phillips had made a name for himself by recording many of the Negro blues artists who, like the Presleys, had migrated to Memphis in search of better times. Phillips started by leasing the master recordings to other, more established rhythm and blues labels, but by 1953 he had begun issuing his own records on the Sun label. He had several rhythm and blues hits, most notably "Bear Cat" by Rufus Thomas and "Mystery Train" by Junior Parker. Phillips was well aware that white teenagers in Memphis were listening to r&b records and radio stations, and he suspected that this was true of much of the rest of the country. In May 1954 Phillips was actively attempting to broaden the acceptability of his company by recording Doug Poindexter's Starlight Wranglers, a local juke-joint country band that featured Johnny Black's brother Bill on bass and Winfield "Scotty" Moore on guitar. Bill was also the band's designated clown. The six-piece band had been together about a year and played weekends at the Bon Air Club, with maybe a Wednesday-night gig thrown in from time to time. Usually they were paid from tips plus whatever they could gather by passing the hat.

One Friday about this time, Phillips received in the mail from Nashville an acetate of a new song titled "Without You." The demo intrigued Phillips so much that he

RCA Victor tie

This RCA Victor tie was worn by Elvis when he signed his recording contract with that company in 1955.

Value: $3,000

Earrings

These EPE earrings match the charm bracelet, but are much more rare today.

Value: $125

Charm bracelets

Among the earliest and most popular of all the items issued by EPE was the charm bracelet. On August 28, 1956, RCA Victor received exclusive rights to distribute the Elvis Presley charm bracelets through dealers who sold both records and RCA Victor phonographs. Originally selling for 69 cents to $1, the bracelet came with a "gold" finish and four charms. After Loving You premiered in mid-1957, the words "Loving You" were added to the display card, but the bracelet remained unchanged. This bracelet was reproduced again in 1977, but though they appear similar, the framed photo of the reproduction is considerably smaller than the original. In the later version, the width of the frame is smaller than the width of the heart.

Value of charm bracelet on display card: $130
Value of charm bracelet alone: $75
Value of "Loving You" charm bracelet with card: $130

"Elvis Presley for President" button

1956 was a presidential election year in the United States. Ike was running against Stevenson, but you'd never know it in the halls of the nation's schools. Here it was "Elvis Presley for President." The Lou Monte reference on the bottom of the button is to the 1956 RCA Victor single, "Elvis Presley for President" sung by Monte.

Value: $25

Good Rockin' Tonight

Which record is the original, and which is the bootleg? It's almost impossible to tell. In this photo, the original album is standing upright. The original 10-inch album was issued in France in 1956 and contains the first eight Elvis songs released by Sun Records. It is extremely rare today. The bootleg, issued in 1978, is a product of American technology. The major difference between the two: the French album has a lightweight laminated cover. The counterfeit has a heavy cardboard cover and no lamination.

Value of French original: $750+
Value of bootleg: $50

wanted to release the record as is. A day on the phone to Nashville failed to turn up the name of the singer, so, without the artist's permission, he was temporarily stumped. Marion Keisker again suggested Elvis' name, and this time Phillips agreed to "give the kid a try." A call was placed to Elvis' home. She later recalled that Elvis came rushing through the front door almost as soon as she hung up. After catching his breath—Elvis had run the entire fifteen blocks—he tried over and over to duplicate the singer on the demo of "Without You." It didn't work. Exasperated, Phillips finally asked Elvis to sing something, anything. What followed was an hour's worth of songs sung in the musical styles that Elvis most admired. This audition almost certainly included pop songs by Dean Martin, Billy Eckstine, and the Ames Brothers and country numbers originally sung by Eddie Arnold, Hank Snow, and Hank Williams. But what most intrigued Phillips was Elvis' versions of the rhythm and blues songs from Hank Ballard and the Midnighters, Joe Turner, and Clyde McPhatter and the Drifters. He even heard something in the more basic country blues numbers. Later, Elvis said, "He mentioned Big Boy Crudup's name, and maybe others, too. We talked about the Crudup numbers I knew, 'Cool Disposition,' 'Rock Me Mama,' 'Hey, Mama,' 'Everything's Alright,' and others." It was a strange audition, but in the end Phillips agreed to put Elvis in touch with Scotty Moore, the only white musician he could come up with on short notice, to see if they could develop anything worth recording.

Elvis dropped by Scotty's home on Sunday, July 4. Scotty vividly remembers, "He had on a pink shirt, pink pants with white stripes down the legs, and white shoes, and I thought my wife was going to go out the back door—people just weren't wearing that kind of flashy clothes at the time. He had the sideburns and the ducktails. Just a lot of hair." Joined by Bill Black, who lived just a few doors down the street, the three spent the afternoon running through a wide variety of material, and Moore was impressed enough to call Phillips and report, "The boy sings pretty good. He didn't knock me out." Phillips and Moore agreed that with the right song the boy might come across on record, and a studio session was set up for the following night.

On the evening of July 5, 1954, Elvis, Scotty, and Bill joined Sam Phillips at Sun Records' studio at about eight for what everyone thought would be an audition just to see how Elvis' voice would sound on tape. The addition of Scotty and Bill was merely meant to flesh out the sound with a little accompaniment. Their sole idea was to come up with a sound or style commercial enough to be released as a single record. Their first few hours together, they ran through several songs in the country and pop vein, including "I Love You Because" and "Harbor Lights." But it was obvious that Elvis' untrained voice just wasn't ready to tackle this type of ballad. It was a hot, stifling night, and the studio was cramped and lacked adequate ventilation, but the musicians continued on, undaunted by their initial lack of success.

Then magic struck. Recalls Scotty Moore: "We were sitting around there drinking a Coke, shooting the bull, Sam back in the control room. So Elvis picked up his guitar and started banging on it and singing 'That's All Right.' Jumping around the studio, just acting like a fool. And Bill started beating on his bass, and I joined in. Just a bunch of racket, we thought. The door to the control room was open, and when we was halfway through the thing, Sam came running out and said, 'What in the devil are you doing?' We said, 'We don't know.' He said, 'Well, find out real quick and don't lose it. Run through it again and let's put it on tape!!'"

The song Elvis had chosen to mimic was Arthur "Big Boy" Crudup's 1947 jump-blues record. Phillips had said repeatedly to all within earshot that if he could discover a white man who could sing like a Negro, the combination would be worth a million dollars. In less than an hour, after at least nine separate takes of the song, the first of which had a decidedly country feel, the trio had waxed the A side of their first commercial release, and Phillips realized that his dream was at hand. "They was just as instinctive as they could be. I let Scotty, Bill, and Elvis know I was pretty damned pleased," Phillips said recently.

In listening to the two versions of "That's All Right," it is evident where Elvis got his version of the song. Crudup's original is rhythmic and shuffling, with a snare drum and bass thumping out a heavy beat. The trio, lacking a drummer, called upon Bill Black to provide a close approximation by slapping his bass with a full hand instead of just picking the strings. Crudup has several additional verses in his song, which Elvis either in his haste forgot to include or chose not to sing, but the trademark "dee, dee, dee-dee" at the end of the song is a Crudup invention. Elvis imitated Crudup's nasal tenor, but imparted his own breathless, out-of-control feeling.

The next night the guys were back at Sun Records, trying to come up with a suitable flip side for their first record. At the end of another long, uneventful session, this time with Bill doing the clowning and Elvis joining in, the trio hit upon another novel idea: reworking the bluegrass standard "Blue Moon of Kentucky." Just how far the song would progress from this brief stroke of luck to the finished product can be heard in the brief outtake of "Blue Moon of Kentucky" that has been around for fifteen years. Elvis still sings in a high register, in a slow tempo, copying the original version of the song by Bill Monroe. Phillips emerged from his control room, obviously excited at what he had heard. "Hell, that's a pop song now, nearly 'bout." By the time they had called it a night, "Blue Moon of Kentucky" had been taken at breakneck speed, with the underlying beat again provided by Bill Black's

Record players

The two models of "Elvis Presley autograph model" record players were first announced in October 1956, and they were marketed by RCA Victor. Both were covered with a dark-blue denim vinyl and a contrasting lighter blue/gray tweed material. The only distinguishing mark on either record player is Elvis' autograph in gold on the top cover. One model could play up to fourteen 45 rpm records automatically and cost $47.95. Teens could buy it on time for $1 down and $1 a week at many participating RCA dealers. This player also came with a special RCA Victor three-record extended play record, Elvis Presley (SPD-23), containing twelve songs, eight from Elvis' first album. The second player was a four-speed model costing $32.95 (75 cents down and

*75 cents a week), which also came
with a special bonus, a two-record
extended play, Elvis Presley
(SPD-22), with eight songs from
his first album.*

*45 rpm record player value: $300
4-speed record player value: $750
Elvis Presley, 2-record EP (SPD-22)
  value: $500
Elvis Presley, 3-record EP (SPD-23)
  value: $1000*

Overnight case

This rare 1956 EPE overnight case was available in at least three colors: pink (Elvis' favorite color), tan, and light blue. The familiar Elvis pose is used along with another photo taken in mid-1956. Inside the case are a plastic tray and a mirror.

Value: $400

Framed color photos

All three of these "autographed" color 5″ × 7″ photos in their gold-and-white plastic frames were issued in conjunction with the November 1956 premiere of Love Me Tender. Fans who attended the movie could purchase each one for only 50 cents.

Value: $125 each
Value of frame without photo: $100

Elvis Presley hats

EPE marketed two different black-and-white gabardine crew hats with song titles in full color. The hat on the right, with Elvis' likeness in the star burst, is more common than one hat on the left, with Elvis holding his hands. Also shown is a floppy hat in blue knit fabric that may have been sold in the 1960s. The price tags for each hat can bring an additional $40.

Elvis Presley hats. Value of hat with star burst: $75
Value of hat with hands: $150
Value of floppy hat: $75
Value of ad-banner for hats: $200
Value of shipping box: $75

Elvis models the EPE crew hat.

Scotty Moore guitar

"The guitar that changed the world" was purchased by Scotty Moore in 1954. Scotty played this Gibson guitar on Elvis' first sixteen songs.

Value: $100,000

Wallets and purses

EPE authorized a number of different wallets and purses for sale in 1956. They were available in an assortment of colors and sold for 59 cents for a cheap plastic wallet to more than $1 for a foldover purse. The less expensive wallets were better sellers in the stores and are somewhat more common today. One of the rarest is the foldover wallet with a photo of Elvis on the front. The other lines of wallets and purses featured only drawings.

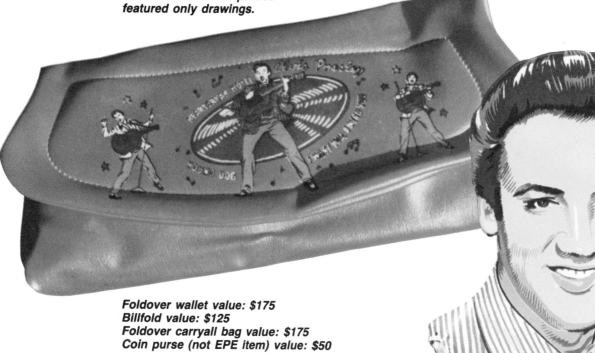

Foldover wallet value: $175
Billfold value: $125
Foldover carryall bag value: $175
Coin purse (not EPE item) value: $50

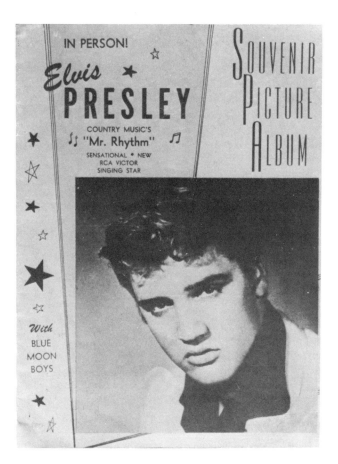

Early 1956 Elvis Presley Souvenir Picture Album

One of the rarest and most sought after of all the Elvis paper collectibles is this souvenir booklet sold while Elvis was touring from January through April 1956. Although only the center three pages feature photos of Elvis (the remainder of the booklet is taken up with the other "stars" who toured with the Elvis Presley Caravan, such as the Louvin Brothers, Justin Tubb, and June Carter), it is both an historical document of the times and a collector's dream.

Value: $250

slap bass. The stage was set. History had been made. Now all that remained was to notify the rest of the world.

By the following weekend Phillips had distributed acetates of his new release to three local disk jockeys, Dewey Phillips (no relation), Uncle Richard, and "Sleepy-Eyed" John Lepley. Memphis was unprepared for the reaction. So was Elvis. On the night his first record was to premiere on Phillips' *Red, Hot and Blue* show on WHBQ, Elvis left the family's radio set tuned to the station. Then he took off for the Suzore 2 movie house nearby for a twin bill featuring Red Skelton and Gene Autry. Meanwhile, when Phillips spun the disk, the rocking had begun. The phones at WHBQ were immediately jammed with requests to play "That's All Right" again . . . and again. There were even telegrams sent to the station by listeners who could not get through on the phone. The deejay immediately contacted the Presleys, wanting to interview this new Memphis phenomenon on his show "Right now!" Elvis was summoned from the darkness of the theater. He may have missed his movie, but he was on the way to the moon.

Dewey Phillips recalled what happened when a breathless Elvis arrived at the studio: "He sat down, and I said I'd let him know when we were ready to start. I had a couple of records cued up, and while they played we talked. I asked him where he went to high school, and he said Humes. I wanted to get that out because a lot of people listening had thought he was colored. Finally I said, 'All right, Elvis, thank you very much.' 'Aren't you going to interview me?' he asked. 'I already have,' I said. 'The mike's been open the whole time.' He broke out in a cold sweat."

Both sides of the record took off instantly, to become local hits. The small Sun Records, which had never had anything other than its few blues hits, found itself with orders for more than six thousand copies of Elvis' record within a few weeks. There were orders from Dallas, New Orleans, Little Rock, and all over Mississippi as more radio stations placed the song on their play lists. In Pleasanton, Texas, a young deejay named Willie Nelson was one of the first to promote the "Blue Moon of Kentucky" side of the record. By the end of July, Elvis was being featured in both of the local newspapers, which reported that his record was receiving "an amazing number of airplays."

All of this publicity led to Elvis' July 30 booking at a major country jamboree featuring Slim Whitman, to be held outdoors at the bandstand shell of Memphis' Overton Park. In Elvis' words, "My very first appearance after I started recording, I was on show in Memphis as an extra added single at an outdoor auditorium. I came onstage, and I was scared stiff. It was my first big appearance in front of an audience. I came out, and I was doing a fast-type tune, one of my first records, and everybody was hollering and I didn't know what they were hollering at. Everybody was screaming and everything. And then I came offstage, and my manager told me that they was hollering because I was wiggling my legs, and I was unaware of it. So I went back out for an encore, and I kinda did a little more, and the more I did, the louder they went." Elvis was a sensation from the very beginning, and his popularity was fueled by his provocative actions onstage. Asked about it later, he replied, "I don't copy my style from anybody. I jump around because it's the way I feel. In fact, I can't even sing with a beat at all if I stand still."

For a short time, Elvis was also hired as an added attraction with the Starlight Wranglers at Memphis' Bon Air Club. He would come onstage in the middle of each set and, backed by Scotty and Bill, would sing his two hits. For this he was paid five dollars a night. Scotty and Bill, on the other hand, were in immediate hot water with the other members of their band, because they were getting to play a special "spotlight" section in the show while the others sat on the sidelines. It wasn't long before they parted ways with the Starlight Wranglers for good.

The first Saturday night in August, barely a month after the first recording session, Elvis, Scotty, and Bill were hired to headline a Saturday-night gig at Sleepy-Eyed John's Eagle's Nest Club, for the princely sum of fifteen dollars—total. The club was a single-story cinder-block roadhouse adjacent to a swimming pool south of Memphis. The trio would return to make a dozen more appearances at the Eagle's Nest through the end of the year. Also in August, they played for the first time outside of Memphis, traveling to East Texas for a few dates.

In September Elvis played to hundreds of fans from the back of a flatbed truck in front of the new Katz Drug Store as part of the festivities celebrating the grand opening of Memphis' first shopping center, Lamar-Airways, while continuing to be a semi-regular at the Eagle's Nest. He also had his second recording session for Sun that month, which produced one of the finest rockabilly performances ever put on wax. It is a safe bet that without "Good Rockin' Tonight" Elvis' career might have folded before it really got off the ground. The song seemed to have been composed just for him, although it had been around the rhythm and blues circles since the late 1940s. This time, instead of aping a previous version, Elvis took the song and made it completely his own. In the two months since his first recording session, Elvis had learned that his audiences wanted more "wiggle" in their music. The single was in the stores by month's end.

On the first Saturday night in October, based solely on his Memphis publicity, Elvis appeared on the *Grand Ole Opry*, the prestigious, nationally broadcast radio show originating live from Nashville's Ryman Auditorium. He was allowed to sing only "Blue Moon of Kentucky," the more country side of his first release, and his progressive style of singing was received coolly by an audi-

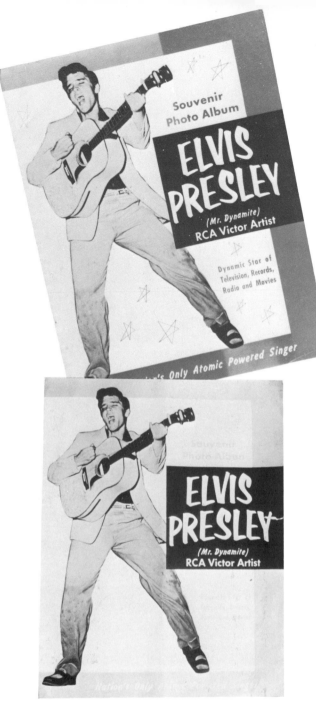

Mid-1956 Elvis Presley Souvenir Photo Album

By the summer of 1956, Elvis was a bona-fide sensation, and the Colonel felt it was time for a tour booklet devoted exclusively to Elvis. This album pictures the marquees of several of Elvis' showdates and includes a number of shots of Elvis exciting the crowds with his stage antics. Notice the misspelled "Albun." Later editions corrected this error.

Value: $125

Third tour book, Elvis Presley

The front and back covers of the magazine-sized tour booklet were printed with full-color portraits from Love Me Tender released in November. Inside are 12 pages of black-and-white portraits. The booklet originally sold for 50 cents.

Value: $75

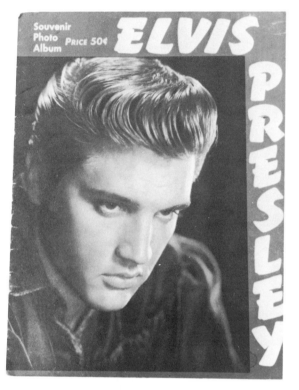

Gold and diamond ring

Elvis gave his mother this 18-carat white gold and diamond ring in 1955.

Value: $15,000

ence accustomed to hearing their country music played without frills or gimmicks. After his performance, Elvis was told by the *Opry*'s talent coordinator, Jim Denny, that he should hang on to his truck-driving job.

Instead, Elvis turned his attention southwest to Shreveport and the CBS radio network's *Louisiana Hayride* show, one of the *Opry*'s prime competitors in the national country radio market, and a show that featured the newer sounds of such younger artists as Marty Robbins, Jim Reeves, David Houston, Slim Whitman, Faron Young, George Jones, Sonny James, Ferlin Husky, and Johnny Horton. This was the show that had first given Hank Williams national exposure before he went on to the *Opry* and an early grave. On October 16, Elvis made a successful first appearance on *Hayride*. According to Elvis, "I went down there to the *Louisiana Hayride* just to try out, more or less. I went down once, and I went back again a couple of weeks later, and the people, they seemed to kind of go for my songs a little bit, so they gave me a job."

Tapes from that first night's performance, the earliest in existence of Elvis performing in front of an audience, show that while Elvis was nervous, he was able to channel this emotions into his singing.

Frank Page, *Hayride*'s emcee, politely introduced him: "He has a new, distinctive style. Elvis Presley. Let's give him a nice hand . . . Elvis, how are you this evening?"

"Just fine, how're you sir," came the hurried response.

"Are you all geared up with your band—"

"I'm all geared up," Elvis interjected.

"—to let us hear your songs?"

An impatient Elvis again stepped on the end of Page's question: "Ah, well, I'd just like to say how happy we are to be down here. It's a real honor for us to get a chance to appear on the *Louisiana Hayride*. We're gonna do a song for ya . . ." Realizing that he was now in charge of the give-and-take, Elvis looked quizzically at Page. "You got anything else to say?"

"No! I'm ready," Page answered, taken aback at the brash enthusiasm of this untried teenager.

After having failed to impress the *Opry* audience and staff, Elvis realized that this was possibly his last chance at the big time. "We're gonna do a song for ya we got out on Sun Records. It goes something like this . . ." and he was off. Grabbing the microphone in one hand, Elvis never once looked back.

His singing came in a high nasal twang, rushing the song to an even faster pace than the version on the record. Scotty Moore lost his place during his guitar break, but Elvis gamely pushed on. It was a performance that was simultaneously amateurish and exciting. It was the break that he needed to take his career beyond Memphis. He was asked to return the next Saturday night, and on November 7, before his third appearance, he signed a contract to appear on *Hayride* every Saturday night for a year. His name appeared in the Shreveport newspaper ad for that evening's show.

Elvis' first manager had been Scotty Moore, who worked closely with Sam Phillips to obtain the bookings on the *Grand Ole Opry* and *Louisiana Hayride*. Now, Memphis deejay Bob Neal was lending a hand to promote the trio, using his popular radio show to advertise their shows. Throughout the fall and early winter of 1954, Elvis, Scotty, and Bill continued to work their day jobs while traveling in ever-widening circles, playing what was often referred to as the "schoolhouse circuit," which included National Guard armorys, VFW halls, high school gymnasiums, and park recreation buildings—any hall large enough to accommodate the crowds. Their travels took them to the neighboring states of Arkansas, Texas, Mississippi, and Louisiana, an area easily covered by Neal's broadcasts on WMPS. To catch the public's attention, Elvis was now billed as the "Hillbilly Cat" and Scotty and Bill were called the "Blue Moon Boys." Through Neal's efforts, Elvis was being mentioned regularly in the national music trade papers, and it was even reported that Elvis was considered the hottest performer on *Hayride*. Crowds, made up primarily of teenagers who eagerly accepted Elvis' singing style, flocked to his shows in increasing numbers. Both of his singles on Sun were selling extremely well in the area, and a new song, "Milkcow Blues Boogie," recorded in December, had received positive reviews. To cap off the year, the nation's disk jockeys voted Elvis the eighth "most promising" country performer in a national poll.

Elvis was on the verge of breaking out of his regional boundaries. Using the money from Elvis' record royalties, the Presley family moved into a larger, four-room home on Lamar Avenue, several miles southeast of the center of the city. In November, Elvis' increased activity forced him to stop driving the truck for Crown Electric. It had been a difficult decision. Vernon had a talk with his son, who remembered the conversation: "My daddy knew a lot of guitar players and most of them didn't work, so he said, 'You should make up your mind either to be a guitar player or an electrician, but I never saw a guitar player that was worth a damn!'" Soon thereafter, Vernon, who was suffering from chronic back problems, quit his job at the paint warehouse to oversee his son's affairs. Elvis later told a reporter, "He's more help for me at home, because he can take care of all my business and can look after things while I'm gone." The burden of supporting the family now rested squarely on Elvis, and he just about had it licked.

The new year found Bob Neal officially holding the title of Elvis' manager. Signing with Neal put Elvis' career full time in the hard-working hands of one of Memphis' most popular radio personalities. Neal's noon broadcasts over WMPS reached deep into the heart of the

Fan club items

Begun in 1956, the national Elvis Presley Fan Club was one of Colonel Parker's strongest marketing tools. At one point the membership numbered above a quarter million. For a $5 annual fee, each member received a membership I.D. card, a button, a "personal" note from Elvis in the form of a postcard, and the three single releases for the year. This last ploy guaranteed that each one of Elvis' 45s would receive an advance sale of a quarter million copies, jumping it to the top of the charts within a week of its release. The "I Like Elvis and His RCA Records" button, pictured here, is the most valuable of all the Elvis Presley Fan Club pins and was issued in Elvis' favorite color, bright pink, and deep black.

Value of "I Like Elvis and His RCA Records" pin: $50
Value of Elvis Presley fan club membership card (1956 ID card): $50
Value of fan club membership greeting: $50

same section of the South that Elvis had already claimed as his own. Elvis generally played in small towns, but now there were more dates at country nightclubs in big cities like New Orleans, Mobile, and Houston. Neal recalled: "He was a sensation everyplace he went, even back in those early days. First playing around Memphis. Then, as a member of the *Louisiana Hayride*, we played a lot of concert tours across Texas. Everyplace he went, even though he wasn't known nationally, he was a tremendous hit and a great favorite. He was also very ambitious at that time."

The miles between shows expanded, reaching as far north as Cleveland and as far west as Carlsbad, New Mexico, where Neal joined with country entrepreneur Colonel Tom Parker in promoting an Elvis show in February. By March, Elvis was appearing on the portion of *Hayride* that was carried live over the 190 stations of the CBS radio network. He was signed to join the last three days of a jamboree headed by Hank Snow, and promoted by Colonel Parker, Snow's business partner in Jamboree Attractions. Elvis thought his chances were so good on a national level that he, Scotty, and Bill flew to New York City to audition for Authur Godfrey's TV talent show. They were politely informed that Godfrey's America wasn't ready for them just yet.

Elvis' fourth Sun single, "Baby Let's Play House," was released in late April. The song was originally written and recorded by Arthur Gunter, a rhythm and blues singer whose musical style was not unlike that of Arthur Crudup. Elvis took the song and ran like crazy. This time, the "babe-babe-baby" used throughout the record is of Elvis' own invention, a vocal bump and grind to accentuate the proposition of the song's title. Also recorded at that ses-

Diary, photo album, record case, scrapbook

EPE used the same likeness of Elvis on all four of these items issued in 1956. The drawing is based on the photo that adorned his first RCA Victor album, Elvis Presley. The hound dog in the background indicates that the design was not completed until after the release of Elvis' smash single, "Hound Dog." Each of these items sports a tan "leatherette" look with black lettering, and the drawings are highlighted in white. The diary is by far the hardest to find.

Diary value: $175
Photo album value: $125
Record case value: $150
Scrap book value: $100

sion was a cover version of Ray Charles' "I Got A Woman," a song that Elvis now included in his live shows. This seems to be the only significant cut from Elvis' days on Sun Records that has never been released, either legitimately or on a bootleg record. Elvis recorded the song again, during his first session for RCA Victor in January 1956, and it would have been interesting to compare the two versions.

On May 1 Elvis started his first extended tour, a twenty-one-day, twenty-city marathon again headlined by Hank Snow. The roadshow started in New Orleans and wound its way through Alabama and Florida, inching up the East Coast through North Carolina and Virginia before closing in Chattanooga. By Jacksonville, Elvis had fallen in "puppy love" with Anita Carter, daughter of Mother Maybelle Carter, and a member of the troupe. After a particularly torrid performance, Elvis feigned swooning and even allowed himself to be taken to the hospital in an attempt to catch Anita's eye. The next morning he was back as though nothing had happened. It was the first of what would be a seemingly endless succession of "co-star" romances.

Elvis continued to return to *Louisiana Hayride* on Saturday nights, often with a week's tour through Texas and Oklahoma sandwiched in between. He joined Snow again in June for a show in Oklahoma, then was on his own for a week through the familiar territory of Mississippi, Missouri, and Arkansas. Red West, Elvis' high school buddy, was now on board as an extra driver and bodyguard. While Elvis was onstage, it was Red's job to fend off the onslaught of females who were driven into hysterics by Elvis' wild abandon. In the parking lot after the show, Red often had to protect Elvis from jilted and jealous boyfriends. Red recalled a particularly fierce fight one night at the Cotton Club in Lubbock. Elvis came on to follow Lubbock's own Buddy Holly (otherwise unknown) and "all hell breaks loose. Suddenly the whole place starts taking sides. Just one incredible brawl with tables and bodies flying everywhere. And now that the men are fighting, the girls start swarming up to the stage. The fight is coming up to the stage and Elvis is still singing away. Some of the guys are dragging the women off the stage. Elvis is now starting to sign autographs! I grab through the circle of women and grab hold of him. When we get out in the open, the fight has spilled out there. I got Elvis to the car and took off like a bomb! As we sped away, Elvis was laughing like a madman!" Inevitably, news of these altercations and hospitalizations reached Gladys at home in their small new house on Getwell Avenue. She was frequently "under the weather" with worry over Elvis' safety. But Elvis telephoned home every night that he was on the road, reassuring Gladys that he was doing just fine and consoling her by telling her how well his singing was being received by all the folks in Texas, or Alabama, or . . .

The Rockin' Rebel, Vol. III bootleg album

This is the third in a series of American bootlegs issued in 1978 and 1979. Each album contained songs from the early days of Elvis' career, concentrating on television and radio appearances as well as live shows. Rockin' Rebel, Vol. III *contains a variety of material, including outtakes from "Loving You," the comedy skit that Elvis performed on* The Steve Allen Show, *his first appearance on* The Ed Sullivan Show, *and two 1956 interviews.*

Value: $50

1956 8″ × 10″ Elvis photos

By the summer of 1956, the photo mills were churning out pictures of Elvis and selling them by the thousands through ads run in movie magazines. Originally costing a dollar or less, today they are fantastic collector's items. None of the photos shown have any indentifying markings.

Value of 8″ × 10″ black-and-white photos from 1956: $15 each
Value of tinted 8″ × 10″ photos from 1956: $30 each
Value of lightweight 8″ × 10″ photo from "Love Me Tender": $15

In the middle of June, having driven Scotty's Chevrolet to an early grave after forty thousand miles, Elvis had a big scare. In a later interview, Elvis related the experience: "The first car I ever bought was the most beautiful car I've ever seen. It was secondhand, but I parked it outside my hotel the day I got it and stayed up all night just looking at it. And the next day, well, the thing caught fire and burned up on the road." It was his first, almost-new Lincoln, bought with money from his record royalties and from six months of personal appearances. The car of his dreams caught fire outside Texarkana. Elvis and a female companion had barely enough warning to escape with the musical instruments. There was no time to stop and mourn the loss; a chartered single-engine plane flew the group to Stamford, Texas, for the evening show. The next week, in a new car, he criss-crossed Texas and Oklahoma before joining Marty Robbins and Sonny James in late June for a tour of the Gulf Coast. From June 9 to July 4, Elvis played a nonstop string of personal appearances.

At home in Memphis, his first real vacation in a year was interrupted by his final recording sessions for Sun, which produced his last Sun single, "Mystery Train." Elvis was now clearly creating his own rock 'n' roll style. The original version of "Mystery Train," by Junior Parker's Blue Flames, had been one of Sun Record's few rhythm and blues hits prior to Elvis' arrival. Elvis took the lyrical idea from Parker's song, but he and Scotty Moore used the flip side of Parker's record, "Love My Baby," as a jumping-off point for a moaning wail of superb rockabilly music.

Elvis was overjoyed to receive the news that "Baby Let's Play House" had done well enough to be his first record to hit the national country music sales charts. He knew this was just the beginning; his career seemed boundless. He relaxed at home, secure in the knowledge that Colonel Parker, working with Bob Neal, was handling his bookings for the rest of the summer and into the fall.

The last week in July, Elvis took Florida by storm. There was a riot in Jacksonville that left Elvis nearly stripped of his clothes as he tried to make his way back to the dressing room after the show. "I accept it with a broad mind," said Elvis, "because they don't intend to hurt you. They just want pieces of you for souvenirs." The tours continued to circulate around Memphis and Shreveport. *Hayride* relented under Colonel Parker's pressure and agreed to allow Elvis to appear on the *Big D Jamboree* in Dallas every fourth Saturday night. There was another car left alongside the highway, fifteen miles south of Texarkana. This time Scotty was at the wheel of Elvis' new pink Cadillac when a farmer in a pickup truck turned left in front of him. Now Elvis had even less time to inspect the damage. Automobiles, which a younger Elvis had devoted hours and hours to loving and caring for, were now only as good as the mileage they could accumulate. He and his trio of musicians (drummer D. J. Fontana had been picked up from *Hayride* and was now a regular member of the act) were putting ten thousand miles a month on their cars. During September, Elvis played twenty-two shows in twenty-four days on a tour that snaked from New Orleans to Roanoke. Part of the time Hank Snow headlined and some of the time Elvis led his own caravan. That same month, "Mystery Train" started its climb to the number one spot on the national country music sales charts after being on the market only six weeks. "Mystery Train" and its flip side, "I Forgot to Remember to Forget," a country weeper, would remain on the charts for an astounding forty weeks, the longest an Elvis 45 rpm record would ever remain on any chart. In mid-October Elvis traveled back and forth across Texas headlining his own show before joining Hank Snow and Bill Haley and his Comets for a show in Oklahoma City promoted by Colonel Parker. Then he and the troupe drove like mad to make his scheduled concerts in Cleveland and St. Louis.

Elvis was now far and away the hottest new performer in country music, and his lucrative contract with Sun Records was on the auction block. The bidding started at $10,000 and quickly rose to $25,000. One by one, the major recording companies dropped out, judging that this talent, as yet untried on the national market, just couldn't be worth the amount asked. Finally it was down to two companies: Atlantic Records, the foremost purveyor of rhythm and blues music and a company that definitely understood the reasons behind Elvis' growing popularity, and RCA Victor Records, a leader in country-and-western music and one of the largest record companies in America. RCA Victor also had close ties to Colonel Parker through his interests in Eddy Arnold, whom the Colonel had formerly managed (and continued to book through 1965), and Hank Snow. RCA Victor, in an unusual joint venture with Hill and Range Publishing Company, won the bidding war by offering $35,000 to Sun Records for the contract, with an additional $5,000 going to Elvis to cover the back royalties owed him by Sun. The deal was struck at the annual disk jockey convention in Nashville on November 20.

It was obvious to everyone that Colonel Parker was holding the reins to Elvis' career and Bob Neal was now riding shotgun. A year later, in one of his rare interviews, Colonel Parker had this to say about taking Elvis under his wing: "I think Presley was a star from the first day he ever started going into show business. I think anyone could have helped him that knows something about show business." Asked for his opinion about his own greatest value to Elvis, he replied, "I think my experience, and, in a small way, handling his future by making contracts where perhaps someone would offer a certain amount of money and I thought this artist was worth more and I held out for my price. I've lost some deals, but I

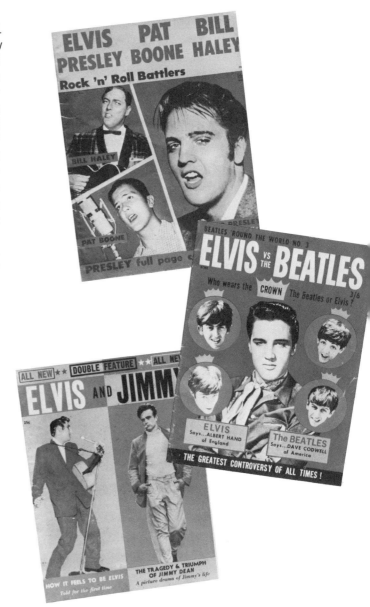

Magazines: Elvis vs. ?

Those at the top must stand off all comers. Just as it is in real life, so it is in the fantasy world of rock 'n' roll. Since the first day he swiveled onto the scene, the media pitted Elvis' popularity against that of other music stars. At first, it was against Pat Boone, the clean-cut singer with whom the middle-of-the-road press corps could readily identify. When Elvis went to Hollywood, he was immediately matched with the image of the sullen James Dean, dead less than a year when Elvis started shooting Love Me Tender. *In 1964, the obvious battle was between Elvis and the Beatles. The competition was always healthy for both the stars and the magazine*

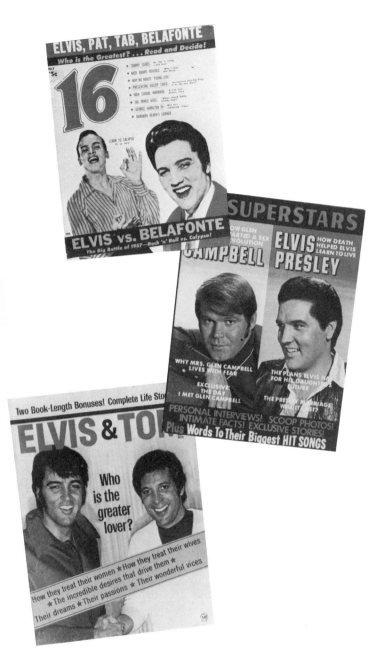

gained some others by waiting." Sam Phillips had been looking for a white man who could sing with the feel of a black in order to make a million dollars. Within a few short years, Colonel Parker said it differently: "Elvis, when I found him, had a million dollars' worth of talent. Now he has a million dollars!"

In December RCA reissued "Mystery Train" on its own label, followed in short order by Elvis' other four Sun singles. As the year came to a close, Elvis was in the enviable position of having two record companies pushing his records, as Sun worked to deplete its inventory. Hill and Range quickly issued the first music portfolio of songs from Elvis, later revising it to include his first hits from 1956. In mid-December CBS-TV announced that, starting next month, Elvis would make four consecutive Saturday-night appearances on *Stage Show,* a television program produced by comedian Jackie Gleason that served as a half-hour warm-up for his very popular *Honeymooners* show. Elvis would receive an incredible $1,250 per show. Eighteen months earlier, Elvis had split fifteen dollars a night with Scotty and Bill at Sleepy-Eyed John's Eagle's Nest Club. Now fortune seemed to be tugging at his heels.

Eagle's Nest Club

At the corner of Lamar and Clearpool, the building housing the Eagle's Nest Club is still a country and western nightclub.

business, and collectors of Elvis memorabilia are the winners. The value of each magazine is affected not only by Elvis' popularity but by that of the other star.

December 1956 Elvis Presley, Pat Boone, Bill Haley *magazine value: $50*
1956 Elvis vs. the Beatles *magazine value: $45*
1956 Elvis and Jimmy *magazine value: $60*
July 1957 16 *magazine (Elvis vs. Belafonte) value: $30*
1970 TV Superstars *magazine (Elvis vs. Glen Campbell) value: $25*
1969 Elvis & Tom *magazine value: $30*

the Phenomenon Explodes

Two days after Elvis celebrated his twenty-first birthday, he was in RCA Victor's Nashville studio to record his first original release for his new label. The result was the *epochal* "Heartbreak Hotel." None of Elvis' Sun singles remotely resembled "Heartbreak Hotel." In fact, nothing in country music or pop music came close. It wasn't even rockabilly. It was pure Elvis. He hiccupped and panted, moaning and wailing so effectively that the listener could almost see the body movements that Elvis had used to accompany the song.

After the recording session, Elvis joined Hank Snow for the last time to tour for a week in Texas. Advertising for the shows prominently featured Elvis as the "hottest new star in 5 years," but, after performing to sellout crowds in cities such as San Antonio and Fort Worth, it was back to Shreveport January 21 to fulfill his contract with *Louisiana Hayride.* Over the fifteen months that he had been a regular part of *Hayride,* the makeup of the audience had changed markedly. His exciting style had driven away many of the older, more conservative members of the Saturday-night gallery. In their place had come hundreds of teens and young adults who were more than ready to rock to the beat of Elvis, Carl Perkins, Johnny Horton, George "Thumper" Jones, David Houston, Johnny Cash, and such lesser-known artists as Werly Fairburn and Slim Rhodes.

Exactly a week later, when Elvis made the first of his legendary *Stage Show* appearances (which were increased to a total of six after the reaction to the original four), the nation got its first live peek at this new phenomenon. He twitched and jerked through "I Got a Woman" and a torrid "Shake, Rattle and Roll" that included a verse from "Flip, Flop and Fly" for good measure and eclipsed the earlier versions by Joe Turner and Bill Haley.

Four weeks after a late-January release, "Heartbreak Hotel" starting climbing the popular music charts. The record eventually went to number one, although it was only in the top ten by the time Elvis made his last appearance on *Stage Show. Stage Show,* hosted by the Dorsey Brothers' bandleader, did not have a large audience of teenagers, the market that everyone agreed was the

Drinking glass

With this item in your cupboard you could always have a drink with Elvis. With a nice overlay of gold, this EPE drinking glass features gold records on the backside and a familiar pose of Elvis on the front.

Value: $85

Coaster/ashtray

Although this porcelain item from the 1950s looks like an ashtray, Elvis wouldn't have permitted it. He never publicly professed to be a smoker, but in private, he often enjoyed those thin, tipped cigars. The EPE coaster/ashtray is 3½ inches in diameter, and the black-and-white photo on the inside is one taken in 1955 while he was still recording for Sun Records.

Value: $65

Million Dollar Quartet bootleg album

It was purely happenstance, but it was also history in the making. The afternoon that Elvis dropped by Sun Records to visit his old friends, Carl Perkins was in the studio, having just finished a session with his band and an unknown pianist, Jerry Lee Lewis. Elvis and Perkins had always been friendly rivals, with the two of them touring together in 1955. A friendly jam session was begun with Perkins on guitar and Elvis soon taking over the piano. Sam Phillips started his tape recorder rolling. Over the next two hours, songs flowed back and forth in bits and pieces. Each man would take the lead, and all would jump in on harmony. The predominant form of music on this 1980 American bootleg is the gospel of the small, grassroots churches of the South. Johnny Cash does not appear on this album as he apparently dropped by later in the day, and no more of this important Million Dollar Quartet session has been released. One of the more interesting items contained on this album is Elvis' rendition of "Don't Forbid Me," which had just been released by Pat Boone and which Elvis mentions was written for him. Another interesting part of this important release is the ability of Jerry Lee Lewis to hold his own with the two, more seasoned rock 'n' roll veterans. Lewis had just recorded his first single, "End of the Road," but was half a year away from having a national hit.

Value: $50

Fourth tour book, Elvis Presley Photo Folio

The fourth and final tour book issued through Colonel Parker's office for the 1950s used a blue-tinted portrait of Elvis from Jailhouse Rock on its cover. Elvis wasn't touring much by this time, so the booklet was sold by mail order as well as at personal appearances. For the folio's second printing, the original back cover, which advertised Jailhouse Rock, was changed to push Elvis' Golden Records issued in March 1958.

Value, with Jailhouse Rock back cover: $90
Value, with Elvis' Golden Records back cover: $60

Elvis Answers Back! magazine

One of the most interesting magazines issued about Elvis is this rare 1956 item with a record pressed into the front cover. Elvis Answers Back! comes in two versions: the one pictured and one in which the record is titled "The Truth about Me!" The 78 rpm records are otherwise identical and contain two minutes and ten seconds of Elvis' answers to the questions he is most asked. The magazine with the record still attached is extremely rare, since the record cannot be played without being cut off the cover.

Value, with record affixed: $200
Value of magazine, with record removed: $50
Record only: $100

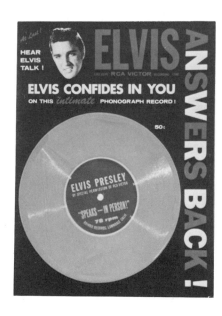

primary target. Not one to dawdle, Parker had a double whammy planned for Elvis in early April. But first he had to get out of that *Louisiana Hayride* contract.

Since signing with RCA Victor in November, Elvis had toured constantly, with weeks of dates tucked between his Saturday commitments on either *Stage Show* or *Louisiana Hayride*. It had become a ball and chain that would not allow him to advance his blossoming career. The time had come time to make his final "regular" appearance on *Louisiana Hayride*. Elvis was still obligated to perform in Shreveport every Saturday night, which drove Colonel Parker to distraction. *Hayride* paid Elvis based on his 1954 contract, and it was going to cost the Colonel nearly a thousand dollars a month in penalties to get him out of an appearance that was paying him $18 a night. Colonel Parker finally bought out the contract for a flat $10,000 plus an agreement that Elvis would play one last concert for *Hayride,* to be broadcast from Shreveport later in the year. On March 31 Elvis made a special, much ballyhooed appearance to a sellout audience of teenagers, and then he and the Colonel were free to pursue loftier goals.

The pair traveled to the West Coast for a meeting with Paramount Pictures' producer Hal Wallis, who put Elvis through a quick screen test and announced a three-picture deal. Elvis' salary would start at $100,000 for the first film and escalate in $50,000 increments. There was a press conference featuring Elvis, who appeared to have just swallowed a canary, flanked by Hal Wallis and Elvis' soon-to-be co-star, Debra Paget, who was, interestingly, not from Paramount Studios but from Twentieth Century–Fox. Later, when he was asked about his new movie contract, Elvis said, "It's a dream come true. It's something I'd never think would happen to me, of all people. It just shows that you never can tell what's gonna happen in life."

Just as important to Elvis' career at this time was his April 3 TV guest shot on the *Milton Berle Show,* which had widespread appeal among teenagers. The show was broadcast from the aircraft carrier USS *Hancock,* docked at the San Diego Naval Station. From the opening beat of "Heartbreak Hotel," it was obvious that this audience of young sailors and their wives and girlfriends was ready for Elvis. And Elvis was ready for them. He immediately followed "Heartbreak Hotel" with a rocking remake of Carl Perkins' "Blue Suede Shoes." The next two nights Elvis played his first West Coast concerts with a pair of shows at the San Diego Arena. The crowd was so unrestrained in its enthusiasm that the navy's shore patrol was called out to protect the star from his adoring fans.

In mid-April Elvis returned to the tour circuit in Texas and the South for two more weeks. It was clear that his popularity had taken a mighty leap since he had played the same area with Hank Snow in January. So had Colonel Parker's publicity blitz. Eddie Fadal, a deejay in

"Stuck on You" sheet music

The boyish photo on the sheet music for "Stuck on You" was taken in the Waco, Texas, home of Eddie Fadal during the summer of 1958.

Value: $20

"Love Me Tender" picture sleeves

"Love Me Tender" had advance sales of over a million copies before it was even recorded! But apparently RCA Victor couldn't decide on which color paper to run the picture sleeve. First, they issued it on green, but that made Elvis look ill, so they came out with pink, a vast improvement. Somewhere in between, a few were released in black and white.

Value of green picture sleeve: $75 pink: $40 white: $150

Love Me Tender theater pictorial

Colonel Parker had thousands of these souvenir photo albums printed up to be sold in movie theaters. But theater owners balked at stocking crates of programs that might remain unsold. Never one to hesitate, the Colonel set up a distribution deal and offered the lot through this clever ad.

Value: $75

Love Me Tender ads

This was the only movie that Elvis made in which he did not star. The veteran leading man Richard Egan and lovely Debra Paget shared star billing, while Elvis was "introduced." The poster carried through the post-Civil War theme of the movie by displaying a charging Confederate cavalry just below Elvis' left knee. In 1962, a reissue of "Love Me Tender" used a different style of poster similar to the 1956 one-sheet (a 27" × 41" movie poster is known as a one-sheet) that had photos of the stars instead of the painting.

Dallas at the time, remembers what happened when Colonel Parker walked into the station: "The Colonel would come in and say, 'I've got a hundred dollars here. I'll buy a hundred spots and you give me a hundred.' That's the way he negotiated." Elvis was generating his own publicity, albeit of a slightly different type. In Fort Worth, the press noted that an "animalistic roar split the coliseum" when Elvis displayed his "sensuous, almost vulgar swaying." In Corpus Christi, following the close of Elvis' show, the coliseum management banned all further rock 'n' roll concerts. In San Antonio he narrowly missed being torn apart by three thousand fans who stormed the stage door after the matinee show. Unable to leave the auditorium, Elvis retired to the keyboard of the large pipe organ and launched into stirring renditions of "Harbor Lights" and "Silent Night." Asked if it was normal for riots to follow his performances, Elvis remarked, "If I said yes, I'd be braggin'. If I said no, I'd be lyin'." His thirty-minute portion of the show normally consisted of seven songs, including "Baby Let's Play House," "I Got a Woman," and "Only You," as well as his first RCA Victor releases.

The first of the rumors that would dog him the rest of his life were starting. Elvis took all of this philosophically: "I hear that I'm about to die in six months. That I've been pushing dope. That I've been to Alcatraz. I don't know how they start, but they're not true. I'm certainly not singing this way because I'm going to die." All of this

27" × 41" one-sheet value: $150
11" × 14" lobby card value: $25

Magazines: Early rock 'n' roll

Of general interest to collectors of rock 'n' roll music, and of Elvis in particular, are the magazines from 1956 through 1958 devoted to this emerging musical style. As might be expected, Elvis usually fills a large number of pages in each magazine, often taking the entire cover story slot. But there are also many stories and photos of the other rock 'n' roll stars of the era such as Gene Vincent, Fats Domino, the Platters, Jerry Lee Lewis, LaVern Baker, Carl Perkins, and Little Richard. These tabloids cover an exciting period in America and are therefore of interest to a greater number of collectors than the magazines devoted purely to Elvis. They also represent the beginning of the teen-oriented magazines such as 16 and Seventeen that have become a staple of the magazine industry.

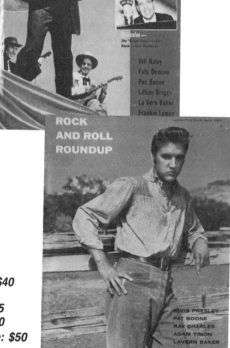

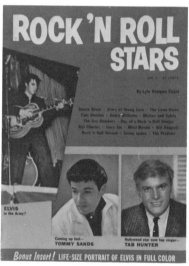

October 1956 Teenage Rock and
  Roll Review *value: $40*
November 1956 Dig *value: $40*
January 1957 Dig *value: $45*
Fall 1956 Rock 'n Roll Jamboree *value: $40*
1956 Rock 'n Roll Stars *value: $50*
1957 Rock 'n Roll Stars, *No. 2 value: $45*
1957 Rock 'n Roll Stars, *No. 3 value: $40*
April 1957 Rock and Roll Roundup *value: $50*
1957 Cool, *Vol. 1, No. 1 value: $50*

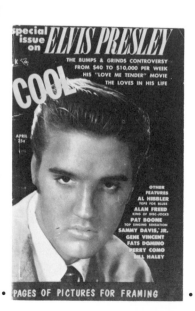

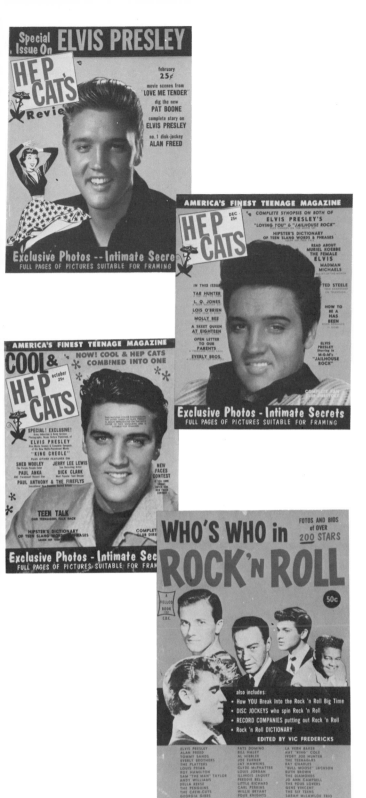

February 1957 **Hep Cats Review,**
    Vol. 1, No. 1 value: $45
December 1957 **Hep Cats, Vol. 2,**
    No. 2 value: $35
October 1958 **Cool & Hep Cats**
    value: $35
1958 **Who's Who in Rock 'n Roll**
    booklet value: $45

publicity led up to his first booking in Las Vegas, starting April 23. It was one of the few bad moves made at the time by Colonel Parker. The two-week engagement, for which Elvis was paid a total of $20,000, was an artistic disaster. The program at the New Frontier Hotel opened with Borscht Belt comedian Shecky Greene. Elvis and his trio followed with a four-song, ten-minute set that presented "our style of singing" to a middle-aged crowd of "music lovers" who sat impatiently waiting to hear the headliner, bandleader Freddy Martin. Elvis fully realized the depth of his predicament. There were no screaming teenage girls. As a matter of fact, there was no screaming at all. The end of each song was greated with a polite smattering of applause. Elvis played out the fiasco in a thoroughly professional manner and survived the two weeks with his sense of humor intact. More significantly, another critical two weeks in front of the nation's teenagers had been lost at a time when Elvis' popularity was just beginning to break nationally. In 1956 the consensus among those in the music business—including Elvis, Colonel Parker, and RCA Victor—was that rock 'n' roll might not last out the summer. It was considered just another musical fad, like "The Yellow Rose of Texas" or "Ballad of Davy Crockett." Elvis was inevitably asked, "What are you going to do when rock 'n' roll is no longer popular?" His usual reply was "I don't think it'll ever die completely out, because they're gonna have to get something mighty good to replace it." But if that fateful day ever came, he said, he'd "go back to driving a truck!"

With Las Vegas behind him, he set about regaining the lost momentum. His new single, "I Want You, I Need You, I Love You," a ballad even further removed from the rock 'n' roll of his Sun Records days, was selling thousands of copies but not generating much excitement on its own. Following closing night in Las Vegas, Elvis was booked on his first tour of the Midwest. It was the tonic that Elvis so desperately needed. Everywhere he played there were mobs of shrieking teenage girls, who quickly restored his self-confidence.

In June Elvis returned to Los Angeles for another guest spot on the *Milton Berle Show.* It was on this show that Elvis offered the television premiere of the 1953 rhythm and blues hit "Hound Dog." With Berle's comic goading, Elvis shocked the nation down to its puritanical toes. That evening, "Hound Dog" started at a slightly slower tempo than the well-known single release. Although Elvis did a little bouncing about the stage while hanging on to the microphone, it was after the song was apparently finished and Berle had returned to the stage to do his famous turned-foot walk that Elvis' humping and bumping began in earnest. The song, which had been added recently as part of his stage act, became an instant rallying point for the country's teenagers. Overnight, Elvis became a *cause célèbre.* There was no mid-

Head scarf

In an era of convertibles and Saturday night cruising, a head scarf was an essential part of each girl's wardrobe. EPE licensed several styles to suit every taste and need. The head scarf measured 32 inches square and featured a four-color print on a blend of rayon and silk. It came in several colors including white and the ever-popular pink and sold for $1.49. A slightly smaller kerchief with the same design was marked $1.29, and a turban-style scarf in white cotton sold for $1. And, of course, there was also a dainty handkerchief.

Value of head scarf: $100
Value of kerchief: $75
Value of turban: $100
Value of handkerchief: $75

dle ground upon which to stand. Either you were for Elvis or you were against him. And the lines were not just based on age. Many teens—mostly boys, to be sure—could not stand Elvis. Elvis caused a stir of controversy wherever he went; and, as always, he allowed the insults to slide off him. "Live entertaining," he said, "is not like you hear it on the radio. When you do it on the stage you have to put on a show for the people. People can buy your records and hear you sing. You have to put on a show to draw a crowd. If I just stood up there and sang and never moved, people would say, 'I could stay home and listen to his records.' You have to give them a show, something to talk about." After the Berle show they had plenty to talk about.

While on the West Coast, Elvis played San Diego again, then Long Beach and Los Angeles before returning to Memphis for a brief vacation and to enjoy the new ranch-style home that he had bought for his parents on Audubon Drive, in a very nice Memphis neighborhood. After years on the edge of poverty, this rambling seven-room house seemed to swallow up the Presleys, even though they were constantly surrounded by friends and relatives. Gladys just couldn't begin to fathom all of the changes the family had been through in such a short time. She continued to keep her flock of chickens in the back yard. The new fence, erected after the neighbors complained about the hundreds of teenage trespassers, just caused her to withdraw further. It was clear that any semblance of a normal home life could not be easily maintained for long.

"Teddy Bear" eau de parfum

The label reads "Elvis Presley's 'Teddy Bear' Eau De Parfum." Rest assured, Elvis never wore this particular scent himself. The original, clear, square bottle with a white cap came in a fake cork box.

Value: $75

Gumball machine pins

An Elvis button for a penny. Each button is about the size of a thumbnail, and all were manufactured by the Green Duck Company for Elvis Presley Enterprises. There must have been millions of these pins sold in gumball machines during the winter of 1956–57 alone. Today the "I Like Elvis" without the photo is the most rare.

Value: $12
"I Like Elvis" pin value: $15

Elvis opened a three-day stand at the Paramount Theater in Atlanta on June 22. It was typical of his concerts at this time. His grueling daily schedule called for him to be onstage three times, at 2:00, 5:50 and 8:30 P.M. Elvis' portion of the entertainment ran a scant twenty minutes and came at the end of a grade B movie and an hour-long review featuring acrobats, magicians, and lesser-known country performers. Once onstage, Elvis and the band were able to maintain control through six or seven songs, until the noise of the frenzied teenage audience brought a thundering end to his portion of the entertainment. The deafening sound of the crowd could be compared only to that of the new jet engines. Offstage, Elvis did his best to relax, and was occasionally spotted at a local pool parlor, where he would graciously sign a few autographs and play a few games of pocket billiards until the crowd became unruly. After this tour, it was time to say good-bye to Red West, who was leaving for a two-year tour of duty with the marines. Red's place as bodyguard-driver-companion would be handled by two of Elvis' cousins, Gene and Junior Smith.

The next scheduled national television appearance was on the July 1 *Steve Allen Show.* Bowing to the immense amount of criticism over Elvis' antics on the previous month's Berle show, Allen toned Elvis down considerably, dressing him in a tuxedo and having him per-

lvis answers his fan mail

lvis' fan mail totally outstripped is attempts to answer it ersonally, so a series of reprinted letters and postcards ere created. Each person writing Elvis (and the letters were equently addressed simply Elvis—Memphis") received a eply, even if it was of the "check e box" variety. Almost all the fan ail was answered by Colonel arker's battery of secretaries in s office in Madison, Tennessee. his was the "headquarters" for e national Elvis Presley Fan Club.

alue: $25

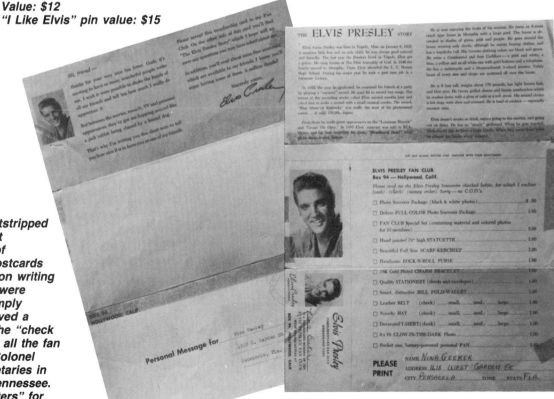

form "Hound Dog" without his guitar, singing to a basset hound. Elvis was also forced to sing "I Want You, I Need You, I Love You" in a stiff, formal manner. The immediate result was twofold. On the one hand, Allen's TV show beat its cross-channel competition in the Sunday-night ratings race. On the other, the fans demanded the return of the "original" Elvis. Allen's television rival was the formidable Ed Sullivan, who had been staunchly opposed to Elvis following the Berle show in June. Now Sullivan had to review his stand against Elvis. After all, Allen might ask Elvis for a return appearance, with even more disastrous results in the ratings race. Sullivan cracked. Within two weeks, he announced that, starting in September, Elvis would be paid the largest fee ever for television guest shots: $50,000 for three shows. Colonel Parker could barely contain his glee.

Elvis hit the road in August for yet another sizzling tour of Florida. This time, it wasn't just Jacksonville that greeted him with mobs of wild teenage girls. Everywhere he performed, Elvis was met by thousands and thousands of fans. And the law followed too, making certain that Elvis did not repeat his burlesque routines in front of any of Florida's impressionable children. A year earlier, it had only been the southern boyfriends of these screaming females who were on Elvis' trail. Now it was an army of adults who saw in Elvis a moral dilemma and a wildness from which they hoped to protect their offspring. Elvis took the teenagers' side: "I don't see any type of music that would have a bad influence on people. It's only music. In a lot of papers, they say that rock 'n' roll is a big influence on juvenile delinquency. I don't think that it is. I don't see how music has anything to do with it at all." He then went on to ask his own rhetorical question: "I mean, how would rock 'n' roll make anybody rebel against their parents?" He shrugged it off, saying, "I've been blamed for just about everything wrong in this country."

"Hound Dog," which Elvis had finally recorded the day after the Allen TV show, was released by RCA Victor and immediately sold two million copies. The record was then flipped over, and the other side, "Don't Be Cruel," racked up another three million sales. It was the largest-selling single release to date, and by summer's end Elvis was unquestionably the most colossal phenomenon that the entertainment industry had ever seen. What was more, his fame was spreading across both oceans. In England, Germany, and France, he was more popular than any local singing idol. In Japan and Australia, his records regularly topped the charts.

RCA continued to pump out songs to satisfy his rabid fans. His first long-play album, *Elvis Presley,* issued in March and combining newly recorded songs and unreleased material from his days with Sun Records, was the nation's top-selling LP from May through July. It went on to become the first album by a solo artist to reach a

P.j.s and tee

The original Elvis Presley tee shirt appeared in 1956. It was white with black trim and a full-color drawing. The girl's knit pajamas sported the same design, but came with either a yellow or a blue background rather than the white.

Tee shirt value: $150
Value of knit pajamas: $175

EPE socks

EPE socks were available in either nylon or cotton in a variety of styles. They were packaged two pairs for $1.

Value: $150

Adjustable finger ring

This adjustable ring features a color photo of Elvis underneath a "crystal" bubble. Licensed in 1956 by EPE, it was "gold" plated and sold for between 49 cents and $1 depending on the source. The cardboard card on which a dozen rings were displayed in stores is actually rarer today than a ring itself and can bring a price upwards of $200. A display card with all 12 rings still attached would fetch more than $1,000.

Value: $75

Hillbilly and Western Scrapbook

This 1957 edition Hillbilly and Western Scrapbook features photos and biographies of many popular country and western stars of that time, including Elvis. Everyone knows that Elvis started his career deeply rooted in country music, but many would doubt that Elvis was a "country" star as late as 1957. However, Elvis was voted the top country male vocalist for both 1956 and 1957 by none other than the jukebox industry!

Value: $75

EPE mittens

This was one way to hold hands with Elvis. The mittens came in red, white, and navy and sold for about $1.50.

Value: $150

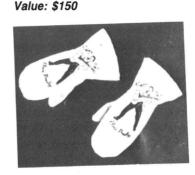

ookends

hese plaster Elvis bookends vould certainly keep a fan's ollection of Elvis books in order. he originals were 7 inches tall nd finished in a lustrous ivory one. Similar items have appeared n the market since 1977, but the arlier bookends were authorized y EPE and are so marked. Many ter versions came from Mexico nd bear no distinctive marking.

alue: for one, $100; for a pair, $225

Record album pins

These small straight-pin buttons were made to resemble gold records, and each came with the name of one of Elvis' hits stamped in the gold outer edge. The center photo, usually a closeup of Elvis shown here, also featured a hound dog (for the record "Hound Dog"), as well as a silhouette likeness of Elvis playing a guitar.

Value: $25

Gumball machine pin, version 2

Although this item is similar to the gumball machine pins, this pin is much more valuable. The drawn likeness of Elvis closely resembles the publicity photos from Elvis' Sun Records days, even though the pin is marked with the EPE, 1956 logo.

Value: $45

million dollars in sales and, for a time, RCA's all-time best-selling album. In late August the record company issued an unprecedented seven singles by Elvis (including all twelve songs from the album plus two new ones), and soon reported that each was selling at the rate of twelve thousand a day. In total, Elvis' records were expected to sell more than ten million copies by the end of 1956. At that rate, Elvis' royalties from RCA would exceed $400,000.

Colonel Parker had not been idle while Elvis was touring and appearing on television. A new company, appropriately named Elvis Presley Enterprises, was set up during the summer to merchandise Elvis' name and likeness. Few consumer goods were left untouched. A teenager could dress from head to foot in "Elvis." There were dolls that looked like Elvis and dolls that looked like hound dogs. There were enough products being sold under the Elvis banner to clothe and entertain an army. And an army it was, with Elvis at the lead.

Meanwhile, Elvis had slipped back to Hollywood to start filming his first picture, not for Hal Wallis and Paramount Pictures (neither of which had a property ready that they thought would fit Elvis), but for Twentieth Century–Fox. Elvis was to make his film debut in a horse opera originally titled *The Reno Brothers*. His part was significantly rewritten to allow him to warble a few tame songs, one of which led to the picture's being renamed *Love Me Tender*. Throughout most of September, Elvis worked hard in front of the cameras. In the evenings he made the Hollywood rounds with a new set of young actors and bohemian friends, including Natalie Wood, Sal Mineo, and Nick Adams. All three had starred with James Dean in *Rebel Without a Cause*, and they had been without a leader since Dean's death in 1955. Elvis, a genuine rebel in the music world, who was struggling with his own instant popularity, was immediately accepted as a peer. It was even rumored that *Rebel Without a Cause* was Elvis' favorite movie and that he could quote entire passages from the film. Some in Holly-

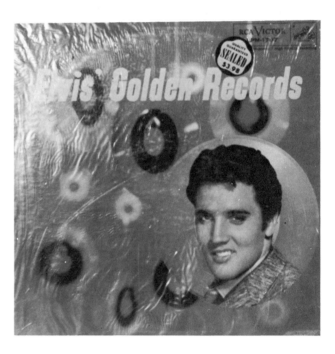

Elvis' Golden Records album

Standing outside the Kennedy Veterans Hospital on the bitter cold morning of March 24, 1958, Elvis was handed a copy of one of his albums to autograph. After careful scrutiny he said, "I haven't seen that one yet." RCA Victor had just released Elvis' Golden Records, and today original copies command a very healthy price. The one shown here has never been opened and is still in the original plastic wrap with the $3.98 price tag!

Value of sealed lp: $300
Value if opened: $80

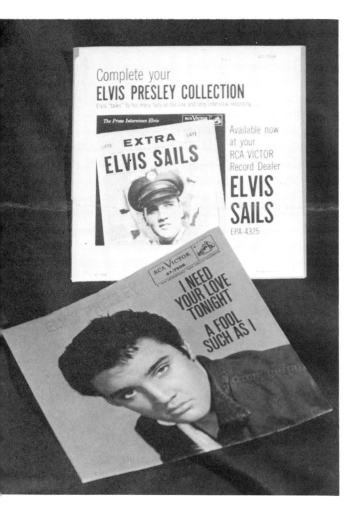

wood thought that Elvis would be perfect for the lead in *The James Dean Story*. Elvis, while obviously pleased by the comparison, had his own views on the subject: "I would never compare myself in any way to James Dean, because James Dean was a genius. I guess a lot of actors in Hollywood would like to have the ability James Dean had, but I would never compare myself to James Dean." Elvis was never asked to play the part of James Dean, and it is no small irony that all of these performers died so young.

While in Hollywood, Elvis recorded material for his second long-play album, to be titled simply *Elvis*. Already, after less than nine months in the national spotlight, his first name was all that was needed for instant recognition. He made his first historic appearance on the *Ed Sullivan Show* on September 9. Sullivan, recovering from an August auto accident, watched the show from his bed while the venerable actor Charles Laughton gamely carried on in his stead. Elvis' portion of the show was broadcast from Hollywood, and he blew away the mostly teen audience with three frantic but, for Elvis, somewhat restrained rockers and the title ballad from his new movie. The money that Colonel Parker had extracted from Sullivan paid off for both parties, as the ratings were the best ever for a variety show. Rock 'n' roll was taking the nation by storm, and the same week that Elvis appeared on the Sullivan show, his old Memphis singing buddy Johnny Burnette was a finalist on Ted Mack's national talent search. (He lost.) Burnette's bass player at this time was Elvis' longtime friend Johnny Black.

On September 26 Elvis took a brief respite from movie work to return to his hometown of Tupelo for a concert at the same annual fair that had been the site of his inauspicious debut in 1945. Tupelo turned out in force, and people came from all over the tri-state area to welcome back the hometown boy who had made good. The arena bleachers groaned under an estimated twelve thousand fans, and Elvis put on two fantastic forty-five-minute performances.

A week later he returned to Hollywood to put the finishing touches on *Love Me Tender*. A new ending was

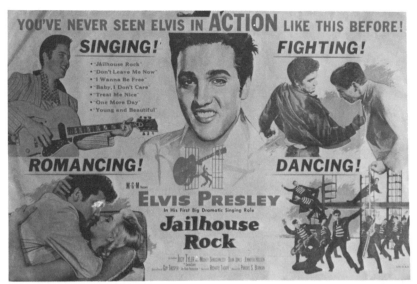

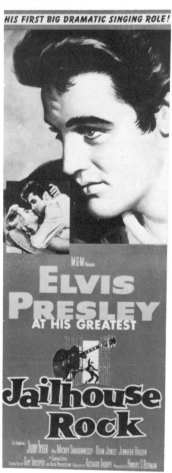

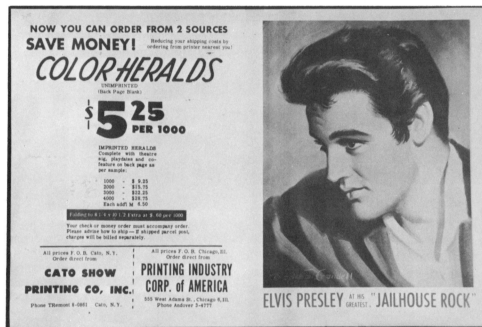

Loving You Recording Sessions

bootleg album

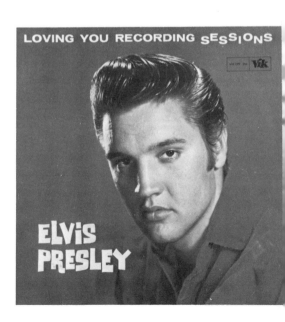

"Rock and Roll Stars" arcade cards

Packages of "Rock and Roll Stars" 4" × 5" cards were sold through arcade machines in packs of three for a nickel. Elvis' card is number 7 in a set of 66.

Value of Elvis' card: $8
Value, complete set of 66 cards: $150
Value of empty box: $150
Value of complete box: $450

Celluloid pins

These pins were manufactured by a different process from those with the likeness or message stamped directly on the metal. These buttons had the information printed on a piece of paper that was then covered by a disk of celluloid before being mounted on a metal back by a machine. Often used to reflect the differing opinions of Elvis during the mid-1950s, these allowed the wearers to proclaim just where they stood on this important issue.

Value of "I Like Elvis" celluloid pin: $15
Value of "I Hate Elvis" celluloid pin: $20
Value of "Elvis the Joik" celluloid pin: $45

produced after sneak previews found that audiences were disappointed when Elvis' character was killed at the end. After much consideration, the original ending was retained, but Elvis was "resurrected" singing a reprise of the title song over the end credits. Elvis was then off on another short round of personal appearances in Texas.

By October, the Elvis Presley Enterprises machine was in full swing, and Colonel Parker's instructions where Elvis played were explicit. No merchandise bearing the likeness or name of Elvis Presley could be sold at any of the concerts except by the "Elvis Presley Concession Department." This included even the area outside the actual coliseums and auditoriums where he appeared. In addition, Elvis' name and names similar to it could not be used for any endorsement on any merchandise or in any advertising other than for the show itself. The Colonel was hard at work in his campaign to close down the many entrepreneurs who were popping up across the country trying cash in on Elvis' popularity without being official licensees of the name.

In Waco Elvis drew 5,000 to the coliseum, which could have held 11,000, but at the Cotton Bowl in Dallas they had to put up chicken wire to keep the 26,500 ecstatic fans off the football field. Elvis entered the stadium riding in a convertible; and his show, according to one report, consisted of Elvis' "staggering, shuffle-footed dance" and "voodoo acrobatics." Caught in the conflict between the fans who dearly wanted to see him perform and the critics who were always ready with their poisoned pens, Elvis and the Colonel were content to allow the live performances (which could easily bring $5,000 or more each night) to become much less frequent as the demands from television and motion pictures crowded his schedule.

Besides the enormous amount of criticism that Elvis constantly received from the nation's newspapers and magazines, he remained the target of attacks of a more personal and violent nature. In late October, while stopping to gas up his Lincoln at a Memphis service station, he traded punches with two of the station's attendants when the always-present crowd of teenagers wouldn't disperse. Elvis was acquitted the next day, but not before the nation had added this incident to its growing list of grievances. A month later, while relaxing in the coffee shop of a Toledo hotel during a short midwestern tour, he and Scotty Moore ended up taking on a nineteen-year-old who was upset because his wife carried Elvis' photo instead of his in her wallet. The police reported that when they arrived, Elvis was pounding the man with his fists as the man tossed Moore over a railing. The arresting officer was quoted as saying, "Presley's no slouch. He was really working over the guy. He knows how to handle himself just fine." Again, it was found to be the other fellow's fault. Through it all, Elvis remained impassive: "I can take ridicule or slander, and I've been called names right in my face and everything, but I've had a few guys that have tried to take a swing at me, and naturally I can't just stand there."

On October 28 Elvis made his second guest shot on the Sullivan show, this time performing from the show's regular studios in New York. His performance was more polished than it had been a month earlier, and Sullivan wisely spread Elvis' four songs over three separate appearances during the hour-long broadcast. Upon returning to Memphis, Elvis welcomed Natalie Wood for a visit. This was his first "Hollywood romance," if one doesn't count his infatuation with co-star Debra Paget, which went nowhere. Wood stayed in Memphis for a few days and then returned to the West Coast. Although the two remained friends, she would never again date Elvis.

Love Me Tender premiered on November 16, to the anticipated reaction: the critics were sour and the fans were ecstatic. The furor boosted ticket sales, and by the end of the month the movie was the second most popular film in release.

On December 4, history was made when Elvis dropped by the studios at Sun Records just in time to catch the end of a Carl Perkins session that featured the young Jerry Lee Lewis on piano. For the next two hours this trio, later augmented by Johnny Cash, jammed on gospel and rock 'n' roll songs, in what became known as the legendary "Million Dollar Quartet." A portion of this session was tape-recorded by Sam Phillips, but it was kept under wraps until 1978, when a scant thirty minutes' worth appeared on a bootleg album in America before receiving an "authorized" release in England.

On December 15, wearing a green coat, blue pants, a white shirt and tie, white shoes with blue soles, and a silk scarf, Elvis played one last time for *Louisiana Hayride*, as a benefit for the YMCA. As Elvis closed his acrobatic performance, rocking wildly through "Hound Dog," the pandemonium inside the youth building of the Shreveport fairgrounds reached a flash point. After each verse of the song, the noise of the nine thousand fans washed across the stage with the sound of gigantic waves crashing on a rocky shore. One reviewer noted, "It was beside the point that the gyrating, rotary troubador was seldom if ever heard by an audience screaming like Zulus every time he moved a muscle. The Pelvis applies more 'Body English' to a song than any baseball pitcher and he has more movements than a well-oiled Swiss watch." It was a triumphant conclusion to Elvis' two-year association with the show that had been the first to recognize his talents.

The *Wall Street Journal* put the icing on Elvis' 1956 cake by reporting that merchandise licensed by Elvis Presley Enterprises had grossed $22 million in just a few months. Included in the figures were sales of 72,000 pairs of black "Elvis" jeans, 7,200 pairs of "Elvis" tennis

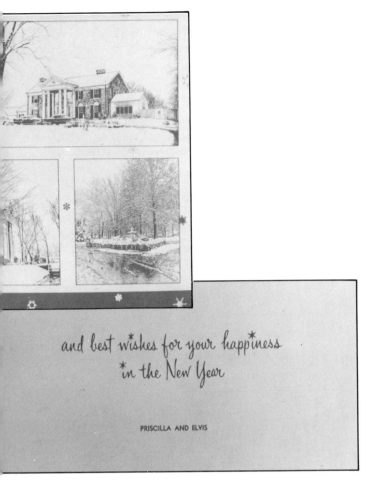

and best wishes for your happiness in the New Year

PRISCILLA AND ELVIS

Personal Christmas cards from Elvis

Being on Elvis' private Christmas card list was an honor few people ever had. The cards came in two basic varieties: those designed specifically for Elvis and commercially available cards. The first variety was usually signed by Elvis, while the commercial cards had the name Elvis, the Presleys, Elvis and family, or Elvis and Priscilla stamped inside the card. Unfortunately, most of the signed Christmas cards were not actually autographed by Elvis. This task was left up to the secretaries in either Elvis' Graceland office or the Colonel's office in Madison, Tennessee.

Value: signed by Elvis: $250
Value, if signed by secretary: $100
Value, if printed only: $50

shoes, and an astonishing 350,000 charm bracelets bearing Elvis' likeness.

Elvis made his third and final appearance on the *Ed Sullivan Show* on January 6. It was his longest television appearance to date—seven songs in three separate entrances. In response to his October performance, when he had wildly danced around the stage, Elvis was filmed "above the waist" when it appeared as though his left knee might break into a wiggle.

At the end of the show, Sullivan was obsequious in his praise of Elvis' personality and manners. Sullivan began, "I want to say to Elvis Presley and the country that this is a real decent, fine boy. We've never had a pleasanter experience on our show with a big name than we've had with you. You're thoroughly all right." The speech sounds as though it came at the prompting of Colonel Parker, who was still exacting his pound of flesh for Sullivan's earlier anti-Elvis comments.

Less than a week later Elvis journeyed to Hollywood to start his second feature film, originally titled *Lonesome Cowboy* and later changed to *Loving You,* after the title of one of the seven songs that Elvis sings the picture. This was the first movie made under the three-picture deal with Hal Wallis and Paramount Pictures. Unlike *Love Me Tender,* this film was tailor-made for Elvis' talents, and the story line presented several seemingly autobiographical scenes that helped to contribute to his growing legend. The songs in *Loving You* were a fine mixture of up-tempo rock 'n' roll and melodic ballads. Unlike *Love Me Tender, Loving You* was photographed in color, and Elvis was even allowed to have his parents appear in the audience as part the climactic final scene. Work on *Loving You* took all of the next two months, after which Elvis and his parents returned to Memphis. There they went house-hunting.

Their home on Audubon had become unbearably inadequate. After only the briefest of tours through an eighteen-year-old house in south Memphis, Elvis bought the house that the previous owner had named Graceland. It was the biggest gift Elvis ever bought for his mother. Later Elvis said, "It's funny. She never really wanted anything . . . anything fancy. She just stayed the same all through the whole thing." Graceland was a two-story house with thirteen rooms sitting splendidly atop a small hill overlooking almost fourteen acres of land. The asking price for the mansion was $100,000 and the Colonel's offer of $40,000 was rejected out of hand. Parker was anxious to sell Presley's Audubon Park home, as well as another property Elvis owned on Union Avenue, so he suggested to Graceland's owner, Mrs. Thomas Moore, that she take those two properties, valued at approximately $60,000, plus the $40,000 in cash. The recently divorced Mrs. Moore wanted a smaller home, and when she found out that the Union Avenue house was across from the Lindenwood Church, which she attended, the deal was struck. She moved to Union Avenue and Elvis moved to Graceland.

With the addition of a head-high stone fence and an imposing front gate with Elvis' likeness in wrought iron, Elvis was finally able to settle in Memphis with a reasonable degree of privacy, after a year of constant harassment by fans and neighbors. "When I first bought the mansion it was like living in the country. There was nothing around my place but a few cotton and sugar cane plantations." Right away, Elvis saw that the house had possibilities. "I got a lot of good decorating ideas for Graceland. I'm always fixing and repairing around the house. I like to do things first class, too. I had one wall knocked out of the first floor of the house to enlarge the room. Then I got a wonderful idea to make the ceiling of my bedroom all velvet. I like bright colors like orange, red, and yellow. They look real nice."

One morning, not long after moving into Graceland, Elvis was treated to some free landscaping. "I looked out my bedroom window on the second floor facing the highway and spotted a man picking up leaves outside the

Medallion

The "Lady-In-Waiting" medallion was a fan club giveaway issued while Elvis was in the army.

Value: $30

Extended plays

Many of Elvis' songs were issued on extended play as well as long play albums. In some cases, this was the only source for tunes sung in his early movies. Consequently, these 7-inch records are among the most highly collected of all Elvis' releases. The ones shown here are all unopened, mint copies. There were a total of twenty-three 45 rpm and two 33 ⅓ rpm EP records available from 1956 through the late 1960s.

Most EPs, value if opened: $50–$75
Value if sealed: $200
Value of Elvis Sails, opened: $100
Value if sealed: $300

The Elvis Presley Story

This was the first book to be published about Elvis Presley, and it made its appearance about the same time that Elvis was landing at McGuire Air Force Base. It was the first time in eighteen months that Elvis had set foot inside the United States. This paperback consisted of a series of articles that had first appeared in the magazine Movieland and TV Time *starting in 1957. The articles are actually quite insightful not only about Elvis but about the times in which he made his biggest impact. Dick Clark even gets into the act by writing an introduction. The full-color photo on the back cover features a wonderful portrait of Elvis from 1956, and it is worth the steep collector's price all by itself.*

Value: $55

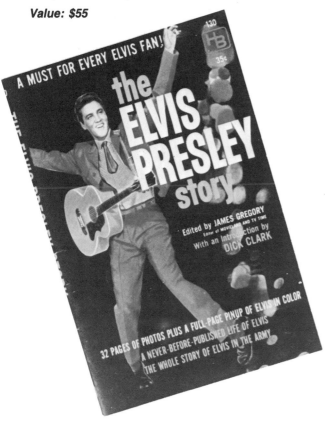

stone fence and stuffing them in a valise. I told my manager, Colonel Tom Parker, and he went out to check on things. He asked the man what he was doing with the leaves, and the man said he'd got a big thing going up in Buffalo, New York, selling the leaves for souvenirs. He was selling them for ten dollars apiece. The Colonel admired the man's ingenuity so much he let him go. The fella kept right on picking up the leaves, just the choice ones, and putting them in his bag. The Colonel got to thinking about the 'leaf gimmick,' as he called it, and he contacted the local Memphis radio stations to come over and rake up ten or twelve thousand leaves, to offer them as prizes in various contests." The leaves taken by the man from Buffalo were now worthless.

In late March Elvis took off on another nine-day tour of the upper Midwest, which brought in a total of $300,000. At Colonel Parker's insistence, Elvis was sporting a new wardrobe commensurate with the title of "king of rock 'n' roll," an honor bestowed upon him by the press and his fans. He appeared onstage in a shimmering gold dinner jacket, and less often in matching trousers, which were guaranteed to drive the already boisterous crowd absolutely frantic. The inside of the suit was made from a very soft leather, while the outside was woven from spun-gold thread that glistened under the stage lights. Elvis hated to perform in the outfit because, with the tremendous amount of energy he expended onstage, the suit was stifling, but the Colonel knew how to generate the headlines, so for most of the year the jacket, at least, stayed a part of the act.

In 1957 Elvis picked up three new aides to assist and befriend him while on the road or back in Memphis. Elvis had first met Marty Lacker, who was now a Memphis deejay, in high school. Lamar Fike from Texas was first spotted hanging around the front gate of the house on Audubon. Weighing nearly three hundred pounds, he was not easily overlooked. Soon he had climbed the low wall, weaseled his way inside the house, and ingratiated himself with Elvis. Alan Fortas was two years younger than Elvis and had been an all-Memphis halfback in high school whom Elvis admired. He had dropped out of Vanderbilt when George Klein brought him by Elvis' home one day, and soon, like the other two new members of the growing entourage, he just stayed.

In late April Elvis, his buddies, and a couple of cousins caught the train from Memphis to Hollywood so he could commence production on his third motion picture in eight months: *Jailhouse Rock* for M-G-M. Everything was going smoothly until Elvis inhaled a cosmetic tooth cap while filming a dance sequence, and had to be hospitalized overnight. The cap was easily removed from his right lung with long forceps, and no permanent harm was done.

RCA Victor released the single of "Loving You" coupled with another song from the movie, "Teddy Bear," and the record immediately sold 1.25 million copies, to become Elvis' eighth gold record. Meanwhile, Elvis was taking a much-needed three-week break in Memphis. He was introduced to a beautiful blond TV personality and movie hopeful, Anita Wood. She quickly became his Memphis steady, a position she held for five years. For their first date, on July 8, the couple attended a late-night sneak preview of *Loving You* just prior to its national release. Critics were a bit more merciful in their remarks on Elvis' acting ability this time, although the film was still generally panned. In the meantime, Elvis and Anita retreated to the safety of the nightlife Elvis most loved. They spent most evenings either at the Rainbow roller skating rink or at the Fairgrounds Amusement Park. At the fairgrounds, Elvis would ride the roller coaster repeatedly while standing up in a death-defying pose. Or he and the guys would chose up sides and play "war" with the electric dodge-'em cars. Elvis became so infatuated with the dodge-'ems that he decided to have his own personal track constructed behind Graceland. That idea was quashed after he was told that the track would cost nearly as much as he had paid for the house.

Elvis also went on a clothes-buying spree that cost him his new three-wheel car. "I've had a German Messerschmitt, a little car, and there's this guy [Bernard Lansky] there in town that's been wanting that Messerschmitt for the past year. He owns a clothing store [Lansky Brothers], one of the top clothing stores in Memphis. So I went up there and told him, I said, 'You've been wanting this car so bad, I want a deal with you. You let me pick out all the clothes I want.' So I was there for about two hours and a half, and the store was a wreck when I left."

Anita Wood was left at the Memphis railroad station as Elvis took the train for his first swing through the Pacific Northwest, on a circuit that covered Spokane, Vancouver, Tacoma, Seattle, and Portland. Elvis returned to Hollywood in early September, not to start a new movie, but to record enough songs to fill up a forthcoming Christmas album. The infrequency of Elvis' short tours and the distances now involved in traveling to his recording sessions added fuel to a problem with his two longtime backing musicians, Scotty Moore and Bill Black, that had been smoldering for some time. Both men were being paid only $100 a week during the long lulls and felt that they needed room to pursue other interests. So, in a move that caught Elvis off guard, they announced that they were retiring from the act. Black stayed in Memphis and soon formed Bill Black's Combo, which had a successful string of instrumental hits starting in 1959 with "Smokie." Moore became a record producer and had a hit, also in 1959, with "Tragedy" by Thomas

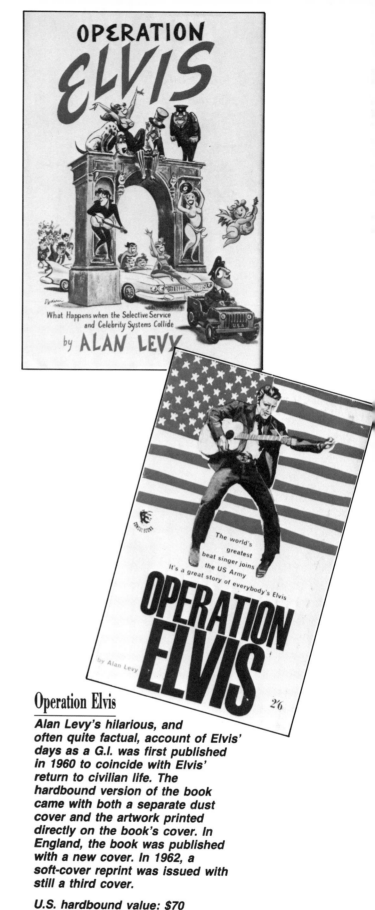

Operation Elvis

Alan Levy's hilarious, and often quite factual, account of Elvis' days as a G.I. was first published in 1960 to coincide with Elvis' return to civilian life. The hardbound version of the book came with both a separate dust cover and the artwork printed directly on the book's cover. In England, the book was published with a new cover. In 1962, a soft-cover reprint was issued with still a third cover.

U.S. hardbound value: $70
U.K. hardbound value: $55
U.K. paperback value: $35

Wayne (Perkins) on Memphis' Fernwood label before moving to Nashville, where he continued to be successful with his own studio. When called upon, Moore continued to record with Elvis until 1969.

On September 27 Elvis made another appearance at the annual fair in Tupelo. Newshounds noticed that he arrived with Anita Wood, so they were lying in wait at the press conference just before the show. Asked if he was engaged, Elvis looked shocked. "Nowhere near it! I just haven't found the right girl yet." The show was a complete success, filling the Tupelo fairgrounds arena to capacity with ten thousand screaming fans. Elvis performed his portion of the show wearing the gold lamé jacket and navy blue pants. The proceeds from his sold-out performance were donated to the city, which had plans to erect an Elvis Presley Youth Recreation Center, to include a meeting hall and swimming pool on the hill next to the small house in which he had been born. Elvis would continue to donate money to the project throughout the next fourteen years. Since 1971, when the complex was finally completed, it has been one of Tupelo's most-used facilities.

Jailhouse Rock was released in October, and both the movie and the title song did outstandingly well. The movie even generated some critical praise for Elvis' improvement as an actor. Elvis returned to California for

The Jailhouse Rock Sessions bootleg album

This 1983 European release has one of the nicest covers to grace any Elvis LP, and it captures the dynamics of the movie much better than the EP released by RCA Victor. Not all the cuts come from the movie, but most of the songs are from the same time period. These come from original studio tapes and retain all the fidelity of a commercial record. Two separate complete takes are offered of the title song as well as "Young and Beautiful" and "Don't Leave Me Now." Three additional songs not from the film include the alternate take of "Old Shep" and completely different versions of "I Beg of You" and "Your Cheatin' Heart." For all these reasons, this is one of the most desirable bootlegs ever made.

Value: $100

concerts in San Francisco, Oakland, and Los Angeles that brought in nearly $100,000 for five shows. In Los Angeles his sizzling style of entertaining once again ran afoul of the courts. After a particularly scorching performance, the police were ordered to film the next night's show to ascertain if he'd broken any laws against lewd behavior. As in the other attempts to tone Elvis down, nothing came of these actions.

A week later he sailed to Honolulu, where he was booked for a November 10 matinee, followed the next day by a show at Pearl Harbor. Elvis fell in love with the Hawaiian life style during his brief visit, and he would return many times, not just for his films and concerts, but also to escape the increasing pressures of his popularity.

Elvis' Christmas Album premiered in mid-November. It was an elaborate package featuring a full-size booklet containing eight color portraits of Elvis inside a fold-out cover. Show business had never seen the likes of the public outcry it generated. The furor seemed to be a throwback to the hubbub of the summer of 1956. Across the country, many deejays felt it was in bad taste that Elvis would even be allowed to issue an album containing Christmas and religious songs. In Los Angeles, Dick Whittinghill spoke for many when he said, "It's like having Tempest Storm [a noted striptease dancer] give Christmas presents to my kids!" Most of the anger seemed to be misplaced, as Elvis actually sang the more sedate carols and hymns with due reverence and "cut loose" only on a few of the bluesier numbers, including "Blue

Just before Elvis boarded the troop train, many of the people who had gathered at his rented home in Killeen posed for this photo. Seen left to right: unknown fan club member from Chicago, Gene Smith (Elvis' first cousin), Dotty Ayres (president of Memphis chapter of the Elvis Presley Fan Club), Arlene Tillman (from Chicago), Earl Greenwood (Elvis' cousin), Eddie Fadal, Elvis, Vernon, Junior Smith (Elvis' cousin), Lamar Fike, Red West, unknown fan.

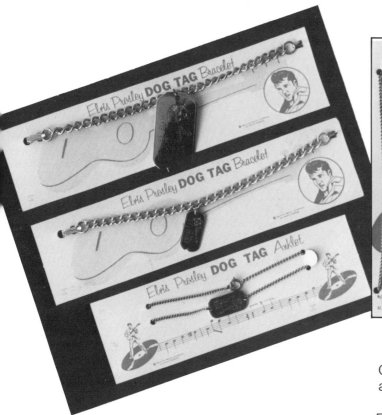

Dog tag jewelry

Elvis was inducted into the Army on March 24, 1958. It was a sad day for all of America's teenagers, and to help them remember Elvis while he was in Germany serving his country, EPE issued jewelry reproductions of Elvis' dog tags complete with his I.D. number, 55310761. All the items carry the EPE 1956 copyright even though they were obviously not issued until 1958. Several were reissued in 1977. Originals have a chrome finish over a brass base, while the newer versions are tinted gold. A few years back, several boxes of the 1958 dog tag jewlery were discovered, and consequently, the current market price for these items is somewhat deflated. The most valuable piece continues to be the sweater holder. The value of all the items is increased if it is on the original display card.

Dog tag necklace on card value: $25
Dog tag key chain value: $45
Man's dog tag bracelet value: $20
Woman's dog tag bracelet value: $20
Dog tag ankle bracelet value: $40
Dog tag sweater clip value: $90

Christmas" and "Santa Claus Is Back in Town." The album immediately rode the fuss to the top of the charts.

Throughout 1957, the military draft had hung over Elvis' head. As early as January of that year, following his required physical exam and his subsequent classification as 1-A, rumors had circulated that Elvis was about to enter the army. The fateful day arrived on December 19, when the chairman of the Memphis draft board hand-delivered Elvis' induction notice. He was ordered to report in thirty days to start a two-year hitch in the army. Because preproduction work had already begun on Elvis' next movie, *King Creole,* a two-month delay was requested and granted. That created a new round of accusations, with many critics contending that Elvis was being coddled. In fact, requests for a delay in reporting were common, occurring most frequently among farm kids, and Elvis certainly had cause. As a sidelight to Elvis' draft notice, one article reported that the U.S. Government would be losing an estimated million dollars or more in taxes on Elvis' lost salary while he was serving his country. Elvis shrugged it off and closed the year with a special New Year's Eve concert in St. Louis.

With the U.S. Army momentarily at bay, Elvis caught the train to Hollywood on January 13 to start work on *King Creole* for Paramount Pictures. After Elvis had recorded the musical soundtrack, the moviemakers shifted their base of operations to New Orleans in early February. This was Elvis' first location trip for a movie outside of the immediate Los Angeles area, and filming continued in and around the Crescent City into March. After his release from the movie, Elvis and his entourage, which now numbered about a dozen, headed for home aboard the train from Los Angeles. Arriving in Dallas, and impatient with the slow progress of the railroad trip, they disembarked, and Elvis rented a fleet of Cadillacs for the rest of the ride back home. There Elvis treated his friends and relatives to six straight nights at the Rainbow Lake roller skating rink, where Red West introduced Elvis to his younger cousin Delbert, whom everyone called Sonny. It would be a few years yet, but Sonny would become another of Elvis' bodyguards. Momentarily at ease, Elvis and his buddies played "snap the whip" at the roller rink with such enthusiasm that sprains and bruises were a matter of course.

On the morning of March 24 Elvis reported for induction at the Memphis draft board, bringing nothing more than his shaving kit. The one officer whom the army had not counted on was Colonel Parker, who was loaded down with a 16 mm movie camera and a box of eight-by-ten glossies of Elvis, which he handed out to fans, soldiers, and passers-by alike. The Colonel led a phalanx of dozens of reporters and photographers, who dutifully reported Elvis' every move during the daylong round of physical and mental tests. In a fit of despair, Lamar Fike even attempted to enlist, but his weight prevented any serious consideration of this. Then it was time for Elvis to raise his right hand and be sworn into the U.S. Army. In the afternoon, obviously weary from the nonstop attention, Elvis had time for a brief private good-bye to his mother and father before he shook hands with all the guys from the entourage and kissed Anita Wood and half a dozen female relatives and fans good-bye. Finally he joined the dozen other inductees aboard an army bus for Fort Chaffee, Arkansas. It was after midnight when they arrived.

At five-ten the next morning, Elvis was awakened by reveille, starting his first full day as a soldier. Guards had been posted at Elvis' barracks to ensure that no unauthorized personnel sneaked in, including Colonel Parker and the press corps, which had followed Elvis so as not to miss even the smallest detail of his continued army induction. Colonel Parker commented that he was on hand "to look after the boy . . . see that he gets everything he needs." The event that received the most attention was, of course, that afternoon's GI haircut. Elvis' famed locks fell unceremoniously to the floor as the civilian barber clipped merrily along, reducing the king's mane to a regulation "butch" in barely a minute. Elvis tried to make light of his new look, commenting, "Hair today, gone tomorrow," but he was so shook up that he got out of the barber's chair without paying the sixty-five-cent fee. During the next few hectic days Elvis was issued his uniform, received various inoculations at the dispensary, and took aptitude tests. On the morning of March 28 he and a busload of other recruits left Fort Chaffee en route to Fort Hood, Texas, where they would begin their eight weeks of basic training. After Elvis arrived on base, the

1950s English Magazines

The Amazing Elvis Presley *and* **Elvis Presley And . . .** *are two examples of the small 5″ × 7″ magazines on Elvis available in Great Britain in the late 1950s. Each is 64 pages long, and both are filled with photos and stories.* **Elvis Presley And . . .** *also has a 24-page illustrated story, "A Letter to Elvis," in romance-comics style.*

The Amazing Elvis Presley 1958 British magazine value: $30
Elvis Presley And . . . 1959 British magazine value: $30

Flasher buttons

Certain to catch the eye, this is the original 1956 flasher button authorized by EPE and apparently issued at the same time that **Love Me Tender** *premiered. The photo moves from a black-white-and-blue closeup of Elvis to a full-length shot of him playing the guitar. It is 2½ inches in diameter and comes with either a dark blue or bright red back. The originals were manufactured by Pictorial Productions, Inc., and say so on the back. Shortly after issuing the three-color pin, Pictorial issued the same pin in black and white only. The full-color flasher buttons were issued right after the original black-and-white buttons, using the same closeup photo, but a different full pose, and carrying the Pictorial Productions logo. Pictorial Productions soon changed its name to Vari-Vue, and later pins carry the Vari-Vue manufacturing marking. A third pin style was distributed under the Vari-Vue logo only and features two full-length poses of Elvis in color. These apparently received very limited distribution.*

Flasher key chains

Along with the flasher buttons, there were also flasher key chains manufactured in two styles in 1956, a rectangle and a disk. They bear no identifying markings, leaving open the possibility that these key chains were bootlegged, using the original artwork from Pictorial.

Value: $18

Value of original Pictorial three-color "Love Me Tender" flasher button: $25
Value of Pictorial black-and-white "Love Me Tender" flasher button: $8
Value of four-color Pictorial flasher button with closeup pose: $15
Value of four-color Vari-Vue flasher button with closeup pose: $8
Value of four-color Vari-Vue flasher button with two full poses: $15

Gold suit photo

This bright, full-color 8″ × 10″ of Elvis dressed head to toe in his gold lame suit was issued by EPE in 1957 while Elvis was touring the Midwest. The photo was sold on tours, and then after Elvis stopped performing live, the photo was part of many Elvis promotions until the stock was depleted. The photo came in two slightly different styles, with either a blue or a pink border.

Value: $25

Elvis' Christmas Album

The most highly sought after of all Elvis' regular commercial releases has to be the 1957 Christmas album. With its album-sized booklet containing eight pages of color portraits, it reportedly sold 100,000 copies. Today they are very scarce, especially in excellent condition. For Christmas 1985, RCA Victor re-released the album with a similar cover. With the original gold foil gift sticker, the album doubles in price.

Value of original: $150
Value of reissue: $10

Kanabe piano

This Kanabe piano originally sat in the Ellis Civic Auditorium in Memphis. Elvis learned to play the piano on this instrument. When Elvis purchased Graceland, he arranged to buy a new piano for the auditorium and had the Kanabe moved to his new home. He had the original mahogany finish changed to white with gold trim. This piano stood in Graceland for twelve years.

Value: $500,000

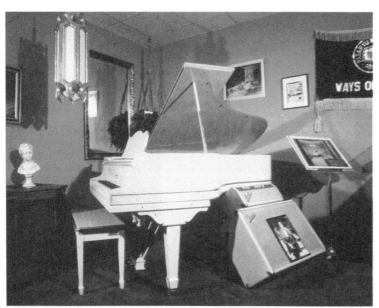

Guitars

Elvis Presley is credited with starting a boom in guitar sales that reached astronomical proportions by 1957. The Emenee Music Company manufactured several different guitars bearing Elvis' likeness. The "Teddy Bear" and the "Hound Dog" models originally retailed for about $12 and came in both four- and six-string models. The "Love Me Tender" guitar, sold exclusively through Sears, Roebuck and Company stores and catalogs, was a more elaborate instrument, featuring a carrying case, small songbook, and an automatic chord player.

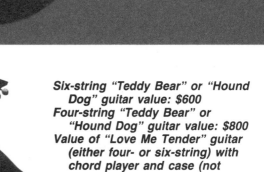

Six-string "Teddy Bear" or "Hound Dog" guitar value: $600
Four-string "Teddy Bear" or "Hound Dog" guitar value: $800
Value of "Love Me Tender" guitar (either four- or six-string) with chord player and case (not pictured): $1,200

A Date With Elvis album

To tide loyal Elvis fans over while Elvis was in Germany, RCA Victor released two collections of recordings that had originally appeared on extended plays on the Sun label. A Date with Elvis featured a 1960 calendar on the back cover with the date of Elvis' discharge, March 24, circled in red. As it turned out, Elvis was actually released on March 5, 1960, because of some unused leave time.

Value, with sticker: $125

1958 Christmas postcard value: $25

1960 Christmas postcard value: $10

Early 1960s Christmas postcard value: $20

1960s Christmas postcard value: $10

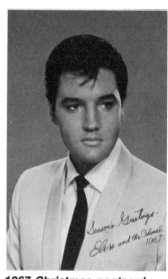

1967 Christmas postcard value: $8

1966 Christmas postcard value: $15

1971 Christmas postcard value: $20

1970s Christmas postcard value: $12

1975 Christmas postcard value: $10

Christmas postcards

These Christmas postcards should not be confused with the greeting cards sent out personally by Elvis or the Colonel. Those cards are extremely rare and very coveted by those fortunate enough to be on either man's holiday mailing list. The postcards pictured here were printed up by the thousands at Colonel Parker's request to be sent to members of the Elvis Presley Fan Club, lesser business associates and acquaintances, members of the press, and anyone else on the Colonel's long list. In the 1960s and 1970s several of these postcards were included in Elvis' albums and tapes as a bonus. Most of the cards were standard size postcards (3½" × 5½"), with room on the back for messages. The most valuable are the two issued while Elvis was in Germany, as well as the ones from the early 1960s. The early cards are also often slightly larger than the standard postal variety.

army put a halt to the circus atmosphere that the press had created, and Elvis was allowed to adjust to army life in relative anonymity.

Eddie Fadal, the Dallas deejay, had returned to his hometown of Waco by the time Elvis arrived at Fort Hood. "I read in the paper where he would be here on a certain day, so I thought I would go to Fort Hood and see if he remembered me. I went through a lot of red tape to get to see him. The gate guard wanted to know what I wanted to do. 'I want to see Elvis Presley.' He looked at me like I'd flipped my lid. 'Oh yeah? So does everybody want to see Elvis ' 'Yeah, but I know him.' "Oh yeah? So does everybody know him!' " Fadal finally got a pass to enter the base and ultimately got to see Elvis. "I told him if he wanted complete privacy in a homelike atmosphere he was welcome to come to our home on the weekend or anytime he could get out. He said, 'I guarantee you I'll do it. I have to stay on the base for two weeks.' So I thought to myself at the time, 'Yeah, he's saying that, but I wonder if he'll come.' I didn't really believe he would. Sure enough, in two weeks my phone rang. He was coming into Waco, and he called on his mobile phone. I told him to meet me at the circle." Fadal finally caught up with Elvis in a small drugstore, buying a tube of Clearasil. Elvis wasn't recognized by the clerk because he was in uniform, with his cap bill pulled down. "From then on it was every weekend he would come down. Sometimes we would go to Dallas, to Ausin, Fort Worth, but he'd always come through here and pick me up."

While Elvis was going through basic training, his latest album, *Elvis' Golden Records*, was not selling particularly well, as the LP put his first twelve hit singles into one package and most of his fans already owned the

Value of 1959 Christmas postcard with message on back: $30
Value of 1959 Christmas postcard without message on back: $20

TV Guide

The TV Guide *cover was the first time Elvis appeared on a magazine that was related neither to music nor to movies. The week was September 8–14, 1956, and the reason Elvis was featured was his much ballyhooed first appearance on* The Ed Sullivan Show *on Sunday, September 9. The magazine ran the first of a three-part interview with Elvis, with the succeeding parts appearing in the issues for September 22–28 and September 29–October 5, 1956.*

Value of TV Guide *cover issue: $50*
Value of next 2 issues: $35 each

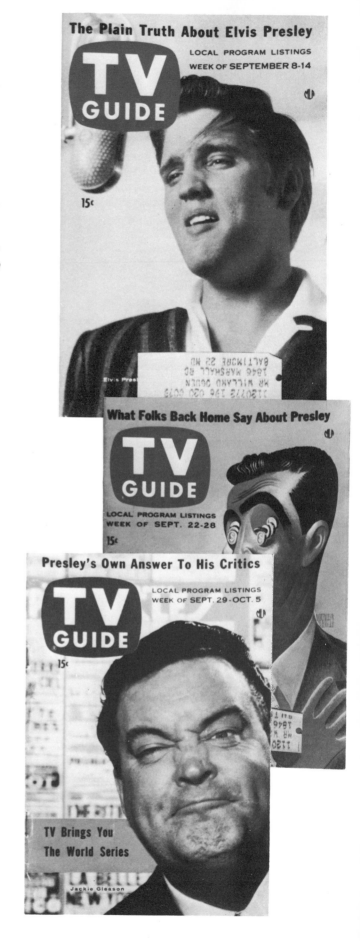

singles. At Fort Hood, Elvis, because of his ROTC training in high school, was appointed squad leader for a fourteen-mile trek and weeklong campout. He was trying to be the best soldier possible and was well liked by most of his fellow GIs as well as his instructors. Away from the spotlight, Elvis, to the amazement of many, turned out to be just a "good ole boy" from Tennessee. According to Elvis, "I never griped. If I didn't like something, nobody knew excepting me. If I'd been what they thought, I'd never have got what was coming to me [in the way of promotions]. I've been treated no better nor any worse than any of the boys, and that's the way I wanted it, because I have to live with the other boys."

Many weekends, Elvis would round up a bunch of buddies, including Eddie Fadal, and they'd set off to see the closest rhythm and blues show. Fadal remembers: "We attended concerts in Dallas . . . Austin. There was this bunch of black artists that he loved. We went backstage at one in Temple, and we stood in the wings. As each entertainer was performing onstage and they'd look in the wings and see him they'd almost crack up. They couldn't imagine Elvis Presley there. The next group would be announced and they didn't want to go out. They were all surrounding Elvis in the wings. Finally the audience found out he was back there, and that's when we had to pull a quick exit. He never got to see a full concert."

Anita Wood was staying near Fort Hood to be with Elvis, and she frequently joined Elvis and his pals on their excursions. Again, Eddie Fadal looks back: "That's the girl Elvis always told us he would marry. On the way back from one of our trips one day we stopped at a service station. Elvis wouldn't stop at the established stations like Esso or Texaco. He'd see a little run-down guy with just one pump and a little hut of a service station and that's where he'd stop. He liked to patronize those people. At this particular time, Anita had to go to the restroom and

Hound Dog

EPE's "You Ain't Nothin' but a Hound Dog" hound dog was a marketing natural. The 10" stuffed toy originally retailed for $2.98 to $3.98.

Value: $150

the only restroom was an outhouse way out in the field. So she made her way through the field to this restroom, and while she was gone Elvis was just dying laughing. He had his foot on the front bumper of his car and just laughing, bending over double that Anita had to go to this outhouse. But while she was gone he said, 'I want to tell you guys. I never told anybody else. When old 'E' gets ready to get married it's going to be to Anita Wood. Y'all keep that under your hat. That's the girl I'm going to marry.' " Fadal reflects, "She would have made a wonderful wife."

On June 1 Elvis was granted a two-week leave, signifying the end of his basic training. He hopped into his convertible Cadillac with Anita Wood, who had been visiting Elvis, and they were off to Memphis for one last round of roller skating or midnight movies—including a sneak preview of *King Creole*. Grudgingly, the critics gave *King Creole* the best reviews of any of his young career, and there were some in Hollywood who thought that Elvis was on the verge of becoming a fine actor after all. Other critics continued to complain about Elvis' music. S. A. Desick of the *Los Angeles Examiner* spoke for many when he wrote, "With such a profusion of music, I wonder whether Elvis' partisans will notice that he has improved somewhat as an actor."

On June 10 Elvis traveled to Nashville for what would be his final recording session for the next twenty months. He recorded only five numbers, which would barely yield two singles—hardly enough to keep an active singing career alive for a year and a half as the Frankies, Bobbys, and Fabians looked hungrily at his rock 'n' roll crown. The

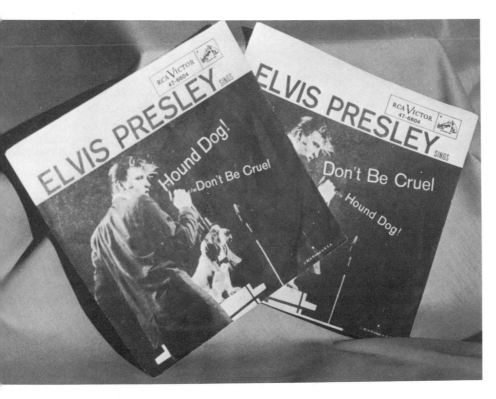

"Hound Dog"/"Don't Be Cruel" picture sleeves

Without question, the most anxiously awaited of all Elvis' single releases had to be "Hound Dog." RCA Victor issued "Hound Dog" in July with a picture sleeve (Elvis' first) that promoted what everyone figured would be the hit. However, the flip side, "Don't Be Cruel," also took off and ultimately became the more requested song, so RCA Victor also issued picture sleeves plugging that song.

Value of "Hound Dog" picture sleeve only: $50
Value of "Don't Be Cruel" picture sleeve only: $65
Value of "Hound Dog"/"Don't Be Cruel" 45 rpm record: $20

Colonel was going to have to hustle to keep Elvis' name in front of the public.

Upon his return to Fort Hood, Elvis was assigned to receive fourteen weeks of advanced training as an armor crewman (tank specialist). Elvis had been eligible for a spot in the Special Services as an entertainer, but Colonel Parker must have nearly passed out at the thought of his million-dollar entertainer singing for army pay.

Elvis soon arranged to live off base with his parents, first in a mobile home near the base, which immediately proved unsatisfactory, then in a house in the neighboring town of Killeen, rented from an attorney. Here he could relax after a day of army life as well as entertain a houseful of soldiers, Memphis buddies, and relatives. Eddie Fadal recalls one weekend when Elvis had a bunch of people down from Memphis to visit him and he took everyone to Fort Worth to stay at a luxury motel. He needed to get away from the base and from his fans, but his plans went a little astray. "There was a beauticians' convention there [at the motel] the next day after we got there, and they just went wild over him. He was very nice about it. He stayed out by the pool and talked to every one of them, and all of these beauticians were around him 'oohing' and 'ahing' and asking him questions. He fielded every one of the questions." Other times, Elvis and Anita would slip away quietly to Waco to visit with Eddie Fadal's family for an evening or a weekend. Fadal's house in Waco became a second home for Elvis and his parents at this time.

As the weeks passed, it became apparent to everyone that Gladys' health had taken a dramatic slide. She had never been a glamorous woman, and after Elvis gained fame, she became acutely aware of her looks. Overweight for many years, she had been a longtime user of diet pills, which were now rapidly destroying her. Eddie Fadal saw her frequently, and remembers, "It came about pretty quick. I didn't know that she was sick before it all happened. They had never said that she was sick. I knew she was fat and bloated. I could see that. She always wore these straight housecoats. Her eyes were swollen and you could see that." When asked about the recurring rumor that Gladys was an alcoholic, Fadal says, "I don't drink and I would have smelled it immediately, beer or liquor. I never did smell it on her—never did see her drink."

In early August Elvis finally persuaded Gladys to visit a doctor in nearby Temple. A few days later, at the doctor's insistence, Gladys and Vernon returned to Memphis, and she was admitted to Methodist Hospital for tests. It was determined that she had acute hepatitis. Elvis requested an emergency leave so that he could visit her, but permission was denied for two days, as her condition worsened. On August 12, at the request of Gladys' doctors, the army finally consented to grant the

Louisiana Hayride bootleg album

Elvis got his first big break when the Louisiana Hayride *radio show welcomed him. Elvis had been rebuffed only two weeks before by the* Hayride's *biggest competition, Nashville's* Grand Ole Opry. *The* Hayride *had a younger audience, and Elvis met with immediate acceptance. The material on this 1985 LP from*

Oil Painting of Elvis

This 1956 study of Elvis is by Loxi Sibley, the artist who painted the portraits sold on Elvis' last tours. One of her studies hangs in Graceland's trophy room, and another is the familiar portrait hanging behind Elvis' last sweetheart, Ginger Alden, when she was interviewed by the press after Elvis died.

Value: $2,500

Europe was first broadcast as part of a tribute to Elvis, and since the bootlegger taped it off the air, it sounds a little like listening to a short-wave radio broadcast. That aside, this is a historically important album. In addition to wonderful music, there are a couple of interviews with Elvis that appear here for the first time.

Value: $30

"Stuck on You" Living Stereo 45

Elvis' first release after serving in the Army was the single "Stuck on You"/"Fame and Fortune." While he was away from the recording scene, RCA switched over to the new stereo sound. As a promotion, the next four of Elvis' 45 rpm singles were issued in "Living Stereo" as well as the regular monaural. Each Living Stereo single is a highly prized collectible today.

Value: $180

leave, and Elvis immediately took a chartered plane to Memphis. He visited the hospital often during the next two days, and it seemed as if his presence lifted Gladys' spirits. The prognosis was for a recovery. But during the early-morning hours of August 14 she suffered a heart attack, and as Vernon sat helplessly by her side, she passed away.

"My mother, I suppose because I was an only child, I was closer to. I mean, everyone loves their mother, but I was an only child and my mother was always with me, all my life. And it wasn't like losing a mother, it was like losing a friend, a companion, someone to talk to. I could wake her up any hour of the night, and if I was worried or troubled about something she'd get up and try to help me."

Elvis was devastated. The most important person in his life had died. Gladys was the only person who could tell Elvis no and make it stick. She had been Elvis' anchor, and now he was adrift. The next two days, leading up to the funeral, were a nightmare for Elvis. He was in a state of shock and exhaustion. At the funeral, he bent over the casket, holding her hands, rubbing them, crying, "Oh, Mama. Those beautiful hands. How you

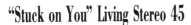

worked. How they worked for me." Eddie Fadal was there and remembers: "Vernon was going through a moan that I've never heard before. I've never heard any goings-on like that. And then he and Elvis embraced and talked little baby talk to one another, like probably things she would say to them." Desperately Elvis was attempting to bring Gladys back from the grave through his own willpower.

But in the end he realized that she was gone forever and he was left alone. "I think of her nearly every single day," he said five years later. "If I never do anything wrong, it's because of her. She wouldn't let me do anything wrong." Even Vernon could be of little help. Rather than drawing the two closer together, Gladys' death seemed to cause a permanent rift between father and son. Vernon was not strong-willed enough to shoulder the family's responsibilities. Everything was left up to Elvis. The two-week emergency leave was extended several times, but finally it was over. For the first time truly alone, Elvis returned to Fort Hood a mournful, lonely young man.

Advanced training was nearly completed as he arrived back in camp, and in mid-September his unit got orders to board the troop train bound for Brooklyn's Military Terminal. That last night in Killeen is remembered by Eddie Fadal: "It was a real sad night. Everybody'd been crying. We'd just said a prayer on the floor. We all made a circle on the floor and everybody's holding hands. We had the sort of prayer where everybody said something as we went around the circle. That must have been the saddest time. First he'd had to give up his career to go into the service. Not only going into the service, but going overseas. That's two blows right there. The next thing, his mother died. Those were traumatic times."

Elvis shared his compartment on the troop train with another soldier, Charlie Hodge, who had been a vocalist with Red Foley's Foggy River Boys and whom Elvis had first met while touring in 1955. Hodge quickly became one of Elvis' closest friends and would forever remain an important part of his life. When the train reached Brooklyn, Colonel Parker had the press waiting for one last interview before Elvis shipped overseas for eighteen months. Elvis and a thousand other soldiers were crammed aboard the USS *Randall,* bound for West Germany. Once at sea, Elvis and Charlie put together a variety show to help speed the passage for the captive audience. True to his word not to sing while on duty, Elvis played the piano while Charlie sang and acted as emcee. After the ship docked at Bremerhaven, the troops boarded a train for the final leg of their journey to Friedberg, the permanent home of Elvis' unit, the Seventh Army.

Elvis was immediately followed overseas by his father and grandmother, as well as two of his body-

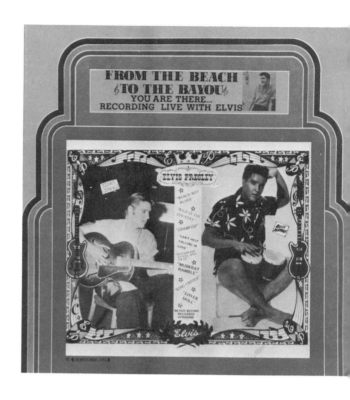

The King Goes Wild bootleg album

The original transcriptions of Elvis' three appearances on The Ed Sullivan Show, *beginning September 9, 1956, exist only as kinescopes (movies made from television). Consequently, the sound quality is not up to even 1956 standards.* The King Goes Wild *is a bootleg album issued in 1975 in England. A year later an American bootleg,* From the Waist Up *contained the same material, but it was not until 1985 that RCA Victor officially released the excellent box set,* A Golden Celebration, *which contains all three shows.*

Value: $100

From the Beach to the Bayou bootleg album

This bootleg not only offers Elvis' seventeen takes of "Can't Help Falling in Love" from Blue Hawaii, but kicks in a full side of outtakes from the King Creole sessions as well. The biggest treat for the Elvis fan comes in the middle of the "Can't Help Falling in Love" session when Elvis totally breaks up over his inability to complete even the first few lines of the song without laughing.

Value: $100 for original yellow cover; $75 for blue cover with tinted photo

guards, Red West and Lamar Fike. The group set up housekeeping at the Ritter's Park Hotel in Bad Nauheim, the hamlet next to Friedberg. Just as he had in Texas, Elvis used the hotel to escape the daily rigors of army life. Surrounded by relatives and friends, he was able to sustain some semblance of normalcy in the midst of a life and culture almost totally alien to him. Unable to speak German, he found even the shortest side trips frustrating. He did make the effort, in late October, to catch Bill Haley's rock 'n' roll show in Stuttgart. On another weekend, he, Red, and Lamar traveled to Munich to visit a German fashion model, Vera Tschechowa, who had once been assigned to a photo session with him. But he usually confined himself to either the army base or the hotel.

The months leading into the deep German winter offered some diversions: Elvis discovered that the German ladies were just as attracted to him as those he had left behind in the States. On a stroll through the park less than a week after his arrival, he introduced himself to a blond local girl, Margrit Buergin, who remained his steady date for almost a year. Every two weeks she'd arrive in a taxi dispatched by Elvis, to spend the evening at Elvis' hotel. Other fans sniffed out Elvis' home away from the army base, and they became such a nuisance at the Ritter's Park that the Memphis group was forced to relocate to the Hotel Grunewald nearby.

In November Elvis' outfit was shipped to an area near the German border for several weeks of winter maneuvers before the weather became too severe for such operations. During his stay in Grafenwohr, Elvis was promoted to the rank of private, first class. When not in the field, Elvis spent most of his off-duty time at the base theater in Grafenwohr, where he met Elisabeth Stefaniak, an eighteen-year-old army dependent. He swiftly became a regular house guest of her stepfather and mother. When he returned to Friedberg, he convinced Elisabeth to come back with him to be his personal secretary. Elvis also brought back his first taste for amphetamines—stimulants that soldiers often used during the long hours of winter field maneuvers to stay awake so they could keep from freezing. Off and on over the next few years, he would keep a quart jar filled with "pep pills" just in case he or his friends needed a quick lift.

By and large, Elvis kept to himself during that first winter. The loss of his mother and the bleakness of his new surroundings must have been very depressing. His two Memphis buddies were often left to their own devices. Red spent hours nursing beers at the local tavern, and got into endless fights defending Elvis' honor against local toughs. Lamar fell in love with a local German girl who was only using him to get close to Elvis. Christmas, normally the happiest of times for Elvis, was dismal without Gladys. The morale of the entourage had sunk so low that they decided to take Christmas dinner at the mess hall on base.

He thought that if he had been stationed in the States his popularity might have continued. Here in Germany, he was sure that his fans would forget all about him while he was in the army. He told Eddie Fadal on the night he left Killeen, "They won't even know me when I get back. They'll forget all about me." With over a year in Germany still spreading out in front of him, Elvis' life was on permanent hold.

On Elvis' twenty-fourth birthday, the U.S. television show *American Bandstand* placed a transatlantic telephone call and interviewed Elvis for five minutes as the highlight of a program devoted to the "king of rock 'n' roll." As the long German winter settled over Bad Nauheim and Friedberg, the Presley entourage had again been kicked out of their hotel. Next stop: a private home at 14 Goethestrasse in Bad Nauheim. Here the fans became an even greater nuisance, surrounding the house at all hours. Posted "rules" had to be instituted, limiting Elvis' autograph sessions to only half an hour each evening. After that, Elvis' life slowly settled into a daily pattern of army work during the days and quiet evenings at the house.

On the home front, RCA Victor released another of the songs that Elvis had recorded before leaving for Germany. "(Now and Then There's) A Fool Such as I" quickly soared up the music charts, but was unable to topple "Come Softly to Me" by the Fleetwoods and failed to reach the coveted number one spot. Colonel Parker routinely issued press releases in a well-orchestrated effort to keep Elvis' image alive. The Colonel reported in March that he was negotiating for a closed-circuit television concert that would be broadcast to one hundred theaters as soon as Elvis changed into civvies. The special never happened.

Returning from an Easter shopping trip, Vernon and Elisabeth Stefaniak were involved in an accident in Elvis' BMW. The car was totaled, and while neither of the occupants was seriously hurt, both required overnight hospitalization. Elvis, suspecting that Vernon was "fooling around" with his young secretary, and apparently unconcerned about any injuries, reached the hospital in a mood befitting the Inquisition. Nothing said by Vernon or Elisabeth quelled his concern. The press, upon hearing that "a Presley" had been in an auto accident, immediately assumed it was Elvis. The ensuing reports were quickly blown out of all proportion, with some declaring that Elvis had been killed. To mollify the newshounds, Elvis allowed himself to be photographed at the local Red Cross center, where he donated a pint of blood "just in case."

Elvis Monthly, No. 1, Vol. 1

The Official Elvis Presley Fan Club Of Great Britain was started in 1957 by Albert Hand, and in January 1960, he began publishing what has become the longest running of all the Elvis fan publications, Elvis Monthly. *The first 5½" × 8¼" issue contained a scant 22 pages. Within three years, the readership had grown from a small band of 7,000 loyal Elvis-ites to a number large enough to support a hardbound book, the* Elvis Annual. *In the spring of 1977, the fan club, which numbered over 100,000, reproduced the first issue so that fans could see what it looked like.*

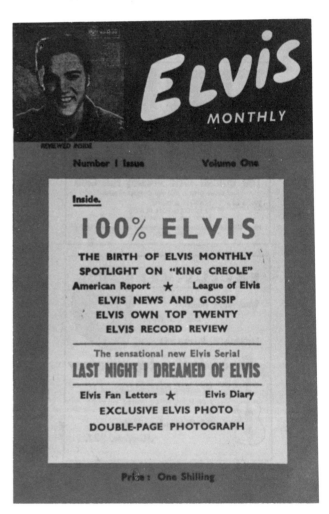

Value of original issue: $200
Value of reprint: $10

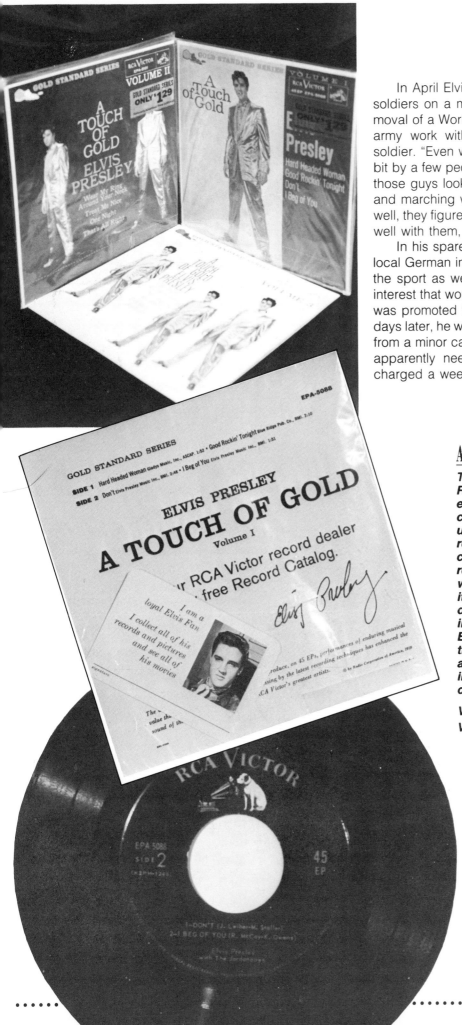

In April Elvis was put in charge of a detachment of soldiers on a mission to Steinfurth to supervise the removal of a World War I memorial statue. This was basic army work with no frills, and Elvis was just another soldier. "Even when I'm a civilian, I get harassed a little bit by a few people, and I was expecting that. But when those guys looked around and they saw me pulling KP and marching with a pack on my back and everything, well, they figured he's just like we are. So I got along very well with them, and they're a good bunch of boys."

In his spare time Elvis began to study karate with a local German instructor. He enjoyed the rough nature of the sport as well as the mental training, and it was an interest that would stay with him for years. On June 1 he was promoted to specialist, fourth class (corporal); two days later, he was admitted to the base hospital suffering from a minor case of tonsillitis. The golden vocal chords apparently needed a few days' rest—Elvis was discharged a week later with his tonsils intact. But for the

A Touch of Gold extended plays

These three EPs were issued by RCA Victor a year after Elvis entered the Army. A very few copies of the records were pressed using the maroon label normally reserved by RCA Victor for its classical music extended play releases. This apparently occurred when RCA temporarily exhausted its supply of black labels with the dog "Nipper" on the top. As an incentive for fans to purchase the EPs, Colonel Parker made certain that some of the copies had an "I am a loyal Elvis Fan" card tucked inside the plastic wrap. Today this can add $50 to the price.

Value of EP with black label: $80 each
Value, with maroon label: $250 each

rest of his life his tonsils continued to be easily infected and caused trouble several times.

In mid-June he went off on a two-week leave, traveling to Paris with Lamar Fike, fellow soldiers Charlie Hodge and Rex Mansfield, and a new face, Joe Esposito. Once registered in the Hôtel de Galles, the quartet frequented most of the city's famed reviews, including those at the Lido de Paris, the Carousel, the Café de Paris, and the Folies-Bergère. Each evening they returned to the hotel room surrounded by a bevy of showgirls. At leave's end, Elvis and his companions returned to Friedberg suitably exhausted.

"A Big Hunk o' Love," the last of the songs Elvis recorded before leaving for Germany, hit the top of the charts in August. For the next nine months the fans would have to make do with reissues of older material from RCA as Elvis stuck with his decision not to record during his time in Germany. By November, for the first time since his Sun singles started to appear on the regional music charts in 1954, Elvis did not have a record on any of the music charts. This situation would remain fairly static until his return.

The Colonel and Paramount Pictures jointly announced that Elvis' first post-army movie would be *G.I. Blues*, with a script that would parallel Elvis' army experiences. Art, for Elvis, again imitated life. A film crew was dispatched to photograph local scenes to be used as background shots.

September proved to be a fateful month, as one of Elvis' air force buddies arranged for an air force dependent to meet America's most famous GI. Priscilla Beaulieu, at age fourteen, made an immediate impression on Elvis, almost ten years her senior, and they became almost inseparable for the rest of his stay in Germany. Four nights a week, Elvis dispatched Lamar Fike in his car to bring her back to the house in Bad Nauheim for a "date" that almost always consisted of sitting in the living room with several members of the entourage and a few army buddies while Elvis entertained by singing and accompanying himself on the piano. Although he continued to see several German lady friends on the other nights, it was Priscilla who was making the lasting impression.

Elvis suffered a recurrence of tonsillitis in October, during army maneuvers near the Swiss border. Bed rest was prescribed, and once more the throat escaped the surgeon's scalpel.

Meanwhile, in Memphis, various civic organizations expressed a desire to honor their hometown boy upon his return to civilian life. There was talk of a monument or a building to be named in his honor. After all, discounting the Mississippi River, Elvis Presley was the biggest attraction in Memphis. Elvis sent a telegram graciously declining any permanent monument, stating that he was

Private Presley photo

This color 8″ × 10″ photo may have been available by mail order while Elvis was in the Army. It is printed on lightweight cardboard and bears no manufacturer's marking.

Value: $15

Good Rockin' Tonight bootleg album

This fine European bootleg album, issued in 1974 on BopCat Records, contains outtakes from Elvis' days on the Sun label on side one and rare material by other Sun artists on side two. Elvis' songs include "My Baby Is Gone" (a slow, bluesy rendition of "I'm Left, You're Right, She's Gone") that Elvis recorded in 1955 along with different versions of "Blue Moon of Kentucky," "I Don't Care If the Sun Don't Shine," and "I'll Never Let You Go Little Darlin' " from 1954. In 1984 these songs were "officially" released by RCA Victor.

Value: $150

Autographed 8″ × 10″

"To Manuela from Elvis Presley."
Outta-sight! Manuela must have
been on a cloud after getting Elvis'
autograph on this 1957 Elvis
Presley Enterprises 8″ × 10″ photo.
The picture is dated on the back
"June 29, 1960," which means that
in all probability, Elvis signed this
picture at the music gates.

Value of Elvis' autograph: $250
Value of EPE photo
  alone: $25

proud to have served his country and did not want to make his service in the army of any more importance than that of all the other GIs. The city commissioners acquiesced, but the idea did not stay dormant for long, surfacing time and time again throughout the 1960s. Finally, in 1971, the highway running in front of Graceland was renamed Elvis Presley Boulevard.

The year ended on a much happier note than the previous one. Elvis had a new girlfriend, his stint in the army was quickly drawing to a close, and all quarters were praising the manner in which he had served his country. Vernon also had a new lady in his life, having stolen a sergeant's wife, Dee Stanley. Christmas found everyone in an expansive mood. Elvis gave Priscilla a gold watch with a diamond set in the lid as a token of his affection for her. She presented him with a set of bongos.

The festivities and happiness at Christmastime continued through Elvis' birthday, when he rented the teen center in Bad Nauheim to throw a lively party for two hundred guests. The same day, he was again the transatlantic guest of Dick Clark's *American Bandstand.* Elvis received his final army promotion, to sergeant, on January 20, and then he participated in the largest American–West German field maneuvers to date, "Operation Winter Shield," at the Grafenwohr exercise area.

RCA Victor released another greatest-hits album, *50 Million Fans Can't Be Wrong,* in mid-February. Those fifty million fans, having already spent their allowance on the singles, steered clear of the album, and its sales dropped off sharply after a few weeks. Concurrent with the release of the new album, RCA issued a report that Elvis had a total of eighteen consecutive million-selling singles, a mark unequaled by any other artist. Colonel Parker was simultaneously launching his own publicity blitz, which would climax with Elvis' release from the army in early March. It was time to find out if the gamble of allowing Elvis to enter the army as a regular soldier had destroyed any hope of reviving his career.

In Germany, Elvis started the necessary outprocessing prior to his discharge. With his paperwork in order, Elvis and seventy-nine other GIs boarded a flight back to the States on March 2. The military plane was followed by an chartered airliner containing Vernon, Grandma, Elisabeth Stefaniak, Lamar Fike, and two dozen trunks stuffed full of Elvis' clothes and several more boxes containing his collection of two thousand phonograph records. Elvis' flight made a brief stopover to refuel at Prestwick Airport in Scotland. This was the only time Elvis' ever set foot on the British Isles.

There was a driving snowstorm in New Jersey as Elvis' plane touched down at McGuire Air Force Base at 7:42 A.M., March 3. Elvis was elated to be back in America for the first time in eighteen months. He and the other returning GIs were taken to the army's Fort Dix, next door to McGuire Air Force Base, for the remainder of their outprocessing. Here, Colonel Parker orchestrated a gigantic press conference for two hundred reporters and photographers. Nancy Sinatra, daughter of Frank, was on hand to present Elvis with a gift from her father. It was soon announced that Elvis had been signed to make an appearance on Frank Sinatra's TV special in May.

Following two final days of soldiering, a civilian Elvis boarded a private railroad car with Colonel Parker's entourage and a few of his own pals for the trip back to Memphis. In small towns along the route, groups of fans lined the tracks to get a glimpse of their returning star. The train finally pulled in to Memphis, where a crowd estimated at two hundred waited in the snow. Elvis disembarked wearing a fancy dress uniform provided by Colonel Parker, which inadvertently promoted him by displaying four stripes on the sleeves instead of the three to which he was entitled. No one seemed to notice. A police escort rushed Elvis to Graceland. He was joyous as he made the rounds through the house, saying hello to the staff and all of the family and friends who had gathered for his return. Later, he walked down to the "music gate" and signed autographs for an hour. He needed that personal reassurance from his fans that his career had not been sacrificed. "I don't just sign the autographs and the pictures to help my popularity or to make them like me. I do it because I know they're sincere."

The afternoon of his return, there was an informal meeting with the local press, this time in the security of Elvis' Graceland office. Asked about recent reports of a new girlfriend (photos of Priscilla's tearful good-bye to Elvis at the Frankfort airport had been published), Elvis was visibly nervous as he attempted to casually brush away any suspicions. With a houseful of girls here at Graceland, more waiting in Hollywood, and Priscilla thousands of miles away in Germany, his reluctance to dwell on the subject was understandable—and pragmatic.

Elvis' vacation was cut short when he traveled to Nashville for his first recording session since June 1958. Elvis and the musicians worked for twelve hours on the night of March 20 and came up with six completed songs, including two for immediate release as a single, "Fame and Fortune" and "Stuck on You."

Two days later he was aboard another train, this time bound for Miami. According to Elvis, "When I got out of the army my first professional appearance was on a television show with Frank Sinatra. Nervous? I was petrified. I was scared stiff. The moving and the shaking I done on that show wasn't from the music, it was from being scared. I wasn't sure I'd make it. Getting back to it wasn't as simple as I thought it'd be. It would've been allright with me if I'd just walked out and walked off. But

Hit Stars bubblegum cards

The Topps Gum Company, seeing the success of the Elvis Presley series, issued a set of rock 'n' roll "Hit Stars" in 1957. Elvis was the 59th card. Other cards in the set are valued at $10 to $15 depending on the singer's popularity.

Value: $25

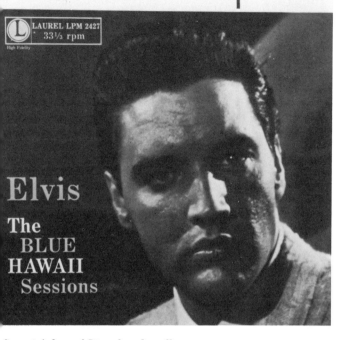

Steppin' Out Of Line | MONO

LAUREL LPM 2427
33⅓ rpm
High Fidelity

Elvis
The
BLUE
HAWAII
Sessions

Steppin' Out of Line bootleg album

In 1984, a European bootleg of Steppin' Out of Line sessions picked up where From the Beach to the Bayou left off, with outtakes of the title song and seven others from Blue Hawaii.

Value: $30

Elvis bought this 1955 pink Cadillac for his mother with part of the $5,000 he received from RCA.

Frank was kind and understanding, and with his help and encouragement we taped the show OK." The show, *Frank Sinatra's Welcome Home Party for Elvis Presley,* was videotaped at the Fontainebleu Hotel, and it would air on May 12 over the NBC-TV network. For his brief performance (he was on camera a total of only nine minutes) Elvis was paid $125,000, ten times the amount that he had received to appear *Stage Show* in 1956, the same year that Sinatra had been very vocal about what he perceived as the evil in Elvis' rock 'n' roll. Sinatra was now more than willing to satisfy the desires of the people, especially with the high rating the show would surely bring. Besides cavorting with Sinatra's Rat Pack—Peter Lawford, Joey Bishop, and Sammy Davis, Jr.—Elvis was seen throughout the show, wearing a tuxedo. He even performed a duet with Sinatra, in which Elvis sang Sinatra's hit "Witchcraft" while Sinatra crooned "Love Me Tender."

RCA Victor pressed 1.3 million copies of Elvis' new single record, "Fame and Fortune," which were hungrily snapped up by his eager fans. In early April Elvis returned to Nashville to finish recording tracks for his new album, *Elvis Is Back.* One of the songs, "I Will Be Home Again," featured Elvis in a duet with army buddy Charlie Hodge, who had been invited to share the hospitality of Elvis' home before returning to stay with his parents in Alabama.

Elvis left Memphis on April 18 in another rented private railroad car, en route to Hollywood and the start of his first movie in more than two years. Along with the usual complement of Lamar Fike, Gene Smith, and several men from Colonel Parker's office and RCA Victor, "the guys," as they referred to themselves, now included Red West's cousin Sonny as a bodyguard. He was temporarily replacing Red, who was working in Hollywood with Nick Adams on the *Rebel* television series and would join everyone at the Beverly Wilshire Hotel as soon as they arrived. Also new to the crew was "Diamond" Joe Esposito, a member of Elvis' army outfit in Germany. Esposito would eventually act as chief of staff for the guys who surrounded Elvis. At the last minute, Charlie Hodge decided to tag along for the ride instead of returning home to Alabama. He was the only member of the group to have a permanent apartment at Graceland, and both he and Esposito would remain loyal to Elvis to the end. Elvis had this to say about his built-in company: "I don't try to surround myself with a group of intellectuals. It's more important to surround yourself with people who can give you a little happiness, because you only pass through this life once. You don't come back for an encore."

Colonel Parker made certain that Elvis was hailed as a conquering hero in each town and city through which his train passed. Finally reaching Los Angeles, Elvis was

Elvis and Richard Lightman after the premiere of G.I. Blues in Los Angeles. Lightman was the executive vice president of Malco Theaters Inc. of Memphis; he frequently opened his Memphian Theater for Elvis after hours, so that the king could enjoy a current movie in relative privacy.

NOW... **AT YOUR FAVORITE THEATRE**
ELVIS IN **"G.I. Blues"**
A HAL WALLIS PRODUCTION-A PARAMOUNT PICTURE

King Creole album and bonus photo

Elvis' fourth movie was the tragic story of a young nightclub singer who got mixed up with the New Orleans mob. Since both the movie and the accompanying soundtrack album were released after Elvis entered the army, the Colonel decided to include an 8″ × 10″ portrait of Private Presley. The **King Creole** *album was one of the first to use an early form of shrinkwrap, which allowed the photo to be placed outside the back cover where it could easily be seen.*

Value of album: $100
Value of photo: $75

G.I. Blues army cap

Just in time for Elvis' first post-army movie, appropriately titled G.I. Blues, *is one of the rarest of all the movie collectibles. The 1960 army cap was made of paper, which probably accounts for why so few are still around today. Like most of the strictly movie items from the 1960s, these were given away at selected theaters.*

Value: $80

greeted by yet another screeching mob waiting at Union Station. If he had any lingering doubts about his popularity, this trip had proven that he was not forgotten.

Production on *G.I. Blues* started immediately. This was the first of Elvis' movies to be in the "musical" genre. Even though he had sung in all four of his first films, the songs had been tailored to fit the story line. In *Loving You, Jailhouse Rock,* and *King Creole* Elvis had even been conveniently cast as an entertainer; his few songs in *Love Me Tender* were set in logical surroundings. In *G.I. Blues* Elvis would break into song at the drop of a salute. During the filming of *G.I. Blues,* Elvis happily reverted to his pre-army habit of dating his co-star. The damsel in this case was the vivacious Juliet Prowse, who was generally thought to be Frank Sinatra's girlfriend. Tension filled the air whenever Sinatra visited the set. Sinatra had a formidable reputation as a man who would not relinquish his woman without a noisy row. The matter was ultimately settled, as were most of Elvis' offscreen romances, when he moved on to his next female co-star.

The album *Elvis Is Back* came out just after Elvis started work on *G.I. Blues.* Overnight, it racked up a million dollars in sales. The Sinatra TV special aired on May 12, and the ratings showed that 40 percent of all TVs in the country had been tuned in to see Elvis' first TV appearance since 1957. On June 21, while working on *G.I. Blues,* Elvis was pleased to be introduced to his first, and only, acquaintances among international royalty, the King and Queen of Thailand, who were visiting the Paramount set as part of a state visit.

On July 3, Vernon married Dee Stanley, the lady friend from his days in Germany, at her brother's home in

Alabama. Elvis, who had returned to Memphis, declined to attend. It's a matter of conjecture whether he was resentful that his father was remarrying less than two years after Gladys' death, or simply wanted to allow the couple the privacy of a wedding without the circus that surrounded his every public appearance. The newlyweds soon moved into Graceland, and Dee brought along her three sons, Rick, Billy, and David, from her previous marriage.

Elvis spent most of July speeding around Memphis' Lake McKellar on his new sixteen-foot motorboat during the day and renting the Fairgrounds Amusement Park after midnight (for fifty dollars an hour) to provide thrills for his friends.

At this time, Elvis became interested in investing in something other than his career. In this area he respected Eddie Fadal's opinion, because of Fadal's successful career in Waco. Fadal recalls one day in Memphis when they went riding around looking for a motel to buy. "He was looking at these big fancy motels and the high-priced properties. I was looking at these shanties but on good land that could be all torn down and something nice built there. I was looking for a location where he was looking for buildings. To me, you can build a building if you have the location, but he didn't look at it that way. So we came to one little motel that looked like a flophouse—just real bad-looking. I said, 'Elvis, this would be a great spot.' He looked at me and exclaimed, 'I wouldn't have that!' I said, 'Elvis, I don't mean that—we'll bulldoze all that. Just look at this land. Just look at this great piece of property.' I said, 'We'll call it Elvis Presley Motel and start a chain.' He just laughed about it. So we got back home and he didn't say anymore about it. He never mentioned it again."

In early August Elvis had a preproduction recording session in Hollywood for his new movie, *Flaming Star,* which was also known at the time as both *Flaming Lance* and *Black Star.* Outdoor filming on the picture took place at Twentieth Century–Fox's Conejo Movie Ranch in the San Fernando Valley. Elvis routinely made certain that as many of his entourage as possible were hired as extras during the making of all of his movies. During work on *Flaming Star* this reached a new comic height when Red West was hired to impersonate an Indian. With his burnt-orange hair and ruddy, freckled complexion, West certainly looked more Irish than Kiowa, makeup and a long black wig not withstanding. *Flaming Star* was Elvis' second feature with a western story line, and, as in *Love Me Tender,* he sang only a few songs, and those within the dramatic context of the film. The movie was directed by Don Siegel, who later enjoyed great success with such action films such as *Dirty Harry.* In an interview with the *Los Angeles Mirror,* Siegel commented on Elvis the actor: "Elvis didn't realize it, but he actually began using

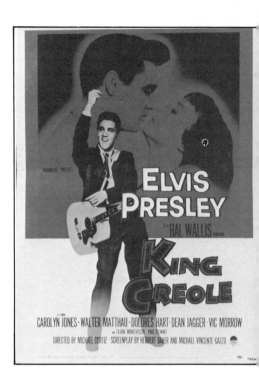

1963 Elvis calendar

To boost Elvis' record sales in 1963, Colonel Parker convinced RCA Victor to include a special bonus with the Girls! Girls! Girls! album in the form of a 12″ × 12″ 1963 calendar. Two other versions of this calendar were issued and all had the same cover. The bonus calendar in the album had a listing of Elvis' movie albums and soundtracks on the back. The version distributed as a giveaway in record stores plugged Elvis' single records on the back. Colonel Parker even had RCA Victor print up a few hundred of the calendars with a Christmas message and a photo of him wearing his famous red Santa Claus suit on the back to be handed out through his office.

Value of 1963 calendar with album catalog: $35
Value of 1963 calendar with singles catalog: $50
Value of 1963 calendar with Colonel Parker in Santa suit: $75

King Creole ads

The window card and one-sheet pictured here for King Creole differ in that the full shot of Elvis in the window card is tinted yellow, while he remains black and white on the one-sheet. King Creole was the last film before Elvis entered the Army. It was also his finest dramatic role.

14" × 22" window card value: $125
27" × 41" one-sheet value: $125

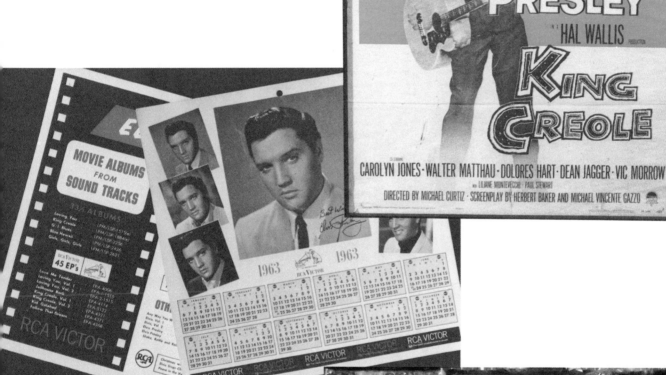

Pencils

The pencil pack, issued by EPE in 1956, contained a dozen pencils in four different colors: yellow, green, orange, and, his favorite brilliant pink. Each pencil was marked, "Sincerely yours, Elvis Presley," and each pack of pencils featured a black-and-white photo. The original price was 39 cents.

Value: $5 each; a package of 12, $75

1956 Elvis bubblegum cards

EPE authorized the Topps Gum Company to add a set of Elvis Presley cards to its line of collectors cards. The cards sold in packets of five for a nickel, bubblegum included, as well as single cards for a penny. The set consists of 66 cards, and like other bubblegum card sets, they were issued in two parts. The "Ask Elvis" set, numbers 1–46, covers Elvis' career up to the middle of 1956 and features a question with Elvis' "answer" on the back. Numbers 47–66 show scenes taken from Elvis' first movie, Love Me Tender, and have details about the movie on the back. All the cards are hand-tinted from original black-and-white photographs. Later reproductions (counterfeits) of these cards were black and white only and are therefore easy to spot. Complete mint sets are very difficult to obtain and consequently fetch a high price in the collector's market, although, because of the number of cards available, a set is worth less collectively ($300) than the total of each card separately ($528).

Value of complete set: $300
Value of each card: $8

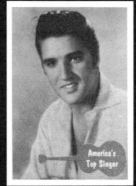

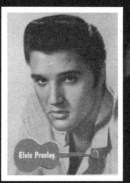

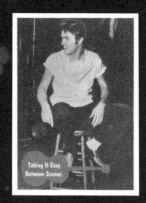

Steve Allen and Elvis

Down on the Farm

Studying the Script

Signing Session

Go, Go, Go, Elvis

Elvis Presley

I Want You, I Need You, I Love You

A Tux for TV

Relaxing at Rehearsals

Love Me Tender

Elvis' Motorcycle

Hound Dog

Clint and Cathy Reno

Farm Chores

Lights, Camera, Action!

Serenade to a Pooch

Elvis with his Fans

Time Out Between Shows

America's Singing Idol

Happy Homecoming

Soft and Mellow

Two Against One

Clint's Plan

Singing Up a Storm

Fighting Mad

Heading for the Fair

"Don't Try to Stop Me"

Porch Performance

Bad News

"I Want an Honest Answer"

Hard Work

'I'm Goin' to Vance

Rescue Ride

New Member of the Family

Elvis at 17

Chow Time on the Movie Set

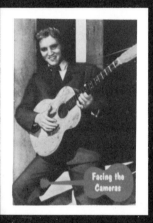

Facing the Cameras

Elvis the Actor

Recording Session

Elvis' Special Shirt

Rockin' on Stage

Radio Broadcast

the Stanislavsky method. When he gets ready to do a serious scene, he closes himself in and is absolutely unapproachable." Siegel also noticed that Elvis was basically shy and inhibited. "That is why he has his buddies around him all the time. Sometimes I found it difficult to get him away from them."

Back in Hollywood, following some September highjinks with the guys, Elvis found himself in trouble with the Beverly Wilshire Hotel, which had served as his home base during his long stays in Hollywood. Elvis decided to rent a palace on Bel-Air's Peruga Way that had been the home of actress Rita Hayworth and her husband the Ali Khan. The enormous home afforded Elvis the same degree of privacy and space as Graceland, and it would be his Hollywood hostel for the next five years.

After returning to Memphis, Elvis suffered a broken little finger during a game of touch football with some of his cronies. It was not serious, but that didn't stop extensive press coverage of the minor accident. Roughhouse football games were one of the few ways in which Elvis could release the tensions of being idolized. In Hollywood, the Sunday afternoon games were typically more organized, with Elvis leading his squad against the friends of such fellow stars as Ricky Nelson, Robert Conrad, and Pat Boone. In Memphis, Elvis' team was apt to take on anyone who ventured out onto the field.

In late October there was another all-night recording session in Nashville, to record songs for a project that was dear to Elvis—his first religious album, *His Hand in Mine.* He had recorded four spirituals in 1957 that appeared first on an extended-play single and later on the Christmas album, but this would be his first full-length album of hymns and gospel numbers.

Elvis' third picture in six months, *Wild in the Country,* found him again on location outside Hollywood, this time in California's Napa Valley. The movie was another attempt at a dramatic role for Elvis, with little singing on his part. While on location, Elvis broke precedent by dating the wardrobe girl, Nancy Sharp. The couple had first met while working on *Flaming Star.* Together they whiled away the many hours of free time that come when making a movie. While in Napa, Elvis also developed a serious case of boils on his posterior. As Napa was the heart of California's wine country, a little juice of the grape was recommended to releive his discomfort. Elvis, who was never a drinking man, got a snootful one night in the interest of medicine. It relieved the pain of the boils, but thereafter he limited his drinking.

His new single, "Are You Lonesome Tonight?" was released in the middle of November and, typically earned gold-record status as soon as it was available. It also brought out a host of records that either parodied the song or answered Elvis' musical question. Among the best were "Yes, I'm Lonesome Tonight" by Dodie

Stevens (who had a 1959 smash hit with the novelty record "Pink Shoelaces") and "Who's Lonesome Tonight" by Redd Dogg.

In his Hollywood office, Colonel Parker read a December 7 newspaper editorial calling for donations to help complete the memorial to the USS *Arizona,* which had been lost during the bombing attack on Pearl Harbor. He immediately set into motion the machinery that would take Elvis back to Hawaii for the first time in four years. Typically, Parker was able to coordinate the benefit concert with the start of a "movin' pitcher" already planned for the following March.

First, *G.I. Blues* and then *Flaming Star* opened in theaters, and Elvis found himself the subject of widespread praise for his movie acting. Said the *Los Angeles Times* of *G.I. Blues:* "Elvis shows a great flair for comedy and acting ability in the more serious moments." The reviews for *Flaming Star* were even better. "This picture should open up a whole new audience for him," said the *Los Angeles Examiner.* Significantly, *G.I. Blues,* with its full complement of songs, did much better at the box office. It was obvious to those in Hollywood, not to mention Colonel Parker, that the paying public wanted Elvis in movies that featured a full musical soundtrack. They wanted Elvis singing, not acting. Elvis had his own thoughts on his acting career: "If I were a good actor I think I would like it a little better. I think I might accomplish something at it through the years. In some scenes I was pretty natural. In others I was trying to act, and when you start trying to act, you're dead."

Elvis slipped quietly out of Memphis around Christmas to celebrate part of the holiday season in St. Louis with the family of Nancy Sharp, the wardrobe girl from *Wild in the Country.* He was back in Memphis so soon that few but the fan magazines had noticed he was gone.

For his work in 1960, Elvis was recognized by the Academy of Recording Arts and Sciences with five nominations, three for the *G.I. Blues* album and two for the single of "Are You Lonesome Tonight?" It wasn't the first time he had been nominated (although he would have to wait until 1967 to actually win a Grammy), but it was the largest number of nominations he would ever receive in a single year. After four years of enormous popularity with the fans but general neglect from the music industry, the recognition of his peers had special meaning for Elvis.

CHAPTER THREE

Follow That Dream

Elvis bubblegum card wrappers

As rare as the Elvis bubblegum cards may be, the original wax paper wrappers are even more scarce. The cards were bought to be saved, traded, and treasured; the wrappers were discarded as worthless.

Value of Elvis 1¢ bubblegum card wrapper: $30

Value of Elvis 5¢ bubblegum card wrapper: $30

Elvis' new album, *His Hand in Mine,* enjoyed excellent sales for a religious LP and soon made its way into the top twenty albums. Less than a year following his discharge from the army, Elvis the artist was becoming a firmly entrenched and accepted member of the entertainment community.

Elvis the individual remained in Memphis for the first two months of 1961. In early February, Eddie Fadal, who was staying at Graceland, was awakened suddenly. "[Elvis had] been up all night—couldn't sleep. He came down and woke us all up and said, 'Get up. Up and at 'em. We're going to Tupelo.' It was cold, man. It was wintertime. He pulls the cover off us. He wanted to see where they were going to build a park [the Elvis Presley Youth Center]. He and Anita sat in the front seat snuggled up, with me and Lamar in the back. All the way down he'd say, 'Wait till you see this place. Man, they're gonna build the most beautiful park.' He was just building it up. And we got there, and the sign had fallen down. Johnson grass was five or six feet tall. And we all just bent over laughing. He did too when he said, 'This is where it's going to be,' and the sign wasn't even there."

Tupelo had changed quite a bit since the Presleys quit the town in 1948, but he tried to keep up with the few remaining friends and relatives in the town of his birth. "The same old crowd that I was raised up with still lives there in the same houses," Elvis recalled. In fact, of the original East Tupelo families who had resided on the knoll when Elvis was born, quite a few remained. But several of the Presleys and Smiths had chosen to move to Memphis at the same time as Elvis' parents. Others had followed as Elvis became more popular, and most now relied on Elvis as their sole source of income. Several uncles on both sides of the family were employed at Graceland as gate guards or maintenance men. Cousins were on the payroll as part of Elvis' personal entourage and were responsible for maintaining his enormous wardrobe and fleet of expensive automobiles. Elvis was the single largest employer of most of his closest kin.

After the holidays, his only break for professional work came in mid-February, when he started warming up with his backing group, the Jordanaires, for a special concert in Memphis on February 25. "Elvis Presley Day" was proclaimed by both the governor of Tennessee and the mayor of Memphis; it started with a luncheon and press meeting. In the middle of the twenty-minute press conference, Elvis waxed philosophical about himself and his career: "I don't like to press my luck too far. I don't like to take chances. As long as I'm doing OK now, why change it until I got reason to change it. If what I'm doing now, if it doesn't go over anymore, then I'll have to change." The day climaxed with two benefit concerts, which raised over $50,000 for twenty-three local charities. In the years to come he would continue to donate at least $50,000 each Christmas to these same charities. In recognition of his generosity, Elvis was made a "Colonel" by the Tennessee legislature. "At last," he joked, "I'm not outranked by Colonel Tom Parker."

Elvis soon traveled to the Nashville studios to record songs for a new album, *Something for Everybody*. Less than two weeks later, he was in Hollywood laying down the musical soundtrack for his upcoming picture, *Blue Hawaii*. Three long days and nights of session work were immediately followed by a flight to Honolulu. Here, Colonel Parker's idea for a benefit concert to help raise funds for the memorial to the USS *Arizona* was ready to roll. On March 25 Elvis gave his second benefit show in a month, raising over $62,000 to ensure that the monument to the sunken battleship would be completed. This was also his last full-scale concert for the next eight years, as movie contracts began to dominate his career.

Production on *Blue Hawaii* began immediately after the benefit show, and filming continued into the middle of April. This was Elvis' second trip to the Hawaiian Islands, and he enjoyed every minute. More and more, he would look to Hawaii—far from both Hollywood and Graceland—as the only place where he could completely relax. All too soon it was time for Elvis and the crew to return to Hollywood. Elvis spent his spare time pursuing Tuesday Weld, his co-star from *Wild in the Country*. One evening at the Peruga Way house, Elvis fired Sonny West when Sonny tried to sneak Weld away while Elvis was ruining Sonny's chances with another girl. Such "firings" were not uncommon. Elvis was under constant pressure, and the men around him often bore the brunt of his short temper. In this case, Sonny was back in the fold by year's end. As it happened, Tuesday Weld was soon out of the picture herself, as Elvis turned his attentions to Joan Blackman, another of his co-stars, who appeared in both *Blue Hawaii* and the upcoming *Kid Galahad*.

Wild in the Country premiered in June, and both Elvis and the film were badly panned. The screenplay was based on a serious novel by Clifford Odets, and the critics found Elvis' treatment of the character "dishonest" and the story line "wobbly." This would be the last attempt to cast Elvis in a purely dramatic role until 1968.

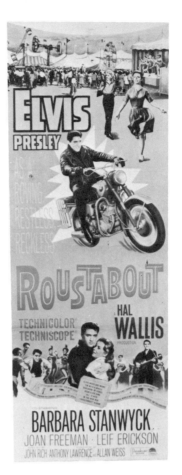

Roustabout ads

This lobby insert and the large one-sheet feature Elvis as a motorcycle dare-devil in Roustabout. *The herald tabloid contains a fine series of comic-book-style photo panels from the movie. Try to guess which of the dancing girls is Raquel Welch in her first movie role.*

14″ × 22″ lobby insert value: $20 (front) (inside) Herald tabloid value: $15

Roustabout Armed Forces album

Several of Elvis' albums were transcribed onto disks for the Armed Forces Radio and Television Service. These disks came in both 12-inch and 16-inch sizes and had all the songs from an album on one side, with songs from different artists on the other.

Value: $100

ROUSTABOUT

Words and Music by Bill Giant, Bernie Baum and Florence Kaye

From The Hal Wallis Production "ROUSTABOUT"
A Paramount Release

Recorded by ELVIS PRESLEY
on RCA Victor

Price 60¢

Elvis Presley Music, Inc.
Sole Selling Agent:
Hill and Range Songs, Inc.
1619 Broadway, New York, N.Y.

"Roustabout"
sheet music

It was rare for a song not issued as a single to have its own piece of sheet music. "Roustabout" broke the rule.

Value: $15

Since before he had sung his first song for Sun Records, Elvis had dreamed of becoming a serious actor. He even said, "I stop thinking about my guitar when I step on a movie stage." Prior to his two-year hitch in the army, two of his four movies, *Jailhouse Rock* and *King Creole,* had shown that Elvis had promise as an actor. Some considered him a serious threat to fill the void left by the death of James Dean, a replacement for the role of the moody, misunderstood young adult. But the poor box office showing for *Flaming Star,* and now for *Wild in the Country,* dashed all hope that Elvis would be placed outside the context of a musical for years to come. The formula had started with *G.I. Blues,* and it would be complete with *Blue Hawaii.* The idea was simply to put Elvis in an exotic location, surround him with gorgeous women, and have him a sing a dozen songs—enough to fill a soundtrack album. To enhance his male image, fistfights would be featured, and Elvis would be given such macho occupations as race car driver, boxer, deep-sea fisherman, and scuba diver. In Hollywood it became known as the "Elvis movie."

Back in Memphis, Elvis spent June relaxing at Vernon's cabin on nearby Lake McKellar. It is often said that Elvis was afraid of the water and had never become a good swimmer, but now he really indulged his passion for water skiing and powerboating. When Red West married Pat Boyd (from Elvis' secretarial pool) on July 1, Elvis escorted Anita Wood. On the fifth he was in Nashville to

"Ain't That Loving You Baby" picture sleeves

Colonel Parker can be credited with using the picture sleeves to promote upcoming albums and movies. Here we have two picture sleeves from the same single.

Value, with "Coming Soon!": $16
Value, with "Ask For": $20

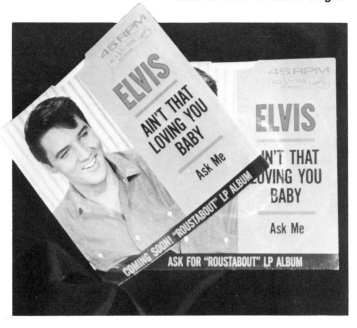

record the songs for the next picture, *Follow That Dream*, and he returned to Hollywood in the middle of the month for preproduction on the new movie at United Artists. Elvis and the film crew traveled to the Florida Gulf Coast for location filming later in July; most of August was spent in and around Crystal River, Florida. Elvis was a big hit with the local Floridians, who set aside one Sunday for a jam-packed picnic in his honor. For hours an obliging Elvis stood in the hot sun and signed autographs for literally thousands of fans.

There were several months of idle time at home before his next project, an October 15 recording date at RCA's Nashville studios. "Good Luck Charm" came out of that session, along with songs that would appear on a new album, *Elvis for Everyone*. Then it was time to report to United Artists to start *Kid Galahad,* in which Elvis was cast as a boxer. Sonny West had been hired by United Artists as a stunt man and soon was back in the entourage, where he would remain as a bodyguard until 1976. Elvis and the moviemakers traveled to the San Jacinto Mountains east of Los Angeles to shoot outdoor locations, but by the end of November the weather had turned sour (the movie was supposed to take place during the summer), and the crew had to return to Hollywood. Because of this delay, production on the picture ran much longer than expected. For the first and last time, Elvis could not travel back to Memphis to celebrate

Elvis Pocket Handbook

Published in England in the summer of 1961 by Albert Hand, this small, 100-page paperback is the precursor of the annual The Elvis Specials. *The Elvis Pocket Handbook has many of the features that would become standard in the later annual, including lists of Elvis' English record releases, details about each song Elvis recorded, a review of his movies, and an "Elvis Diary." Containing 32 pages of publicity and movie stills from* Flaming Star *and a full-color pin-up, this little book is highly sought after by fans worldwide.*

Value: $75

Other fan club pins

Two other fan club pins are of interest to collectors. One sports the familiar "guitar pose" stamped in blue-and-gold metal. The other is from about 1963 and features a black-and-white portrait of Elvis from It Happened at the World's Fair with red lettering.

Value of fan club pin with guitar: $15
Value of fan club pin/portrait: $12

Christmas and New Year's with his family. He compensated by dating starlet Connie Stevens and stealing Sonny West's latest girlfriend for a weekend tryst in Palm Springs. Elvis apparently wanted to make certain that Sonny knew who was boss.

Blue Hawaii was released in the fall, and both the movie and the accompanying soundtrack album were enormously successful. The movie became Elvis' biggest-grossing film at the box office, and the soundtrack was his best-selling album. To top it off, a song from the movie, "Can't Help Falling in Love," was released as a single and became number two on *Billboard*'s chart. According to the Jordanaires, Elvis confessed during the recording session, that the song made him think of a little girl in Germany. This song, always one of Elvis' favorites, would become the closing number during most of his 1970s' concert shows.

In early January, much to his personal displeasure, Elvis was still in Hollywood working on *Kid Galahad*. By his reckoning, he was supposed to be back in Memphis for the year-end holidays, and he didn't let anyone around him forget it.

Back in Memphis, in anticipation of Elvis' return, Vernon and Dee decided to move out of Graceland; they rented a house on Hermitage Way while a new home was being built for them on Dolan Street, adjacent to the back of the Graceland property. Even though Graceland was large, the space was more than a little cramped as Dee's sons approached their teens.

Gold Standard picture sleeves

RCA Victor started reissuing Elvis' hit singles on their Gold Standard label in March 1959. Five years later, in a special promotion, they placed five of them in special picture sleeves for a short time.

Value: $75 each

Though his records would still show strength on the charts, the March release of "Good Luck Charm" marked Elvis' last number one single for the next seven years. Most of Elvis' singles and albums were now related to his current motion picture. In the world of popular music rock 'n' roll was still going strong, but changes were brewing. Just over the horizon was the sound of Detroit's Motown, California's surf music, and the British beat invasion. Those closest to Elvis and Elvis himself seemed to miss the fact that his days of effortless domination of the music industry were at an end. It had been six years since "Heartbreak Hotel" and "Hound Dog" swept aside the pop vocalists, leftovers from the big band era of the 1940s and early 1950s. There is nothing more certain in the faddish world of popular music than that there is a new fad waiting just around the next corner.

Immediately after work was completed on *Kid Galahad,* Elvis and the entourage left Hollywood aboard their newly refurbished touring bus. When they reached home, Christmas lights and decorations still adorned Graceland, a reminder of the holidays that he had missed at home. It was quite a sight. The large bus blared its mighty horn as it swept up the curving Graceland driveway, illuminated by a hundreds of blue Christmas lights all ablaze . . . in February. There was even a late snowfall that year, and Elvis, ever the child, enjoyed sledding down the Graceland hills.

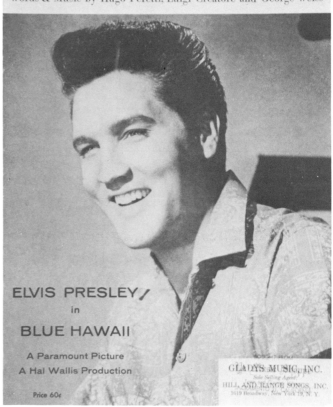

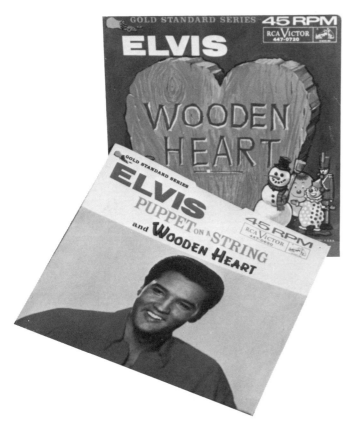

"Wooden Heart" singles and picture sleeves

The song "Wooden Heart" first appeared in the movie G.I. Blues in 1960, but was not released as a single until November 1964. It appeared on a Gold Standard issue paired with "Blue Christmas." A year later, it was issued once again on a Gold Standard single, this time backed with "Puppet on a String" from Girl Happy.

Value, with "Blue Christmas": $55
Value, with "Puppet on a String": $30

"Can't Help Falling in Love" sheet music

The photo of a grinning Elvis on the cover of the sheet music for "Can't Help Falling in Love" was taken on the set of Blue Hawaii.

Value: $18

"You're the Devil in Disguise" sheet music

The sheet music for "You're the Devil in Disguise" shows a happy shot of Elvis taken in 1961.

Value: $15

Eddie Fadal recalls his frequent visits to Graceland in those days, especially an incident that involved Elvis' favorite Memphis clothing store. Fadal was looking for an excuse to return home to Waco, so he told Elvis that he'd run out of clothes. "Well, that didn't work. 'Come on,' Elvis said, 'we'll do something about that.' We got in the car and we go down to Lansky Brothers and he buys everything in that store. And I kept saying, 'I don't want it . . . I don't need it. I've got plenty of clothes at home.' He bought me a suit and he bought the slacks and a sport coat and he bought me an assortment of shirts—one of every color in the store. He had my monogram put on them. I kept saying, 'I don't want it.' The Lansky brothers were just gloating over it. They loved it. It was a big sale for them. He walked out of the store to get his shoes shined by one of the little black boys that were shining shoes on Beale Street out on the sidewalk, and he turned to Bernard Lansky and said, 'Give Eddie anything in the store he wants.' He started out the door and turned around and said, 'Give him the whole damn store if he wants!' That's the kind of guy he was. So how could I go home after all that? I had to stay a few more days."

After a few weeks of relaxation, Elvis had a recording session in Nashville and waxed a few new songs for his next non-movie album, *Pot Luck*. Then it was off to Hollywood and Hawaii again to film *Girls! Girls! Girls!* This time there would be no benefit concert, only weeks of movie

Follow That Dream medallion

To promote Elvis' 1962 release, Follow That Dream, EPE had a special medallion issued as both a necklace and a bracelet. Elvis' likeness is inset in blue against burnished steel.

Value: $20

work on Oahu and the big island of Hawaii. By late April the company was back at Paramount Studios putting the finishing touches on the picture.

Elvis had barely completed work on his latest Hawaiian opus when he had a special visitor. After more than two years of cajoling, Elvis had finally been able to convince Priscilla's stepfather to allow her to fly from Germany to the States for two weeks. Upon her arrival in Los Angeles, Elvis and Priscilla, now sixteen— accompanied, as usual, by a handful of Elvis' cronies— hopped into Elvis' bus and drove to Las Vegas for a few days of vacation. Their time together was short, and soon Priscilla was back in Germany. Elvis returned to chasing Hollywood starlets. For some, "absence makes the heart grow fonder." For Elvis it was more like "out of sight, out of mind." Priscilla's visit had also set off a chain reaction back in Memphis, with Anita Wood calling it quits after five years without any prospect of a permanent life with Elvis.

Follow That Dream was released and did good box office business. It was the finest light comedy of Elvis' career, and while it featured relatively few songs, the fans and the critics were forgiving. Said the *Hollywood Reporter,* "Presley is not, of course, basically a comedian, but the laughs play about him and he comes off with disarming simplicity and sympathy." A movie industry trade poll even voted Elvis the top box office draw. The Colonel took all of this into account and upped Elvis' asking price for any new contracts to one million dollars per picture plus 50 percent of the profits. Elvis was now the highest-paid entertainer in Hollywood.

Elvis' next motion picture was set at the 1962 Seattle World's Fair, which served as a topical backdrop for a little romancing and ten songs. After a late-August recording session in Hollywood, Elvis and the M-G-M film crew flew to Seattle. Several days of the inclement weather typical of the Pacific Northwest stalled the production schedule, but in less than two weeks it was a wrap and everyone was back in Hollywood to complete work on *It Happened at the World's Fair.*

Elvis was able to spend the rest of the year relaxing back in Memphis. He got great pleasure from his new pet, a chimpanzee named Scatter. Elvis had purchased the chimp after it was seen performing on a local television show, and Scatter was given the run of the house during the day. It was even taken back and forth with Elvis whenever he went to Hollywood to work on a movie. Scatter was full of humorous antics and high energy, and brought a smile to Elvis when it was dressed in one of its small suits. Scatter was also an alcoholic, and the chimp became wilder as the years went by. It finally had to be kept in a pen at Graceland. Other pets that Elvis collected over the years included a spider monkey named Jayhu, a mynah bird, and a pair of peacocks.

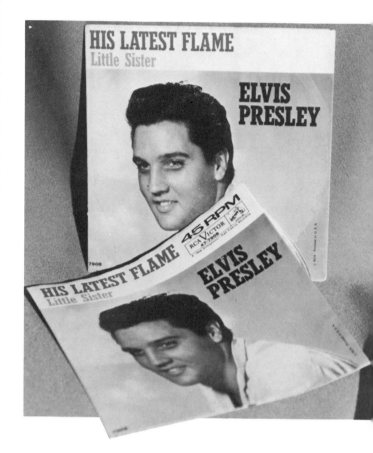

His Latest Flame picture sleeves

As collectibles, mistakes are often worth more than regular issues. A case in point is shown in these two picture sleeves from "His Latest Flame." The upper sleeve is missing the imprint of the RCA logo and record number, while the bottom sleeve is the regular commercial issue.

*Value of picture sleeve without logo: $100
Value, with logo and number: $24*

"Please Don't Drag That String Around/Along" single

Here's an error made at the printing plant that turned out record labels for RCA Victor. The correct title is "Please Don't Drag That String Around."

"Please Don't Drag That String Around" single value: $8
"Please Don't Drag That String Along" single value: $100

February 1961 benefit show program

After Elvis returned home from serving in the Army in Germany in March 1960, he performed only twice on the concert stage until 1968. Both of those shows were 1961 benefits. This program is from the February 25, 1961, show in Memphis, which raised over $50,000 for local charity organizations. As a historic collectible, this program rates very high.

Value: $75

During the winter Elvis also fielded his own personal team, dubbed the Elvis Presley Enterprises, in the play-offs of the Memphis touch football league. The second week of December, his team lost to the squad from Delta Automatic Transmission. "I have a great ambition to play football. I have had, and I still have. I have a touch football league. I like rugged sports. I'm not knocking people who like golf and tennis and the other things, but I like rugged sports such as boxing, karate, and football."

Girls! Girls! Girls! hit the theaters in November, and Colonel Parker used the opportunity to order up a special sport shirt for himself with the movie's title imprinted all over the material. He wore the shirt daily on his trips around Hollywood for a little free advertising. The movie needed all the publicity it could get, because the critics were beginning to see the "Elvis movie" for what it was. *Variety* recognized the key component of the formula when it reported that the movie required Elvis to sing thirteen songs "regardless of whether they fit smoothly into the action." The *Los Angeles Times* said that the movie was "no better or worse than previous Elvis epics. It's just a matter of whether you can take it."

On December 20 Priscilla arrived in Memphis to spend the holidays at Graceland. This was a very special Christmas for Elvis, but the holiday season was always his favorite time of year. Employees at Graceland started to decorate the house as soon as the table had been cleared from the Thanksgiving meal. If Elvis was out of town filming a movie, the trimming of the tree waited until he returned from Hollywood. This was the first year that a full-size Nativity scene, built by Hardie Phipps, was erected on Graceland's front lawn; over the years it would win numerous civic awards. Gifts for Elvis from his worldwide cadre of fans started arriving by mail even before Thanksgiving, and many Christmas Eve gift openings ran well past midnight, as he attempted to open every package. This year Elvis hosted a special party for seventeen-year-old Priscilla on Christmas Day and on New Year's Eve there was the first of what would become almost an annual holiday routine—a private party at Memphis' Manhattan Club followed by an enormous fireworks "battle" back at Graceland.

As the allotted two weeks of her second vacation with Elvis neared an end, Priscilla pleaded with her stepfather by telephone for an extension. She was denied, much to her chagrin, and shortly after the first of the year she returned to West Germany.

Elvis left Memphis shortly thereafter for Hollywood, to begin work on *Fun in Acapulco*. The setting for the picture may have been the Mexican seaside resort, but Elvis never left the back lot at Paramount. Another new low had been established for the "Elvis movie." Now the star could remain in Hollywood and lip-sync the dozen songs and woo the female stars in front of scenic footage shot on location. It was less bothersome for the film company that way, and less costly, to be sure.

In February Priscilla returned to Elvis, this time accompanied by her stepfather, who was being transferred from Germany to an air force base in California. Elvis and Major Beaulieu agreed that Priscilla would finish high school in Memphis under the auspices of the Catholic Church, and that Priscilla would take up residence with Vernon and Dee at their home adjacent to Graceland, where she could be chaperoned. After a few days in Hollywood, while Elvis wrapped up production on *Fun in Acapulco,* everyone returned to Memphis to make the arrangements. As soon as her parents left Memphis, Priscilla moved out of Vernon's house and into Graceland. From then on, whenever Elvis was in town, she stayed with him. When he was in Hollywood, she moved back in with Vernon and Dee.

Eddie Fadal remembers Graceland with and without Elvis around: "I've been there when it was so lonely. Elvis would go on the road. That place is like a graveyard when he's not there. It's just terrible. You can't imagine how everything drops off when Elvis is out of town. And how everything speeds up when Elvis is there. When he's there that place is just full of activity. I've stayed there thirty, forty days at a time. On the other hand, I'd go planning to stay a week and I'd want to leave in two days. It's just such a pace that you couldn't keep up. He wouldn't let you sleep. You're sitting in the living room and fans are in there and he's inviting people up from the gate and everyone's having a ball and in awe of Elvis. If one of the people that is staying with Elvis dozes off, he'll shake him and wake him up. If you doze off, brother, you've had it! And you're dying for sleep. Sometimes when he goes to bed and you're settled down in your bed real comfortably and just about to nod off, he decides he can't sleep so he comes down and wakes everybody up and off you go to get a hamburger."

Pocket watch

The photo on the face of this pocket watch shows Elvis from 1965's Girl Happy. This is not a licensed product of EPE. In the 1970s a similar watch was released, but it is easy to tell the two apart. The background of the earlier watch is a light pink; the later version is more reddish. The later watch also has a slightly pebbled back, while the original's back is smooth.

Value: $75

Girl Happy ads

This bit of fluff opened just in time for the annual spring migration of college students Ft. Lauderdale. The setting for the movie is that resort town in southeastern Florida.

14″ × 36″ lobby insert value: $20

Triangle watch

Elvis wore this Hamilton triangle watch during the filming of Blue Hawaii. *The watch is 14-carat white gold.*

Value: $12,000

Easy Come, Easy Go ads

This press book for Easy Come, Easy Go *contains newspaper ad mats in different sizes for the movie theater manager to use in the local advertising campaign. The booklet also contains radio spots as well as hints to generate word-of-mouth advertising. A similar book was issued with each of Elvis' movies, and each is a collector's item valued on par with the one-sheet.*

Press book value: $25

After his return to Los Angeles, Elvis was involved in an ugly incident that later received much publicity. As it involved a woman, Sonny West, as usual, was in the middle of it. West had invited a girl out to Elvis' home on Belagio Way for the evening, and while Elvis was playing a game of pool with one of the guys, she started berating Elvis for not paying her any attention. Elvis asked her to leave him alone several times. When she became irate and called him a "son of a bitch," Elvis hurled his pool cue at her, and it smacked her in the chest. That was the one word of profanity which Elvis, due to its literal implications, would not stand to be called. No one was more surprised at his actions than Elvis. He was immediately apologetic, and insisted that the girl receive medical attention. The extent and seriousness of any injuries were never made clear. Elvis had a quick temper, much as the men he played in the movies, and often his actions preceded any logical thought about the consequences. Afterward he almost always felt sorry for any hurt, physical or otherwise, that he might have inflicted. In a later interview, Elvis had this to say: "When I am pushed to a certain point I have a very bad temper, but it doesn't happen very often, and then I don't like myself later."

It Happened at the World's Fair opened, and although it did as well as expected, raking in several million dollars on its initial release, the single from the film, "One Broken Heart for Sale," did not crack the top ten, and the album did only marginally better. Elvis' stranglehold on the pop charts was clearly at an end. *Daily Variety's* review of the movie echoed others when it said that the ten songs in the movie were little more than "interuptions [that] upset the tempo of the yarn, frivolous as it is, and prevent plot and picture from gathering momentum." After the soundtrack album was released, there was some hue and cry among the fans over its brevity. The usual long-play record at this time had twelve songs. *It Happened at the World's Fair* had only ten and played for a scant twenty minutes. As a result, when future soundtracks came up short, they were padded with leftovers from Elvis' various recording sessions. The quality of these "bonus songs," as can well be imagined, was substandard even when compared to the dismal songs from the movies.

While in Los Angeles, Elvis took receipt of a car that was special even for him. A Rolls-Royce Phantom V Touring Limousine had been specially customized according to his instructions by a dealer in England and then sent to Los Angeles by boat. The twelve-foot-long auto was powered by an enormous 6230 cubic inch V-8 driving a four-speed automatic transmission. The exterior paint was midnight blue, and there was a gray cloth interior, which featured such amenities as a sterling silver ice thermos with two cut-glass decanters and five crystal glasses. This Rolls-Royce remained Elvis' auto of choice

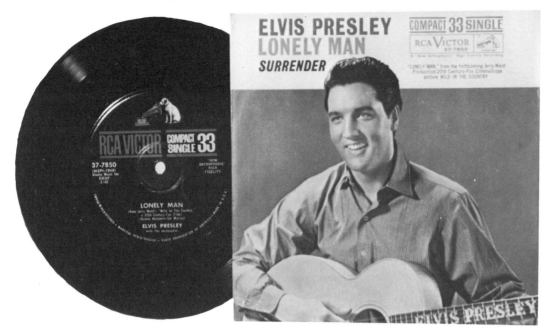

until he bought a Stutz Blackhawk in 1971. He was so happy with his new toy that when he arrived back at Graceland in April, he had new cars distributed to all of his employees, including the maids and cooks, who received either a Ford or a Buick.

The only business for Elvis during his three months of vacation at Graceland came on May 26, when he traveled to Nashville for another session, recording songs that would be released over the next few years on singles or used to fill upcoming soundtrack albums.

In June Priscilla graduated from Immaculate Conception High School. During her Memphis schooldays, she was ferried daily to and from classes in Elvis' limousine. Elvis did not attend the graduation ceremonies, for fear that his presence would detract from Priscilla's day of honor. Priscilla was now eighteen, and following graduation she enrolled in a finishing school to learn modeling and modern dance. Elvis felt that she could use the extra training. His intentions, it seems clear, were to shape Priscilla into an image of his own design. If he liked dark-haired women with bouffant hairdos, she dyed her long light brown hair black and wore it teased higher than anyone else. If he liked dark eyeshadow, she wore enough to make her deep blue eyes disappear into bottomless inky pools. She tried desperately to please Elvis. She understood that part of the gentleman's agreement between Elvis and her stepfather that had allowed her to come to Memphis was that, when the time came, Elvis would marry her. But she was just beginning to see that her hold over him might never be complete, for Elvis was easily swayed by the pleasures of Hollywood She held him completely only when he was near at hand.

In early July Elvis returned to Hollywood to start filming *Viva Las Vegas* with Ann-Margret. This was the first time since *Loving You* that Elvis shared billing above the title with another star, and was a tribute to Ann-Margret's

"Lonely Man"/"Surrender" Compact Single

In the early 1960s, RCA Victor was attempting to capture a larger share of the record-buying public through the introduction of "Compact Singles," which, while the same 7" size as a regular single, played at 33 ⅓ rpm. The idea was just too novel to catch on. As a result, the experiment ended with only five of Elvis' 1961–62 releases issued as Compact Singles.

Value of record and sleeve: $400

"Ask Me"/"Ain't That Loving You Baby" sheet music

Both sides of Elvis' late 1964 single release, "Ask Me"/"Ain't That Loving You Baby" had sheet music issued. "Ask Me" was tinted blue; "Ain't That Loving You Baby" came with a red tint.

Value: $15 each

growing appeal. After recording the soundtrack, Elvis, Ann-Margret, and over two hundred members of the M-G-M film crew traveled to Las Vegas for two weeks of location work. Elvis, who routinely made a romantic play for his female co-stars, was instantly smitten by Ann-Margret. On and off the set, they saw each so frequently that they became an item for the gossip columnists. So torrid was their apparent affair that it was the subject of much hype and speculation; even the local Memphis papers, unaware that Elvis had a secret teenage house guest at Graceland, picked up the story. Priscilla, who had been left in Memphis, heard all the rumors and innuendoes and was infuriated.

After completing the location work, Elvis, Ann-Margret, and the crew returned to Culver City, where the indoor scenes were shot at the Goldwyn Studios through August. Then the time came for Elvis to return to Graceland to face Priscilla. She was possessive but at the same time very insecure. She was so eager to please Elvis that, even in the face of repeated stories about a "blossoming" affair between Elvis and Ann-Margret, she accepted his story that the whole mess was a press ploy of Ann-Margret's design.

In October Elvis started work on another movie, *Kissin' Cousins.* Taking no chances, Priscilla accompanied him to Hollywood. She quickly found out that being close to Elvis was no guarantee of fidelity. The reports of the affair between Ann-Margret and Elvis, whether true or false, were repeated with such frequency that Priscilla finally left in a huff and returned to Memphis two weeks early. By then Elvis was too busy with the movie to take much notice. Besides, Priscilla's constant complaining about Ann-Margret was getting on his nerves.

On the set of *Kissin' Cousins,* Elvis was quick to learn that his long-standing desire for an acting career with legitimate overtones had been tossed out the window. The new picture was being produced by Sam Katzman, less than affectionately known around Hollywood as the "king of the quickies." Katzman had made a name for himself during the 1940s by turning out an endless stream of twelve-part movie serials and cheap B pictures. *Kissin' Cousins,* which had the added benefit of casting Elvis to play dual roles, was budgeted at only $800,000, of which half went for Elvis' salary. Outdoor locations were filmed at Big Bear Lake in the hills close to Los Angeles. The entire shooting schedule for *Kissin' Cousins* was only two weeks, but it ran an inexcusable two days over. Another low mark had been set for the "Elvis movie."

Just before Thanksgiving, *Fun in Acapulco* was released to justifiably lukewarm reviews. *Variety,* acknowledging its shoddy nature, said, "Presley has come a long way and is deserving of better material." The single from the movie, "Bossa Nova Baby," was a halfhearted attempt to ride the current wave of "dance songs" hooked to the watusi, the mashed potato, and the twist, but it failed to generate much action. Elvis took all of this in stride and returned to Graceland to smooth Priscilla's ruffled feathers.

The first Nashville recording session of the year, on January 12, went poorly, and only three songs were waxed. The best of these was a rolicking version of Chuck Berry's classic "Memphis, Tennessee," which, because of the implications of the title and the story line, should have been a natural tour de force for Elvis. Feeling little guilt over his scant recording output, Elvis left

RCA record catalogs

In 1965, Colonel Parker convinced RCA Victor to actively promote Elvis' records by issuing annual catalogs of the currently available Elvis records and tapes. Each catalog was in the form of a small booklet, and there were issues each year through 1973. From 1965 through 1969, they are printed vertically and stapled in the spine. From 1970 through 1973, each booklet was spiral-bound and printed horizontally. The covers of the 1965 and 1966 catalogs are identical except that the 1965 booklet has a red band at the bottom and the 1966 booklet has a blue band.

Value of 1965–1967 catalogs: $15 each
Value of 1968–1973 catalogs: $12 each

"Milky White Way" and "Joshua Fit the Battle" singles

For Easter 1966, RCA Victor released two religious singles at the same time. All four songs had been recorded in October 1960 for the His Hand in Mine *album.*

Value, with picture sleeves: $85 each

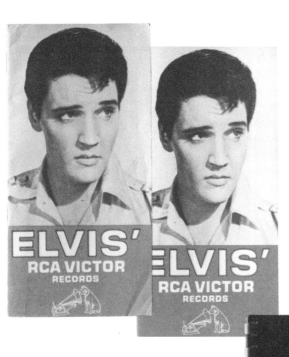

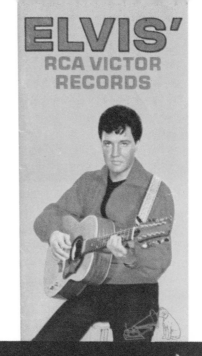

Elvis fabric

This 30"-wide, lightweight cotton cloth has Elvis' likeness along with "hip" sayings such as "the most" and "flip your wig."

Value: $25 per yard

Blue Hawaii lei necklace

What is more appropriate than a lei to promote a movie set in the beautiful islands of Hawaii? Colonel Parker just added a color promotional photo of Elvis from 1961's Blue Hawaii, and before you could say "aloha," here was another novelty to collect.

Value: $65

Elvis (Elvin) tee shirt

This tee shirt of unknown origin has an image of Elvis, which is labeled "Elvin." Song titles printed on this colorful tee shirt include "Don't Be Cruel," "Loving You," "Love Me Tender," and "Jailhouse Rock."

Value: $125

Blue Hawaii postcard

This jumbo 6″ × 9″ postcard was sold in the Hawaiian islands during the 1960s. It has no identifying markings.

Value: $25

Blue Hawaii ads

Blue Hawaii *did more to restrict the type of movie Elvis would make for the next five years than any of his other films. Its overwhelming financial success virtually forced Hollywood to lock Elvis into "travelogs" with beautiful scenery, gorgeous women, and a dozen songs. The one sheet from* Blue Hawaii *offers three separate views of Elvis, while touting the 14 songs in the soundtrack.*

27″ × 41″ one-sheet value: $60
11″ × 14″ lobby card value: $15 each

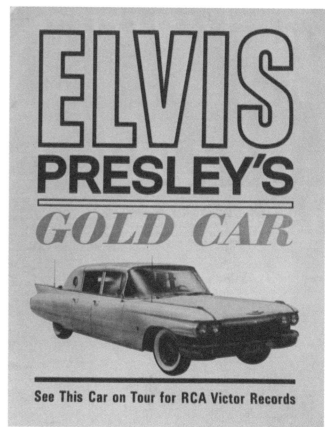

Spinout car

This 1958 Cobra was driven by Elvis in Spinout. It is interesting to note that this car actually entered and won several races after the film was completed.

Value: $100,000

Elvis' "Solid Gold" Cadillac

Elvis' "solid gold" cadillac is now on display at the Country Music Hall of Fame in Nashville. The 1960-series limousine was altered and customized by George Barris. Much of the exterior is plated in 24-carat gold, and the rest is painted with forty coats of diamond and pearl dust mixed in a liquid plastic base. Duplicates of some of his gold records adorn the car. The interior "lounge" features an entertainment center with a gold-plated television and telephone and a gold vanity with a gold electric razor. The car has 43,735 miles on the odometer.

ELVIS' GOLD CAR ON TOUR FOR RCA VICTOR RECORDS

shortly thereafter for Las Vegas and a brief vacation before returning to Los Angeles.

Elvis often vacationed in Las Vegas while staying on the West Coast. He enjoyed the bustle of the city's nightlife, and caught many of the lounge acts, as opposed to the lavish shows in the larger rooms. His favorite performers at this time included Fats Domino and Chuck Berry, with whom he shared a musical comradeship. He also loved to listen to songstress Della Reese entertain with her brand of blues and torch songs. His favorite comedian, interestingly, was Don Rickles, and the two of them were genuinely friendly with each other. Rickles respected Elvis because of Elvis' deep love for his mother, a trait they both shared. In Vegas, Elvis and the boys always stayed at the Sahara Hotel, because it was owned by Colonel Parker's good friend Milton Prell.

Back in Los Angeles on January 30, Elvis (probably at Colonel Parker's insistence) had a patriotic urge and bought the yacht *Potomac* at auction for $55,000. The yacht had previously belonged to President Franklin Roosevelt, and it was Elvis' contention that the presidential yacht should be maintained as a national treasure. Roosevelt had suffered from a severe case of polio and been confined to a wheelchair, so it was natural for Elvis to offer it to the March Of Dimes society as a donation. A week later, the March of Dimes gracefully declined, stating that it was a health agency and did not have any inclination to get into the yacht-restoration business. Now it appeared that Elvis would be stuck with the boat. Elvis offered to donate the yacht to a Miami coast guard auxiliary, but that was nixed when it was learned that the

Elvis' "Solid Gold" Cadillac on tour

In the mid-1960s, Elvis was too tied up with movie contracts to go on the touring circuit. So the Colonel, ever alert to unconventional methods of keeping Elvis' name in front of the public, sent Elvis' famed "solid gold" Cadillac off to meet the fans. Of course, there had to be a "tour book." And there were postcards showing the car in all its splendor, which the Colonel tied to Elvis' latest movie, Harum Scarum. Today, it is a major attraction at the Country Music Hall of Fame in Nashville.

Tour book value: $30
Postcard value: $10

Harum Scarum ads

The three pieces of advertising for Harum Scarum shown here are interesting in that the one-sheet and the lobby insert are virtually twins, while the window card has a totally different design.

27″ × 41″ one-sheet value: $40
14″ × 36″ lobby insert value: $20
14″ × 22″ window card value: $18

Harum Scarum album and bonus photo

Original copies of the Harum Scarum album, issued in October 1965, contained a bonus album-sized color portrait of Elvis in costume. Harum Scarum is universally considered to be Elvis' worst movie, and the soundtrack reflects the Arabian setting. The album is so weak musically that no song was issued from the film as a single record.

Value of album: $40
Value of photo: $25

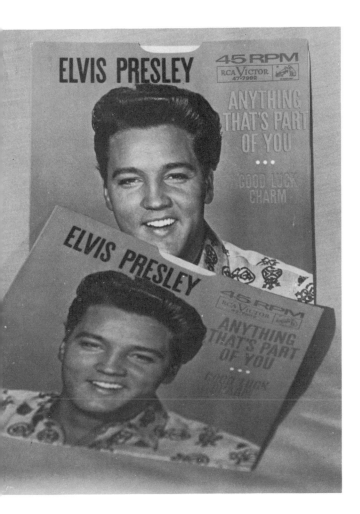

"Good Luck Charm"/"Anything That's Part of You" picture sleeves

For some unexplained reason, the picture sleeves issued for "Good Luck Charm" came with the two distinct color variations seen here. Differences like these, however, are what makes collecting Elvis' records so much fun!

Value of blue and pink printing: $30
Value of rust and purple printing: $20

auxiliary planned to cut the boat up for scrap metal and use the money to build a clubhouse. Elvis finally found a taker. In Long Beach on February 13, at a ceremony covered by the press corps, he presented the yacht to actor Danny Thomas, the national spokesman for St. Jude's Hospital in Memphis. Largely through the efforts of Colonel Parker, a near fiasco had been converted into a first-rate piece of publicity.

Elvis was on the West Coast to report for work on *Roustabout,* which was filmed at Paramount Studios, with location work for the carnival sequences photographed at Hidden Hills and Thousand Oaks, forty miles northwest of Los Angeles. Elvis' co-star in *Roustabout* was movie veteran Barbara Stanwyck—in this case, there was no movie-set romance—who reportedly embarrassed Elvis with her strong language. Elvis liked the women in his life to be genteel, and Stanwyck could tangle with even the most rugged of movie stagehands. Later, upon closer examination, film buffs noticed that one of the otherwise forgotten dancers in *Roustabout*'s tent show was a very young Raquel Welch in her movie debut.

Outside of Elvis' tightly controlled circle, the world of pop music was undergoing the most radical change since 1956, when Elvis had first burst on the scene with such an overpowering fury. Nineteen sixty-four was the year the Beatles conquered America. They made their first American appearance on Ed Sullivan's TV show on February 9. To gain a little free publicity and goodwill, Colonel Parker sent them a welcome-to-America telegram from "Elvis and the Colonel," which Sullivan read during the program. In two months, records by the Beatles completely dominated the music charts in this country. The Beatles led a virtual British Invasion that included other such shaggy-haired groups as the Rolling Stones, the Animals, the Kinks, the Searchers, Herman's Hermits, and the Dave Clark Five.

During the deluge, Elvis' songs remained firmly rooted in the silly movies he was making. The lack of adequate material harkened back to the original 1955 recording contract with RCA, which was partly financed by Hill and Range Songs. Now, virtually all of the songs written for Elvis' movies came from the same handful of writers working through Hill and Range, who were hopelessly out of touch with the rock 'n' roll market. For *Roustabout* there were songs with such titles as "Carny Town," "Poison Ivy League," and "Wheels on My Heels." But the movies continued to gross better than $2 million each during their initial release, and both Elvis and Colonel Parker frequently said that it would be foolish to tamper with success. For the time being, the easy way out for Elvis was business as usual.

In the meantime, *Kissin' Cousins* had been released, and the critics had a field day thinking up new phrases with which to castigate it. *Variety* called it "a pretty dreary effort," while the *Los Angeles Herald-Examiner* noticed that "acting demands upon the singing personality are kept to a minimum." All agreed, however, that the movie would probably be another financial hit.

Late in April, Elvis had just finished working on *Roustabout* when Albert Hand, the president of Elvis' most loyal British fan club, paid him a visit. It was unusual for Elvis to "officially" greet any of his fans, including fan club presidents. The entourage of friends and relatives that Elvis had formed in 1960 had by now become much more than a source of companionship. The Memphis Mafia, as the Hollywood press had dubbed the dozen or so hangers-on, now acted as Elvis' buffer against the outside world. Visitors were screened carefully, and few were allowed to enter the hallowed inner circle of Elvis' life. Most days were spent on movie sets, with nightly parties in the house in the Bel-Air hills. And everywhere that Elvis went, his front guard followed en masse.

The newest member of the group was Larry Geller, a Hollywood hairdresser who would bend Elvis' ear with religious teachings of mystical and metaphysical Eastern philosophies. Elvis was a willing student, having always been eager to learn more about the supernatural and the occult and the various religions of the world. Over the next three years, Geller would become the guru for Elvis and the group. Elvis always had an inquisitive mind. While he was never one to excell in school, this didn't mean he didn't thirst for knowledge. "I read a lot of philosophy and some poetry," he told one interviewer. "Have you ever heard of a book called *Leaves Of Gold?* It's by different people. Just different men's philosophies on life and death and everything else. Well, that kind of stuff interests me, to get different people's opinions on different things."

Viva Las Vegas opened in May, just in time for the summer movie audience, and the much-discussed romance between Elvis and Ann-Margret was up on the screen for everyone to see. The *Los Angeles Herald-Examiner* noted that the stars were "an explosive pair of dynamite performers." The stars certainly did sizzle, but the movie still received mixed reviews. *Variety* said the

1960's Elvis photos

The business of selling stars' photos continued unabated through the 1960s. This is the type of photo a fan would receive when responding to an ad that read "8 photos of Elvis for only $1.00." The set of eight photos is 5″ × 7″ on a nice sepia-tone paper.

Value: $5

Wild in the Country ads

Elvis had three love interests in Wild in the Country, *and the one-sheet from the movie captures Elvis locked in a passionate embrace with each lady. There's also a fist fight, a speeding car, and Elvis picking a guitar. The poster certainly has more action than the movie did.*

27″ × 41″ one-sheet value: $75

Girls Girls and More Girls bootleg album

This 1985 bootleg album is one of the second generation of European bootlegs that appeared after the American record industry and various legal branches of the government closed down the bootlegging of Elvis albums in this country. This album took the songs from Girls! Girls! Girls! directly from a copy of the film. The only item of genuine interest here is an acetate of "Plantation Rock," a song recorded for the movie, but shelved. An earlier bootleg, titled "Plantation Rock," had included the first issue of the song, but this version is much longer.

Value: $25

movie was "a pretty trite and heavy-handed affair, puny in story development and distortedly preoccupied with anatomical oomph." Nevertheless, it was money in the bank for all concerned, grossing $5.5 million, about double for Elvis' films at this time, which made the Colonel exceedingly happy.

In June Elvis reported to M-G-M Studios in Culver City to start work on *Girl Happy.* The songs were, if anything, worse than those for *Roustabout.* The setting for the movie was to be Fort Lauderdale, Florida, during the annual migration of college kids looking for a party in the sun; Elvis's scenes were shot on a back lot at the Goldwyn Studios. Elvis also suffered a blow to his ego when he tried to start up a little romance with his co-star, Shelley Fabares. She was friendly, but that was all. Elvis soon switched his attention to Mary Ann Mobley, a supporting actress and an ex–Miss America. She would weave through Elvis' life in an on again, off again romance through her second movie with Elvis, *Harum Scarum,* a year later. After six weeks' work on *Girl Happy,* Elvis returned to Memphis (and Priscilla) in late summer. He had been away for eight months, his longest absence from Graceland since returning from Germany. Priscilla had calmed down considerably, and the separation had created an even stronger bond between them.

Police work had always fascinated Elvis. It was one of the careers that he had seriously considered following graduation from high school. In September, now that he was Memphis' most famous person, he decided to take advantage of his position. After letting it be known that he had a deep desire to aid the local sheriff's department, he was graciously made a permanent deputy sheriff of Shelby County. Not an honorary deputy sheriff, but the real McCoy. This was only his first badge. There would be more over the next few years as he worked his wiles in many of the cities that he visited. Elvis took each of these awards seriously, even stopping an occasional speeding vehicle to chastise the driver, or helping to investigate an

Sheriff's badges

These represent only part of Elvis' collection of sheriff's badges. The badges in the middle of the top row were four of six given by Jimmie Velvet to Elvis for members of his personal entourage. Each was engraved with a name and number, but three of the names were misspelled. Velvet has managed to reclaim these four; he is still searching for the other two.

Value: $10,000 for any badge

accident. Possession of the badge also meant that he could carry firearms as a peace officer without worrying about breaking any local laws. His love for guns had originated in Tupelo during childhood hunting trips with his father or an uncle. Now that he could afford to fulfill his heart's desire, he amassed a large collection of fancy firearms. Engraved pistols were his favorite weapon, and he often gave away a special piece to someone as a token of his favor.

Production work on the year's third movie, *Tickle Me,* could best be called "cheap." It was another movie cast in the *Kissin' Cousins* mold. *Tickle Me* was a joint financial effort between Colonel Parker, Elvis, and Allied Artists Pictures, which was having money problems at the time. Allied Artists had been the started by several of Hollywood's better-known actors, including Sidney Poitier and Paul Newman, as a company that would cater to the needs of the actors and produce pet-project films. By 1964, after several pictures had lost money, the movie company was in need of a financial boost. Enter Colonel Parker, who agreed to cut Elvis' current asking price from a million dollars to $750,000. That left only another $750,000 in the budget to cover all of the other expenses, which meant that Elvis recorded no new songs for the movie. The musical soundtrack consisted of numbers culled from his previous albums. The entire look of the film was "bargain basement," but, just like all of Elvis' other movies, it made a handsome profit for everyone. This, of course, was the only reason for its existence.

Elvis, still trying to be the optimist, strained to see the bright side of his dismal movie career. "I have people say to me all the time, 'Why don't you do an artistic picture? Why don't you do this picture and that picture?' I would like to do something someday where I feel as if I've really done a good job as an actor in a certain type role. But I feel that it comes with time and a little living and a few years behind you. I think that it will come eventually. That's my goal. In the meantime, if I can entertain people with the things I'm doing, well, I'd be a fool to tamper with it. It's ridiculous to take it on your own and say, 'I'm gonna change. I'm gonna try to appeal to a different type audience.' Because you might not. And if you goof a few times you don't get many more chances in this business. That's the sad part about it. You're better off sticking with it until just time itself changes things. That's the way I believe, really."

The year opened with Elvis' latest soundtrack album, *Roustabout,* topping the charts. Though some later albums did chart well, it would be his last number one LP for eight years. By 1965, the metamorphosis of rock 'n' roll from its earliest heyday of the 1950s was complete. The style of popular music had fractured into a myriad of musical pathways, each with rock 'n' roll as its parent.

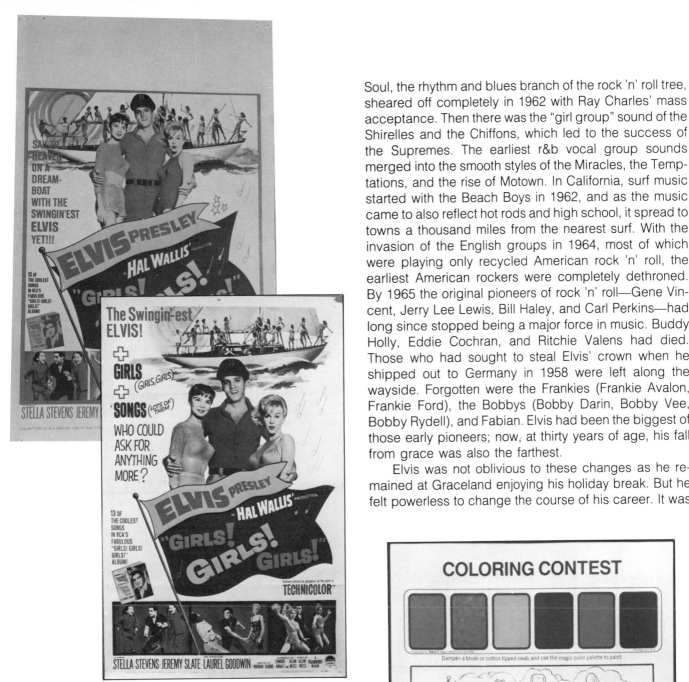

Soul, the rhythm and blues branch of the rock 'n' roll tree, sheared off completely in 1962 with Ray Charles' mass acceptance. Then there was the "girl group" sound of the Shirelles and the Chiffons, which led to the success of the Supremes. The earliest r&b vocal group sounds merged into the smooth styles of the Miracles, the Temptations, and the rise of Motown. In California, surf music started with the Beach Boys in 1962, and as the music came to also reflect hot rods and high school, it spread to towns a thousand miles from the nearest surf. With the invasion of the English groups in 1964, most of which were playing only recycled American rock 'n' roll, the earliest American rockers were completely dethroned. By 1965 the original pioneers of rock 'n' roll—Gene Vincent, Jerry Lee Lewis, Bill Haley, and Carl Perkins—had long since stopped being a major force in music. Buddy Holly, Eddie Cochran, and Ritchie Valens had died. Those who had sought to steal Elvis' crown when he shipped out to Germany in 1958 were left along the wayside. Forgotten were the Frankies (Frankie Avalon, Frankie Ford), the Bobbys (Bobby Darin, Bobby Vee, Bobby Rydell), and Fabian. Elvis had been the biggest of those early pioneers; now, at thirty years of age, his fall from grace was also the farthest.

Elvis was not oblivious to these changes as he remained at Graceland enjoying his holiday break. But he felt powerless to change the course of his career. It was

Girls! Girls! Girls! ads

The one-sheet tells just about all that the average fan might need to know about the movie: Girls! Girls! Girls. Elvis has two love interests and plays the part of a fishing boat skipper. There is some fighting and dancing, and the songs are available on a soundtrack album. The coloring sheet was a free promotional item available at the theater.

27" × 41" one-sheet value: $40
14" × 22" window card value: $20
Coloring sheet value: $15

COLORING CONTEST

Dampen a brush or cotton tipped swab, and use the magic color palette to paint.

HEY, KIDS! COLOR THIS SCENE FROM "GIRLS! GIRLS! GIRLS!"...
YOU MAY WIN TICKETS TO SEE THE NEW ELVIS PRESLEY MUSICAL
...PLUS OTHER PRIZES!
See how good an artist you are! Return your completed picture
to RECORD LANE no later than October 30, 1962

very frustrating to be locked into long-term movie contracts, but it was also very lucrative. And so, in late February, just as he had for the past four years, he started work on another picture, traveling to Nashville to record the soundtrack for *Harum Scarum*. The quality of his movies reached an all-time low with this terrible M-G-M release. Songs such as "Golden Coins," "Animal Instinct," and "Wisdom of the Ages" (the last two were, mercifully, cut from the film's final print) did little to endear Elvis to the teenagers of the day. By now, Elvis was heartbroken over the decline in his movie career. While his feelings seem to be concealed in his remark "I try to do the best that I can in the movies, with the experience I've gotten," by now he knew that he was never going to become the actor of his dreams.

En route from Memphis to Los Angeles with the usual gaggle of hangers-on, Elvis had a "spiritual experience." While crossing the southwestern desert, he saw a cloud formation that, everyone in the bus agreed, showed the bust of Stalin and the likeness of Jesus. The group's guru, Larry Geller, made a bigger deal of this than was probably necessary. After all, clouds can look like many things to different people. Still, the incident seemed to dog the entourage, for shortly thereafter the tour bus caught fire, forcing its abandonment while Elvis and his bedraggled buddies continued on to Los Angeles in a fleet of rented cars.

Production on *Harum Scarum* started on March 15 at the Goldwyn Studios in Culver City. This was to be Elvis' first "costume epic." The idea was to have Elvis in a role more appropriate for Rudolph Valentino. The story line was as thin as water, and Elvis complained loudly to anyone within earshot. How low had the "Elvis movie" sunk? Consider only Colonel Parker's suggestion of using a talking camel. The idea was subsequently dropped, which too bad, as some lively patter certainly couldn't have hurt the finished product. Fortunately for Elvis, he didn't have to endure the humiliation for long, as the picture was completed in a brief eighteen days.

Girl Happy had been screened by the Hollywood press in late January, to generally upbeat reviews, but

Stay Away, Joe ads

In the movie ads for Stay Away, Joe, *Elvis appears to be almost overrun by a rampaging bull ridden by half-a-dozen frolicking folks as a square dance takes place on the brim of his cowboy hat. Whoopie!*

14″ × 22″ window card value: $18

Kid Galahad ads

This window card from Kid Galahad *differs from the one-sheet only in that it doesn't have the top banner with two photos of Elvis. Unless one examines the movie ads closely, the fact that this movie is concerned with the boxing profession might be lost.*

14″ × 22″ window card value: $25

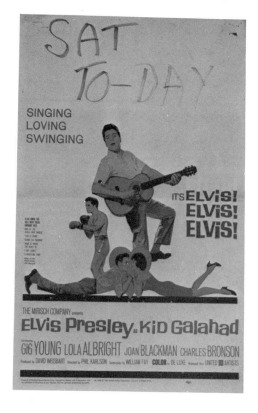

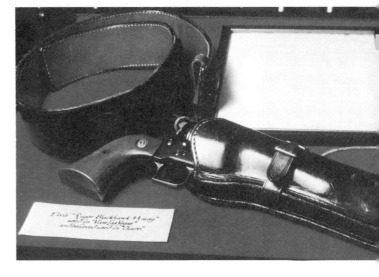

Magnum 44

Elvis carried this Ruger Blackhawk Magnum 44 in Viva Las Vegas, but it was also one of his favorites for personal use.

Value: $20,000

It Happened at the World's Fair ads

The choice of Seattle's 1962 World's Fair as the location for one of Elvis' movies was ideal. It allowed him to romance co-star Joan O'Brien against the much larger spectacle of the Space Needle.

27″ × 41″ one-sheet value: $40

the film itself was held for release until April and the academic spring break, when it went merrily along to earn another million dollars in profit. Elvis was in the middle of a five-week vacation when *Girl Happy* hit the theaters. He was deeply into the study of yoga and self-realization, and spent many of his free hours on Mount Washington near Los Angeles, meditating at the ashram of Sri Daya Mata. His deepening involvement in the various religious activities brought up by Larry Geller had a profound effect on Priscilla. Elvis wanted her to experience the same inner peace that he was striving to achieve, but Priscilla found the required teachings boring and the endless sessions tedious. She felt threatened and confused. Her suspicions were shared by other members of the inner circle, who were always uncertain of their exact place in the group. An intense struggle for Elvis' attention had begun in the entourage.

For the Easter season, RCA Victor went back into the vaults and resurrected the song "Crying in the Chapel" for release as a single. Elvis had recorded it back in 1960. To everyone's amazement, this spiritual sold well enough to garner another gold record. Colonel Parker, no slouch when handed such an opportunity, promoted the single and Elvis' *His Hand in Mine* album as a natural for radio stations to air on Mother's Day.

Elvis was hard at work waxing the songs for his second movie of the year, another costume flick, *Frankie and Johnny*. The songs were as forgettable as usual, and included "Petunia, the Gardener's Daughter" and a bastardized version of the folk classic from which the movie took its name and story line. Although the movie was produced by United Artists, it was filmed at Elvis' new home studio, M-G-M. Colonel Parker had moved into his own spacious building on the back lot of the Goldwyn Studios, where he entertained one and all with practical jokes and regaled listeners with yarns of his early carny life. The walls and ceilings were always plastered from top to bottom with advertising for Elvis' latest movie. Upon entering the hallway leading to the Colonel's office, one was inundated with a blizzard of Elvis publicity.

Tickle Me, surprisingly, met with little resistance from the nation's film critics upon its release in July, a possible indication of how little was now expected from an "Elvis movie." *Variety* noted, "Presley takes his character in stride, giving a performance calculated to appeal particularly to his following." On the other hand, the *Los Angeles Times* saw through the "lousy color, cheap sets and hunks of stock footage, painted scenery and unconvincing process work."

At the end of the month Elvis was fêted at a Hollywood to-do as he donated $50,000 to the Motion Picture Relief Fund. This was the largest private donation that the fund had ever received. Frank Sinatra and Barbara Stanwyck lent an air of dignity to the proceedings, and Colonel Parker made certain that the press was invited en masse.

On the last day of July, Elvis, feeling adventurous as well as generous, ordered a dozen Triumph motorcycles to be delivered to his Bel-Air home within the hour. There was a motorcycle for every member of the entourage, several of whom were outwardly hesitant about joining Elvis in a spin through the neighborhood. The boys were immediately tagged "El's Angels," and the neighbors complained loudly about the noise as a dozen cycles rumbled through the normally placid lanes of suburban Bel-Air.

Magazines: Movie rags

As a group, the movie fan magazines are among the least desirable of all Elvis collectibles produced while he was living. The stories are almost always based on some piece of fiction and are mostly misleading. The better ones, from a historical point of view, are Screen Stories, *with its synopsis of current movie plots and copious photos, and* Movieland and TV Time. *The latter issued the 1960 paperback book on Elvis which contained quite a few early stories that are generally reliable. The other movie magazines must be taken with a grain of salt if they are read at all. In fact, if the magazine doesn't have good photos of Elvis, then it is generally next to worthless.*

MUST READING! A CONFIDENTIAL REPORT ON RICKY NELSON

MOTION PICTURE

OCTOBER 25¢

GIANT PHOTO*
OF ELVIS
IN UNIFORM!
IN COLOR!
AUTOGRAPHED!
ABSOLUTELY
THE LARGEST
PIN-UP OF ELVIS
EVER PRINTED!

*Twice the size of
this magazine

Kim Novak

biggest color pin-up of
Elvis ever printed!
perfect for framing!

Early in August, Elvis began work on the soundtrack for his next movie, *Paradise—Hawaiian Style*, his third Hawaiian tale for Hal Wallis and Paramount Pictures. He was noticeably overweight when he arrived in Honolulu. Elvis' enormous appetite was his worst enemy. His eating habits were bred from years of southern-style cooking, which meant lots of fried foods. He had previously been able to keep his weight under a semblance of control by using over-the-counter diet pills to curb his appetite, but this time even they didn't work. In the movie industry time really is money, and there was no time to wait for Elvis to shed the extra pounds. Looking puffy around the face and midsection, he started shooting his scenes soon after his arrival.

Back in Los Angeles at the end of August, Elvis played host to the Beatles, the reigning kings of the musical world, who were in town on their second American tour. Elvis invited his rock 'n' roll rivals out to his home for a relaxing evening of musical jamming and friendly talk. Brian Epstein, the Beatles' manager, and Colonel Parker were there too, so it was not surprising when news of the summit leaked out to the press. Traffic was snarled throughout Bel-Air as thousands of teenagers and reporters converged on Elvis' home to wait in vain for a glimpse of either Elvis or the Beatles. It is unfortunate for the history of rock music that there are no known tape recordings or photographs of this memorable jam session. By all accounts, a splendid time was had by all.

Driving the tour bus and followed by his entourage in five trailing cars, Elvis arrived at Graceland on October 7. Elvis was seen frequently thereafter riding around the grounds in his new go-cart. The go-cart had started as a regulation model, but it was quickly souped up to cruise at over sixty miles per hour around the driveway leading up the hill to the house. He was also spotted tooling around Memphis in his new Oldsmobile Toronado or one of the new front-wheel-drive autos, or on one of his motorcycles.

If Elvis wasn't doing any more tours, then Colonel Parker would send out the next best thing to meet his fans: the "solid-gold" 1960 Cadillac "75" limousine. The car had been customized by George Barris' Kustom City in North Hollywood—the same outfit that had overhauled his bus. The top of the Cadillac was covered with white pearl Naugahyde, and all metal trim was plated with 24-karat gold. The exterior received forty coats of "diamond-dust pearl" lacquer, which consisted of crushed diamonds and fish scales imported from the Orient. The interior of the automobile was styled after the bridge of a yacht, with gold lamé drapes covering the "portholes" cut into the side of the car. There was white Naugahyde upholstery, a record player, tape recorder, and TV, and a refrigerator with a freezer. Overhead there were replicas

"VIVA LAS VEGAS"

Viva Las Vegas ads

This lobby card from **Viva Las Vegas** *offers terrific insight into not only the movie's plot, but the off-screen interplay between Ann-Margret and Elvis. She seems determined to hold on to Elvis, while he is just as eager to slip away. Lobby cards, in sets of eight, were issued for all of Elvis' movies.*

11″ × 14″ lobby card value: $12 each

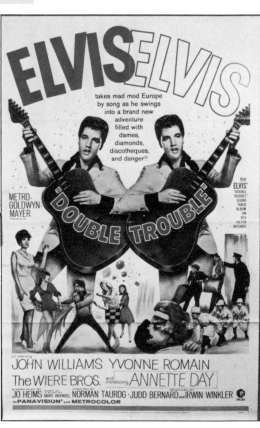

of all of his gold records. By the early 1970s the car had been seen by thousands of sightseers all over the world.

Harum Scarum received the anticipated pans from the movie critics. The movie failed to entertain because of a "lack of imagination in providing the star with a substantial showcase," complained *Variety*. Without even one song from the film considered strong enough for release as a single, RCA Victor reached back to *Girl Happy* for "Puppet on a String," pairing it with "Wooden Heart," from 1960's *G.I. Blues*. Amazingly, the record sold half a million copies. It was during this holiday season that the stereo reissue of Elvis' 1957 Christmas album pushed its total sales to over 300,000 copies. Recycled Elvis was still able to ring cash registers.

Elvis was disturbed by the lack of challenge that his career seemed to offer. His frequent outbursts about the

Double Trouble ads

The one-sheet and the window card for **Double Trouble** *are similar in most respects. The movie had its best moments when the bumbling trio of detectives, played by the Weir Brothers, are on-screen, and they are given a prominent place in the advertising.*

27″ × 41″ one-sheet value: $30
14″ × 22″ window card. value: $18

Elvis for Everyone albums

Although it would appear that Elvis for Everyone is all stereo, four of the songs ("Your Cheating Heart," "In My Way," "Forget Me Never," and "Sound Advice") were originally recorded in monaural and do not sound right when heard in "stereo." "Tomorrow Night," a track originally recorded by Elvis during his days with Sun Records, was "rediscovered" and overdubbed by Chet Atkins, and several other Nashville musicians with the Anita Kerr Singers on March 18, 1965. Therefore the complete collector requires a stereo and a monaural copy of Elvis for Everyone to hear the pure sound of the songs.

Value of stereo LP: $40
Value of monaural LP: $60

simple songs and slipshod films were often leveled at the ever-present entourage. It would seem that they were also a part of the problem. The pressure of living up to the image of "Elvis Presley" was enormous, and while his buddies tried to protect him from outside pressures, they also encroached on the very privacy they were supposed to secure. The problem with his weight, first apparent on the set of *Paradise—Hawaiian Style*, was now constant. When he was depressed, Elvis did as so many other people did: he ate. Now his career and his life style worked together to depress him. His thirtieth year had proved to be the worst in terms of fulfilling his needs as an artist. He complained to everyone in earshot that he felt a growing need to return to the basics of his career. It had been four years since his last concert, the Hawaiian benefit for the memorial to the sunken USS *Arizona*. After that he had been on a treadmill, making three movies a year. Now each was worse that the last. Lamentably, the end of this uncontrollable nonsense was nowhere in sight. The seven-year movie deals with the studios had him tied up for three more years.

For Christmas, Priscilla tried to cheer Elvis up by giving him a slot-car racing set. He immediately fell in love with it, and expanded the track layout to such monstrous proportions that an addition had to be built onto Graceland. Everyone had a special car, and Elvis spent hours on end racing the tiny vehicles round the track. As with most of his toys, Elvis' enthusiasm for slot cars lasted only a few months after the expensive room was completed. The track was eventually dismantled and the room was used to store his many awards and trophies. Elvis had little patience for most of the material items with which he surrounded himself. When something became old, it was thrown out or put in storage. "I had enough antiques to last me a lifetime when we were living in Tupelo."

Elvis celebrated the New Year with a massive fireworks fight on the grounds of Graceland. By this time, the holiday pyrotechnics had become much more than a mere display. As with everything that Elvis undertook, the fireworks became an outlet for his boundless energy. "War" was declared, and the guys divided into two teams. Football helmets, motorcycle jackets, gloves, and other heavy clothing were the regulation dress for the games. Roman candles were used as mortars; two-inch firecrackers became hand grenades. Exploding rockets and screaming devils whizzed through the air wildly. No one who was found outdoors was excluded. The timid hid behind locked doors and peeked through parted curtains. Thousands of dollars' worth of fireworks went up in an inferno of airborne incendiaries and hole-digging blasts that lasted for hours. Injuries were frequent but minor, and Elvis got a much-needed release from a year's worth of pent-up frustrations.

June Kelly poster

This 16″ × 20″ color poster of a painting by June Kelly was manufactured by RCA Victor to be given away by record stores with the purchase of Elvis albums during the mid-1960s.

Value: $30

Spinout ads

"With his foot on the gas and no brakes on the fun!!!" At least that's what the one-sheet and the window card say. But this movie gave the audience gas, and the brakes should have been applied before the first frame was shot.

27″ × 41″ one-sheet value: $35
14″ × 22″ window card value: $15

Early in 1966, RCA Victor announced that Elvis had sold an astonishing total of 78 million records, up from 49.3 million only two years before. To anyone looking only at the accountants' books, Elvis' career appeared to be in full swing. But a closer examination of Elvis' success as measured against that of other superstars of the day showed an ever-widening gap, with Elvis' record sales consistantly dropping behind his contemporaries'.

After two months of leisure, Elvis returned to Hollywood in mid-February to start filming *Spinout* for M-G-M. The recording of the soundtrack was followed by some location work in Santa Barbara and at Malibu Lake north of Los Angeles. Most of the movie, as usual, was shot back at the Goldwyn Studios. Elvis' frustrations rose to the surface over a delay in one day's filming, and he blew up at the director, Norman Taurog. The incident was over in a flash, and might have been forgotten except for its ferocity. This public emotional tirade was something rare for Elvis. He took professional pride in being able to hide his discomfort with his movies while on the set. His screaming at the director caught everyone by surprise.

Taurog, ever the diplomat, quickly soothed Elvis' feelings. Taurog had started directing Elvis with *G.I. Blues*. *Spinout* was his sixth Elvis movie, and he was fully aware of Elvis' temper. As if to show that everything was alright, that evening Elvis took his entourage on a spree of Cadillac buying, purchasing a total of nine, giving each man a new convertible. He also paid all of the taxes (including the federal gift tax), so that each man would own the car outright. It wasn't the first time that he had used his generosity as a means to quell his inner demons. It wouldn't be the last.

As Elvis arrived back in Memphis in late April, *Frankie and Johnny* opened in theaters across the country, to mediocre reviews. "Elvis is Elvis," said the review in *Variety*. "He sings and acts, apparently doing both with only slight effort."

It only took a few days of rest from the rigors of Hollywood before he once again started the rounds of midnight movies. He viewed over forty films during his two-month vacation. He also rented the amusement park several times for late-night parties. He still enjoyed a rugged game of "war" in the "dodge-'em" cars, and would follow that up with dozens of exhilarating rides on the roller coaster. In the early morning, everyone would return exhausted to Graceland.

He had two recording sessions in Nashville in May and June, to lay down the songs for his second religious album, *How Great Thou Art* and record the single "If Every Day Was Like Christmas." A fully decorated Christmas tree was delivered to the studio to liven up the latter title.

Spinout album and bonus photo

The album Spinout *was issued in October 1966 to coincide with the release of the movie, and original copies contained an album-sized, full-color portrait of Elvis as a bonus. The songs are a cut above other Elvis mid-1960s movie soundtracks, and he even gets a passable rocker in "Stop, Look and Listen." The lasting interest in the album lies in the three bonus songs. "Tomorrow Is a Long Time" is an early Bob Dylan number that lasts more than five minutes, Elvis' longest song up to that time. Another is "Down in the Alley," a 1954 rhythm and blues hit for the Clovers. Finally, there is the beautiful ballad "I'll Remember You" by Kui Lee, the Hawaiian songwriter who's death from cancer sparked Elvis' 1973* Aloha from Hawaii *worldwide satellite TV show.*

Value of album: $40
Value of photo: $25

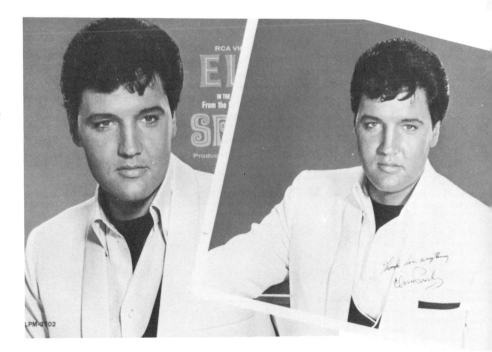

Paradise—Hawaiian Style was released for the summer trade. Remarked the Hollywood *Reporter,* "It is not one of the best Presley films, but it should satisfy the fans." Obviously, the movie industry considered the level of acceptance by his fans quite low.

During his stay in Memphis, Elvis came down with a flu bug that he wasn't able to shake. When he couldn't reach his regular family doctor, his old friend George Klein suggested that Elvis visit Dr. George Nichopoulos, for whom Klein's wife worked as a receptionist. It wasn't long before Dr. Nick, as he was called, was a full-fledged member of the entourage.

Elvis' next movie had its setting in Belgium, but Elvis never left the M-G-M back lot in Culver City. The few scenes actually shot in the Belgian countryside were filmed by a second unit using a double for Elvis. Work on *Double Trouble* was wrapped up in early September, followed by the immediate start of *Easy Come, Easy Go* for Paramount Pictures. The movies were becoming a blur, one blending into next with monotonous regularity. *Spinout* was released for the winter vacation, with *Time* magazine speculating that the picture might be aimed at a possible adult audience—"adult chimpanzees." The magazine went on to offer an unflattering but fairly accurate view of Elvis' appearance at age thirty-one: "Eleven years of living high on the hawg . . . has porked up his appearance. His cheeks are now so plump he looks like a kid blowing bubble gum—and his mouth is still so squiggly that it looks like the bubble had burst." In a final slap at Elvis, *Time* fired a parting shot at Elvis' hairstyle, the pride of his permanent hairdresser, Larry Geller: "What's more, he now sports a glossy something on his

Tape recordings

Starting in 1960 with **Elvis Is Back,** *all of Elvis' albums have been made available on tape. First, it was reel to reel, then 8-track, and now cassette. As a new tape format was introduced, the older ones were gradually phased out. The value of tapes is tied to their availability as well as to the number of copies sold.*

Clambake album and bonus photo

Released in November 1967, **Clambake** *was a half-baked idea for a movie in the first place, and the soundtrack shows it. The bonus songs are the most interesting. "Guitar Man," Jerry Reed's classic, highlights Reed's superlative acoustical guitar work. Then there's "Big Boss Man," again featuring Reed's guitar and some blues on the harmonica from Charlie McCoy. The bonus photo is an album-sized snapshot of Elvis and Priscilla taken on their wedding day. A monaural copy of this album is valued above the stereo version because RCA, along with the rest of the industry, was cutting production of monaural at this time.*

Value of monaural album: $150
Value of stereo album: $50
Value of photo: $25

Value of reel-to-reel tape
    recordings: $40 average
Value of 8-track tape recordings:
    $20 average
Value of "Savage Young Elvis"
    1984 Radio Shack cassette on
    12" × 12" card: $15

Clambake ads

*The artwork for Clambake reflects
the late 1960s turn away from the
more traditional ad. There is a
switch to pale purples and
aquamarine from the customary
deep red and bright yellow. The
tag line has Elvis apparently
"bikini-ing." Fans certainly could
be forgiven for flocking to local
theaters to catch Elvis modeling
one of those brief swimsuits; there
is little else to recommend
Clambake.*

27" × 41" one-sheet value: $30
14" × 22" window card value: $18

Elvis Presley in comic books

These two romance comics were issued in 1966, and each contained a story about Elvis. Elvis never had his own comic book, though Ricky Nelson did.

Value: $75 each

Elvis, The Swingin' Kid

This 1962 British paperback by Charles Hamblett covers Elvis' career through Blue Hawaii. There are eight pages of black-and-white photos in the middle of the book from his tour of duty in Germany and from the set of Follow That Dream.

Value: $35

Elvis Full Color Folio

One of the nicest items issued by RCA Victor is this full-color, 16-page magazine with an 11″ × 21″ fold-out poster from 1963. Several pages are taken up with listings of Elvis' albums and singles, but there are 19 color photos of Elvis, several of which are full-page portraits.

Value: $30

Red jacket, black leather vest

The red jacket with black leather trim pictured here was worn by Elvis in the last one third of Double Trouble. The black leather vest is an item from Elvis' personal wardrobe. In the 1960s a radio station in Chicago sponsored a contest in which participants had to fit as many Elvis song titles as possible into an essay of a limited number of words. First prize was this vest.

Red jacket value: $10,000
Black leather vest value: $5,000

Easter postcards

Just as with the Christmas postcards, these cards bearing Easter greetings were another of the Colonel's tactics to keep Elvis' name in front of the public. For four years, from 1966 through 1969, special Easter postcards were distributed to record stores through RCA Victor as a "freebie" for customers. Each card, except the first, is dated.

Value: $10 each

Tickle Me ads

Tickle Me, *according to the inside of the colorful packet of* Tickle Me *feathers, starred "Elvis as a singing, swinging wrangler on a dude ranch—for girls!" The feathers are an obvious advertising gimmick. Also available announcing the movie was this 8 ½" × 11" single-page herald printed on lightweight cardboard.*

Tickle Me *feathers value: $40*
Herald value: $15
Value of quill pens: $50

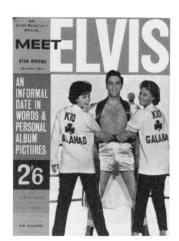

Meet Elvis, Star Special #1

Meet Elvis, Star Special #1 *is a 1962 publication of Albert Hand. Throughout the 52-page booklet, the "meet" theme is followed with stories such as "Elvis Meets the World," "Meet G.I. Elvis," and "I Meet Elvis." Most of the photos used are stills from Elvis' movies.*

Value: $75

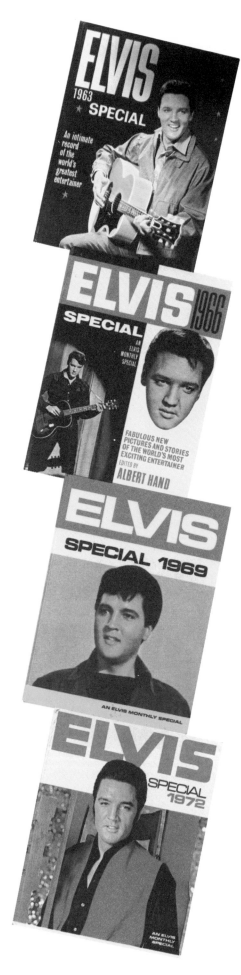

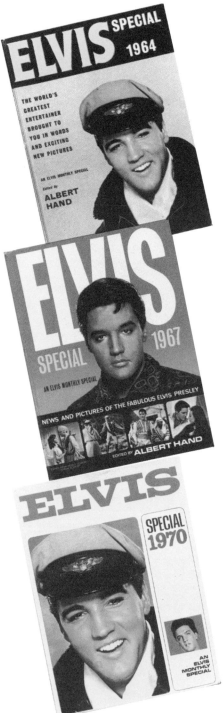

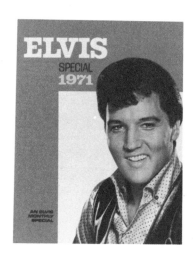

Elvis Specials, 1963–1982

*Beginning in 1963, the Elvis
Presley Fan Club of Great Britain
began issuing a yearly hardbound
"annual" covering Elvis' career.
Each is full of rare photos ("Elvis'
Personal Album #8, 1969),
cartoons ("Elvistoons," 1965),
poetry ("A Date with Elvis," 1964),
quizzes ("Here's a Double Puzzle
to Give You Double Trouble" from
1964), stories ("The Story of Count
Elvis and the Bloated One," 1967),
trivia (lists of Silver Disc awards
presented by the English Disc
magazine are in each volume), and
lists of every Elvis song, album,
single, and EP issued in England.
The books are 112–116 pages in
length. The earlier issues are the
most valuable.*

Value: $15–$50

Pocket calendars

Starting in late-1962, pocket-sized calendars with Elvis' picture on the front appeared in local record stores each year. They were given away to customers as long as the supply lasted. The tradition of issuing annual Elvis pocket calendars continued through to 1980. In 1981, Boxcar Enterprises reissued the set in a special cardboard sleeve. The reissues in most instances are photocopys of the originals and are easily spotted.

Pocket calendar value, by year:
1963, $60; 1964, $45; 1965, $25;
1966, $20; 1967–69, $15;
1970–72, $12; 1973–76, $8;
1977–80, $4; Boxcar set, $15

summit that adds at least five inches to his altitude and looks like a swatch of buttered yak wool." Elvis fled back to Graceland's relative security. Another year had passed, another three movies were in the can, and Elvis was more in the dumps than ever. He must have asked himself if the endless tripe disguised as movie scripts would ever go away.

To assuage his pangs of insecurity, he started giving away expensive gifts as soon as he was home. He was told of the plight of an elderly black woman who lived in a run-down house not far from the area of Memphis that had first been home to the Presleys when they moved from Tupelo. She had lost the use of her legs and could not afford to replace her dilapidated wheelchair. Elvis bought the woman a top-of-the-line electric wheelchair and delivered it personally, leaving $200 in cash to help out further. Still feeling generous, Elvis stopped by an auto dealer's showroom, where he bought George Klein a Cadillac. Elvis then took Klein's almost new Chevy convertible and delivered it to Gary Pepper, the invalid who was president of Elvis' Memphis fan club. One car purchased, two people happy. Elvis was working miracles. Topping both of those generous gestures, his annual donation to Memphis charities and the Tupelo youth center was doubled to $100,000 for the first time in 1966.

One night near Christmas, Elvis formally proposed to Priscilla. It was a day that both of them had always known would come, although Priscilla had privately wondered if Elvis would manage to put it off forever. In fact, it appears that the timing of the marriage may have been mostly Colonel Parker's idea. The Colonel was a prudish man, and Priscilla's staying with Elvis at Graceland, whether or not there was anything going on, rankled him. There was a limit to just how long the story of Elvis and Priscilla's living arrangement could be kept from the fans, much

Frankie and Johnny album and bonus photo

Issued in April 1966, the soundtrack from Frankie and Johnny is a schizophrenic mix of rock and ballads and a few throwaway songs that desperately attempt to fit the setting of the movie, a turn-of-the-century showboat. The bonus photo is a portrait of Elvis in costume painted by June Kelly, the artist who did the painting of Elvis in the red shirt which RCA Victor distributed in the 1960's. Frankie and Johnny was deleted from RCA Victor's catalog soon after its release because of poor sales. Because the rights to the songs were deeded over to the Pickwick Record Company in the 1970s, the album was never reissued in its original form.

Value of album: $75
Value of photo: $30

Frankie and Johnny ads

Now here's an interesting twist: the main line from the ads for Frankie and Johnny plugs the RCA Victor album! Admittedly, the movie wasn't much to shout about, but surely the publicity department at United Artists could have come up with something more appropriate.

27" × 41" one-sheet value: $40
14" × 22" window card value: $18

less the press. The final nudge for Elvis came during a private talk with Colonel Parker, who issued an ultimatum in no uncertain terms: "Either marry Priscilla or kick her out of Graceland." When her stepfather had allowed her to come to Memphis to live as a teenager five years earlier, it was understood that one day she would become Mrs. Elvis Presley. Now that she was twenty-one, that time had arrived. No official date for the marriage was set at this time, but the inside money was on a spring wedding.

Just after the start of 1967, Elvis and Colonel Parker renegotiated their contract to include a fifty-fifty split on all of Elvis' entertainment fees and record royalties. Previously, Colonel Parker had received 25 percent of Elvis' earnings. Up until 1965 the Colonel had continued to book his previous star, Eddy Arnold. Now he felt that the new contract was justified because he represented no other artist except Elvis. Elvis, ever loyal to the Colonel, went along with little or no discussion. As if to show that there was enough money to spread around, M-G-M announced that the seven movies made for them by Elvis, starting with *Jailhouse Rock* in 1957, had grossed over $76 million. M-G-M also released an item reporting that Elvis' next two films would be *Bumble Bee, O' Bumble Bee* and *Pot Luck* (Neither title was ever used.)

Early in 1967 Elvis had his bedroom at Graceland redecorated in a Spanish motif. Included in the renovation were two television sets (supplied free by RCA Victor, of course) embedded in the ceiling so that he could watch TV lying in bed. While Graceland was the permanent home that he loved, he had his eye on a 163-acre ranch just across the Mississippi stateline. He had first spied the property on an afternoon's drive through the countryside, and when it came up for sale in February he quickly pounced at the chance to spend $300,000 to claim it for his own. He named the ranch the Circle G, but later had to redub it the Flying Circle G when he discovered that there was already a ranch registered with the first name. Here he could stable the seventeen horses that he had recently purchased, which had been temporarily pastured at Graceland. The favorite of his horses was the golden palomino quarterhorse, Rising Sun; others included his Tennessee walker, Bear, Red West's Big Red, Vernon's Midnight, a Shetland pony named Boolaloo, and Priscilla's mount, Domino. With much enthusiasm, Elvis immediately set about to improve the ranch so that he and his friends and relatives could spend weeks on the property without leaving. A dozen mobile homes were bought and erected as living quarters. He liked this idea so much that he moved into one of them, instead of staying in the ranch house. There was a mobile home for Vernon and one for each of the guys. The neighbors were quick to complain that Elvis was starting a mobile home park, and a special permit was required to hook up the electricity and the twelve septic tanks. He purchased an astounding thirty-three pickup trucks, with the total bill coming to $98,000. Again, every member of the Memphis Mafia got a truck, as did relatives, other employees, and even a few total strangers. In fact, there were so many trucks that their owners' names had to be painted on the door just to keep them straight. Vernon was beside himself. He had put up Graceland as collateral on the original loan to buy the ranch, and it fell to him to pay the bills as Elvis bought implements, tack, hardware, and machinery. He went to Elvis, pleading that the spending at least slow down to a manageable level. "Daddy," Elvis replied, "I'm having fun for the first time in ages. I've got a hobby, something to look forward to getting up in the morning for." They spent weeks on end at the ranch, and when show business called Elvis away, Alan Fortas was named ranch foreman.

Films and Filming magazine

The August 1966 issue of the prestigous English Films and Filming magazine featured a cover story on "The Changing Face of Elvis" that discussed his 10-year, 22-film career. In the story it was reported that the gross from his first 18 pictures topped $175 million.

Value: $10

Kissin' Cousins ads

This was a silly movie, so it's fitting that the poster should be as well. In the drawing, which is the poster's main feature, Elvis looks almost embarrassed.

27" × 41" one-sheet value: $40
14" × 36" lobby insert value: $20

Fun in Acapulco ads

The most "fun" in Acapulco was pairing Elvis with the voluptuous Ursula Andress. Both the one-sheet and the lobby insert play down Ursula Andress, concentrating instead on co-star Elsa Cardenas. The passport is an 8-page, photo-filled pamphlet that was given away free to movie patrons.

*14" × 36" lobby insert value: $20
14" × 22" window card value: $15
Passport value: $25*

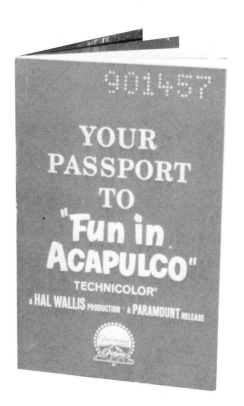

In early March, just before he left Memphis to start work on *Clambake,* Elvis got the idea that the old three-room cottage behind Graceland (which had once served as a home for his uncle Travis Smith and his family) should be destroyed to make room for a horse arena. He tried to do the job himself, with the small tractor that was used for grounds work, but it proved to be woefully inadequate. A wrecking crew with a full-size bulldozer was called in. Elvis soon decided that they were working much too slowly, and commandeered the machine and attacked the house in a frontal assault. Wearing only a football helmet for protection, Elvis crashed repeatedly into the wood-frame structure. After the house had been reduced to mostly rubble, he set fire to it, causing an enormous blaze that summoned the fire department. Elvis hadn't enjoyed himself so much in weeks.

Production on *Clambake* ground to a quick halt when Elvis slipped on an electrical cord in the bathroom of his Bel-Air home and suffered a mild concussion. Colonel Parker took this opportunity to regain some of the control over Elvis that he had lost to the entourage in recent years. Up to that time, several members of the group had been acting in a manner that the Colonel felt was confusing to Elvis. After a long private meeting with Elvis, the Colonel put the clamps on the group, particularly Larry Geller, and the study of mysticism and numerology came to a temporary halt as Geller decided to leave. The Colonel saw to it that most of the books on Eastern religions were removed. In one further step, Colonel Parker set up a formal chain of command within the Memphis Mafia—Joe Esposito became chief of staff—designed to limit direct access to Elvis. Throughout the incident, Elvis refused to step in and defend either himself or the Memphis Mafia. This was one of the rare occasions on which he let Colonel Parker handle his personal life.

Work on *Clambake* began after Elvis recuperated, but it was obvious that his heart wasn't in making "Elvis movies" anymore. After *Clambake,* his sole remaining movie obligation was the contract with M-G-M, which had two more years to run.

The release of the *How Great Thou Art* LP was a bright spot amid the usually dreary soundtracks. The album even went over well with those in the music industry, garnering Elvis' first Grammy award for best sacred performance. *Double Trouble* also found the critics eager to overlook its flaws. *Variety,* as always, summed up the general opinion: "Elvis, as usual, gives a pretty fair account of himself despite what's handed him." Elvis, it seemed, was at last becoming respectable.

And what better way to capitalize on this new respectability than for the world's most eligible bachelor to wed his sweetheart of seven years? After their engagement had been announced, the location and date of the wedding remained a matter of speculation even among those closest to Elvis. The planning for the upcoming marriage, like everything else, was left up to Colonel Parker.

Under a tight blanket of secrecy, Elvis and Priscilla, along with both sets of parents, met at Elvis' Palm Springs hideaway. The Hollywood press immediately smelled the bacon. Luring the reporters to Palm Springs, Colonel Parker issued an announcement that there would be a special press conference at the Aladdin Hotel in Las Vegas at 1:00 P.M. the next day, May 1. But at 3:00 A.M., Elvis and Priscilla sneaked into Las Vegas aboard a rented Lear jet and quickly obtained a marriage license. (In this gambling town, the business of issuing marriage

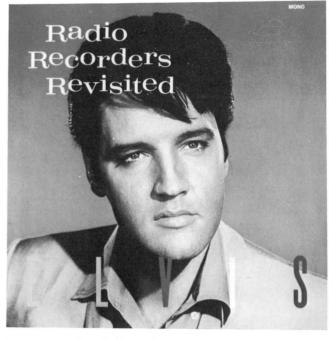

Radio Recorders Revisited bootleg album

This European album from 1985 contains quite a few outtakes of the six songs in the film **Kid Galahad.** *The outtakes are quite different from those that appeared on the soundtrack. The title of this album refers to the studio on Santa Monica Boulevard in Hollywood that Elvis most frequently used to record his movie soundtracks.*

Value: $30

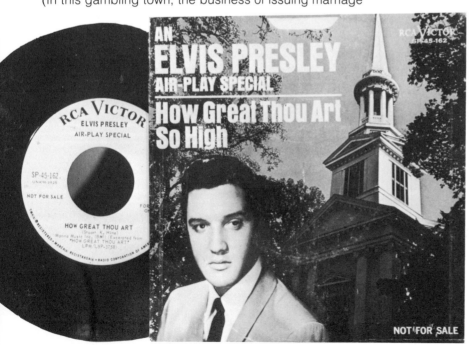

"How Great Thou Art" promotional single

This single should not be confused with the April 1969 RCA Victor release of "How Great Thou Art" (74-0130). This special, limited promotional single with picture sleeve was sent to radio stations on February 21, 1967, to plug Elvis' upcoming religious album with the same title.

Value, with sleeve: $300

Double Trouble album and bonus photo

The Double Trouble album was issued in June 1967 and contained a bonus 8" × 10" portrait of Elvis. Elvis portrayed a nightclub entertainer in the movie, and most of the songs from the soundtrack have a 1960s cabaret sound.

Value of album: $40
Value of photo: $15

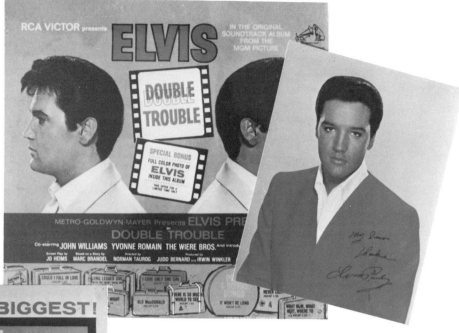

Paradise-Hawaiian Style ad

If this movie were made today, it would have been named "Blue Hawaii 2." The very colorful and exciting one-sheet is also unintentionally funny: Is there really such a word as "luau-ing"?

27" × 41" one-sheet value: $40

licenses is a twenty-four-hour-a day operation.) At 9:41 A.M., in the private suite of Milton Prell, who now owned the Aladdin Hotel, they were married by a Nevada State Supreme Court justice. The secrecy surrounding the wedding had worked both for and against the couple. Most of the Hollywood press had played into the Colonel's hands, arriving with egg on their faces. On Colonel Parker's orders, most of the members of Elvis' personal entourage had also been excluded, but only Joe Esposito and Marty Lacker, who acted jointly as best men, were on hand. The rest of the guys were told that they wouldn't be able to attend the ceremony due to "space limitations" in Prell's apartment. Although Elvis, Esposito, and Lacker were not at fault, the ill will created by this incident lasted a long time. A few of Elvis' most trusted aides left the hotel in a huff, without even staying for the sumptuous reception at the Aladdin. That afternoon, following the meeting with the press, the newlyweds, along with their parents and the few remaining friends, boarded Frank Sinatra's private jet for the flight back to Palm Springs. (Sinatra was probably happy to see Elvis safely out of the bachelor ranks. After all, he might have lost Juliet Prowse to Elvis six years earlier.) Elvis and Priscilla soon returned to Graceland, where they donned their wedding attire for a second reception held for the relations and friends who had been unable to attend the first one.

In mid-June Elvis and Priscilla left Memphis in their motor home for a leisurely cross-country honeymoon trip. Meanwhile, in Hollywood, working through real estate agents, Elvis had purchased a split-level French Regency style house on Hillcrest, in the exclusive Trousdale Estates section of Los Angeles. Once settled in his new house, it was time to report to the Goldwyn Studios to start work on *Speedway*. The setting for the story was the Charlotte Speedway, home of one of the country's largest annual stock car races. As usual, Elvis shot all of his scenes in Hollywood. On July 13 the studio happily announced that Priscilla was pregnant. The baby was due the following February.

The warm summer days were spent either at the new ranch or back at Graceland, where the happy couple could be spotted playing badminton, pitching horseshoes, or speeding through the neighborhood on one of Elvis' motorcycles.

A recording date in Nashville on September 10 marked a true departure for Elvis from the soundtrack grind of the past five years. These two days brought Elvis closer to his rock 'n' roll roots than he had come in years. Songs such as "Guitar Man," "High Heel Sneakers," and "Big Boss Man" signaled a change in musical direction that had been long overdue. The addition of one of Nashville's hottest guitarists, Jerry Reed, was also a stroke of genius. "Guitar Man" was Reed's composition. More than any other song Elvis recorded at this time, the lyrics allowed him to dig into his own emotions. Elvis felt as if the song had been written with his life story in mind.

Elvis' next movie was also to be a departure from the normal formula. *Stay Away, Joe*, a comedy, featured almost no songs, and none out of context of the story, in which he played a Navaho Indian in the modern West. Filming called for three weeks of location work in the desert near Sedona, Arizona, starting in mid-October. Elvis hadn't worked on a movie outside the Los Angeles area since *Viva Las Vegas* in the summer of 1963.

On one of the last Sundays of the year, Elvis and Colonel Parker bought time on three thousand radio stations to air a special Christmas show featuring Elvis singing a half hour's worth of Christmas songs. Most were taken from the 1957 album, which had received so much criticism upon its initial release. Ten years later, they were considered tame. It was an excellent public relations move, while at the same time it helped foster the idea that Elvis was finally "wholesome."

Elvis was later than usual arriving back at Graceland for his Christmas vacation, finally driving up on December 7. These days were among the happiest he had known. Priscilla was now noticeably pregnant, and the time spent awaiting the birth of their first child was filled with sweet (if anxious) anticipation.

Movie poster

Movie Ad Corporation was licensed by EPE in 1985 to produce this "collage" movie poster.

CHAPTER FOUR

Viva Las Vegas

NOW! ELVIS NOW!

LAS VEGAS HILTON
THE INTERNATIONAL HOTEL

Thru Labor Day Sept. 6th

Hear Elvis

Las Vegas post cards

No stone was left unturned when it came to the Colonel's promotions on behalf of Elvis. Postcards were sold at both the souvenir stands and the hotel's gift shops. They were also placed on each table before the shows, and hundreds were given away to guests of the hotel. Thousands would flood the mail each week while Elvis was performing.

Value: $5

January 1968 was spent in eager preparation for the arrival of Elvis and Priscilla's child. There was repeated practice so that everybody at Graceland would know his specific function when the baby finally arrived. From the mansion to the hospital, there were timed drives to determine the quickest route. On January 15 Elvis took a day off from all the preparations for a quick trip to Nashville to record some more rock 'n' roll, but his preoccupation with the upcoming birth interfered with his concentration, and only one usable song, "Too Much Monkey Business," was recorded. The session was cut short at midnight. Two days later, at RCA's insistence, he returned to Nashville; but once again only one number, "U.S. Male," was waxed.

On February 1, exactly nine months to the day after Elvis and Priscilla were married, the big day finally arrived. Priscilla's labor pains brought a flurry of activity inside Graceland, and a convoy of cars was brought around to the front of the house. Elvis was too nervous to drive, so Charlie Hodge got the call. They arrived at Baptist Memorial Hospital at 10:40 A.M., and police guards quickly sealed off the maternity ward to afford the famous couple security. Elvis and his buddies took over a waiting room for a daylong wait. Later that day, at 5:01 P.M., Lisa Marie Presley was born; she weighed six pounds, fourteen ounces and measured fifteen inches. The press got its first brief glimpse of the baby a few days later as Elvis and Priscilla took Lisa Marie back to Graceland. Elvis was beaming brightly, an obviously proud papa. He was also slim and trim. Married life appeared to be just what he had needed.

On February 8 it was announced that Elvis had been elected to *Playboy* magazine's Music Hall of Fame. Since 1956, Elvis had regularly won as "best male vocalist" in music polls in such movie magazines as *Hit Parade* and *Photoplay,* on TV's *American Bandstand,* and in the trade journals *Billboard, Cashbox, Variety,* and England's *Melody Maker.* But the *Playboy* award was his first recognition from a mainstream magazine, outside the show business community. The award was also indicative of the newfound recognition that rock 'n' roll music was attaining as an American musical art form. It was now being mentioned in the same breath as Dixieland and modern jazz.

Elvis' time at Graceland was cut short; accompanied by Priscilla and Lisa Marie, he flew from Memphis to Hollywood on February 25 to begin work on M-G-M's *Live a Little, Love a Little.* Elvis spent March filming the new picture at various locations around Los Angeles. The story line had Elvis playing a fashion photographer, and the soundtrack included at least one passable song, "A Little Less Conversation."

In April "U.S. Male" became the first song by Elvis to make the country charts in seven years. His new respectability was opening up new markets. Today Elvis is often thought of as a singer with country roots. This, of course, was not always so. In fact, after his incredible ascension in the mid-1950s, the country community was divided by the idea of Elvis and rock 'n' roll. Traditional country artists saw in Elvis a threat to their share of the music market. Other, generally younger country singers with more modern viewpoints gave rock 'n' roll a try. While it is generally recognized that such rock 'n' roll pioneers as Bill Haley, Jerry Lee Lewis, Carl Perkins, and Buddy Holly emerged from country backgrounds, there were established country singers who tried the style with varying degrees of popularity. The most successful was Marty Robbins, who had a year of hits covering songs such as "Maybelline" and "Long Tall Sally" before returning to Nashville's mainstream. George Jones sang rock 'n' roll under the name "Thumper" Jones. Johnny Horton issued a few records with a rock 'n' roll beat; Eddy Arnold put out "Hep Cat Baby"; and Red Foley covered Chuck Berry's "Thirty Days." Eventually, all of these country artists returned to the fold; later, most of the rock 'n' roll singers who had come from a country base returned to the style when the nation's tastes in rock 'n' roll passed them by. The most successful at the turnaround has been Conway Twitty, who issued several hot rockers under his real name, Harold Jenkins, as well as his pseudonym. Now, in 1968, Elvis was crossing back over into the country market. Even though he still regularly placed records on the pop charts, his greatest successes were now labeled country. Similarly, the foundation of his listening audience would hereafter prefer country music.

In April Elvis and Priscilla took a short vacation in Las Vegas, where they attended a casino show starring the popular Welsh rock singer Tom Jones. Afterward, Jones invited them to his suite, where they spent the night swapping stories. Elvis had few pals within the entertainment industry, choosing to distance himself from what he considered the "Hollywood" life style. His friendship with Tom Jones, as well as with Sammy Davis, Jr., and Rick Nelson, was the closest he had come in years to admitting another entertainer into his inner circle. Elvis and

Speedway ads

After Elvis' first two movies, his place as the sole star in his films was assured. Only twice did he later share top billing with anyone. The first time was in 1964's Viva Las Vegas, *and the second was* Speedway *with Nancy Sinatra. Starting in 1965, Nancy Sinatra had released a number of hits, including two which topped the pop charts, "These Boots Are Made for Walking" and "Somethin' Stupid" (a duet with her famous father).*

14" × 22" window card value: $18

Live a Little, Love a Little ads

Elvis portrayed a professional fashion photographer in this light comedy. The plot was skimpy and so were the bathing suits worn by most of the ladies on Malibu Beach where much of this film was photographed. The herald pictured here is much more interesting than the rest of the artwork for the movie.

14" × 36" lobby insert value: $20
Herald value: $10

Value of monaural album: $600
Value of stereo album: $40
Value of photo: $20

Speedway album and bonus photo

The interesting thing about the soundtrack album from Speedway is that, for the first time, there is a solo number on the album not sung by Elvis. Nancy Sinatra, Elvis' co-star, sings "Your Groovy Self," and although it is not up to the quality of her mid-1960s hits such as "Lightning's Girl" and "Summer Wine," it is almost the best thing on this album. Elvis' finest number, is a bonus song, "Suppose." Given a fine spiritual treatment by Elvis and the Jordanaires, it is a glimpse of the combination of power and tenderness that Elvis would begin to impart to his songs at this time. The best song from the movie is a hot number, "There Ain't Nothing Like a Song," belted out by Elvis with help from Nancy Sinatra and the Jordainaires. The worst number has to be the improbable "He's Your Uncle Not Your Dad." The bonus photo is a full color 8″ × 10″ portrait from 1963. Monaural copies of Speedway were produced by RCA Victor in very small numbers.

Priscilla continued their vacation in late May, when they flew to Honolulu. The couple was invited to attend a professional karate tournament featuring Chuck Norris and Mike Stone. Elvis, who had begun his study of karate in Germany in 1959, was one of the sport's most enthusiastic supporters. Chuck Norris, of course, went on to become a major star of action movies. Mike Stone would later play a very different role in the future of Elvis and Priscilla.

During the lull following the completion of *Live a Little, Love a Little,* Colonel Parker negotiated with NBC for an Elvis television special to be aired the following December. Elvis had never appeared in an hour-long special before; what was more, his last TV appearance had been in 1960, with Frank Sinatra. The Colonel's initial thought was to have Elvis, dressed in a tuxedo, singing a selection of Christmas songs. Elvis and NBC's producer-director Steve Binder had other ideas. They planned to build around the story line of the song that had been released in early 1968, "Guitar Man." Immediately there was a nasty confrontation between Elvis and the Colonel. Rarely did Elvis stand his ground against his manager, but on the direction of the TV special he was firm. Fortunately for everyone, Elvis persevered, and rehearsals began in mid-June.

Finally the time came for Elvis' moment of truth. On June 27 Elvis performed in a "pit," surrounded by a live studio audience of about two hundred fans. Elvis was accompanied only by Scotty Moore and D. J. Fontana, two of the three members of the Blue Moon Boys from his days with Sun Records. The music they made was raw,

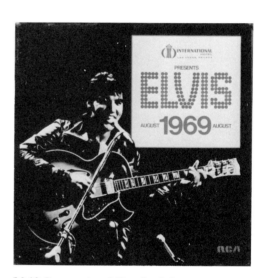

1969 International Hotel gift box

Those staying at the International Hotel during Elvis' premier engagement received a complimentary album-sized box with such promotional items as the latest pocket calendar and Elvis record catalog, the soundtrack from the Elvis TV special, and a letter from Colonel Parker.

Value of empty gift box: $250
Value of complete package: $300

From Memphis to Vegas/From Vegas to Memphis album and bonus photo

This two-record package features one disk recorded live in Las Vegas during Elvis' premier month-long engagement at the International Hotel in August 1969 and one disk of songs from Elvis' historic Memphis session in January 1969 that had not been released on From Elvis in Memphis. *There were two bonus photos included, both black-and-white 8″ × 10″ stills from Elvis' 1968 TV special. The live side is as close to a straight showroom concert as RCA Victor ever released by Elvis. The Memphis sides suffer slightly when compared with the original album from the January 1969 sessions. After all, this material had been passed over once in favor of other songs. The original double album was issued in November 1969, and a year later it was split into two separate albums without any bonus photos.*

Value of album: $30
Value of photo: $10 each

Leather jacket

This hand-tooled leather jacket was one of Elvis' favorite pieces, one which he wore frequently during the late 1960s.

Value: $2,500

bare-bones rock 'n' roll; the two mini-concerts taped that night were electrifying. Sheathed in black leather (which he never actually had worn during the 1950s), Elvis was the epitome of the king of rock 'n' roll. Two days later, he performed in another pair of half-hour concerts, this time working alone from a small stage in the round and singing with a pretaped orchestra augmented by a live four-piece rock band. Elvis, again dressed all in black leather, prowled the small enclosure like a caged panther. The television special also featured several set pieces, including the one that opened and closed the show, in which Elvis fronted a huge *Jailhouse Rock*-type of set filled with dancers. There was also a scene featuring a gospel medley, and another long piece included a dance routine in a bordello. The bordello portion, which would have certainly been one of the show's highlights, was cut from the final special, as it was considered too risqué to be broadcast. It took ten strenuous days of work before the show was completed. The project represented a gigantic risk for Elvis, one that was probably not apparent to those close to him. The seven-year movie contracts that had locked Elvis into making three pictures a year were coming to an end. This TV special would act

as a bridge to the next phase of his career.

Elvis' next movie, *Charro*, a western, was a complete change of pace from everything he had previously attempted. The only song would be heard as the opening credits rolled, and there would be no onscreen singing by Elvis. Elvis would appear throughout the movie with a week's growth of scrubby beard and several layers of trail dust. This character would be a western gunman of dubious background, a character initially patterned after the "Man With No Name" from the very successful spaghetti westerns starring Clint Eastwood. However, the film company, National General, under pressure from the board of censors, kept reducing the amount of violence in the original screenplay, so that the final cut of the movie was pretty tame. Location filming started in the middle of July at a movie ranch outside Phoenix and continued through the first few weeks of August. The interior scenes were filmed back in Hollywood at the M-G-M studios during the remainder of August.

In September Elvis suffered another bout of tonsillitis; he recuperated in Palm Springs before returning to Memphis after a seven-month absence. Back home, he and Priscilla spent quiet days on the ranch in Mississippi or made their usual round of midnight movies back in Memphis. *Live a Little, Love a Little* bombed when it was released. *Variety* called it "one of his dimmest," and the *Hollywood Reporter* noted that it was "musically anemic" as well. The single, "A Little Less Conversation," didn't even crack the top forty.

After a month at home, Elvis flew to Hollywood to start his third movie of the year, *The Trouble with Girls (And How to Get into It)*, for M-G-M. While it is clear that Elvis was now more actively attempting to influence the type of movies in which he appeared, this was one of the strangest of all. The movie had almost no recognizable plot and no songs worth remembering. Elvis barely appeared on screen until the flick was more than thirty minutes into the story, such as it was. Even the title was confusing, having nothing to do with the plot. Work on *The Trouble with Girls* took up all of November and ran into early December.

In anticipation of the airing of the TV special, RCA released the powerful anthem of hope "If I Can Dream," sung by Elvis as the show's finale. The song struck a responsive chord and became Elvis' biggest-selling single in three years. The special was aired on December 3, to the largest TV audience of the year. This one television show was seen by as many people as had seen all of his movies, and its impact was astounding. The nation was obviously hungry for a closer look at Elvis, whose image was perceived to be at the same time both new and old. In an instant, Elvis was forgiven for all of the years of mediocre pictures. It was clear that in front of a live audience he was still a performer of immense physical power. The king of rock 'n' roll had returned! It is not

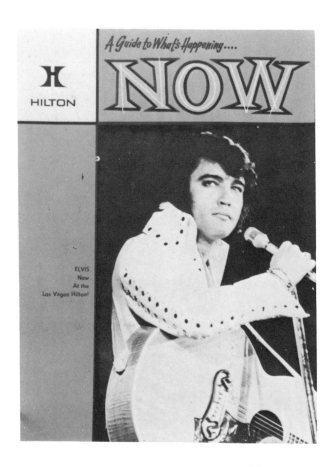

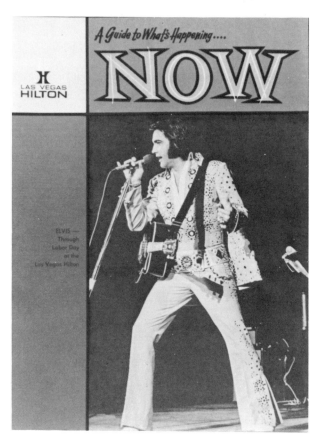

From Elvis in Memphis album and bonus photo

Generally regarded by critics and fans alike as Elvis' best studio album from the 1960s, this collection of country and soul shows off Elvis' many-faceted vocal talents. In January and February 1969, Elvis entered the American Studios in Memphis for several weeks of sessions. When he was finished, he had enough songs to fill several albums, and his music had taken a dramatic turn in direction. After years of flippant movie soundtracks, Elvis now faced the various musical trends of the day head on. American Recording Studios was the home to many of Memphis' finest black soul singers and instrumentalists, and the best songs on this album are those that allow them their freedom. "Only the Strong Survive," which would soon be a hit for Jerry Butler, and Elvis' punchy rendition of the country classic "I'm Movin' On" are the best examples. As a bonus, original copies of the 1969 album came with a color 8" × 10" photo of Elvis posed for his 1968 TV special. In 1982, this album was one of the first chosen to be re-recorded by Mobile Fidelity Sound Labs using techniques that ensure that the sound on the record is as close to that heard in the studio as possible.

Value of original album: $20
Value of MFSL album: $25
Value of bonus photo: $10

Now Vegas magazine

It is not surprising that Elvis was featured many times on the cover of Now, the weekly guide to events in Las Vegas. What is surprising is that he wasn't the cover story every time he was in town. It just goes to show how jaded even Las Vegas became to Elvis' twice-a-year schedule of month-long engagements.

Value of Now with Elvis on cover: $5 each

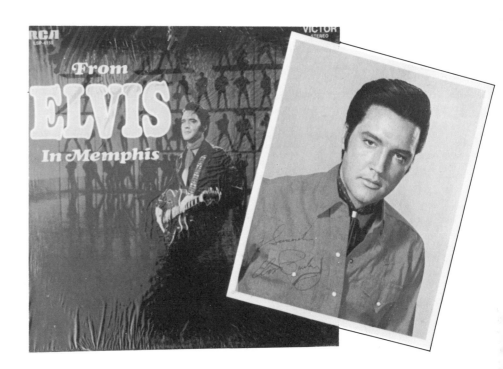

surprising, considering the path of his subsequent career, that the TV show is often referred to as the "1968 Comeback Special."

Once back at Graceland for the holidays, Elvis could hardly contain his joy. This was Lisa Marie's first Christmas, and everyone was in a wonderful mood. Vernon was even coerced into dressing up in a Santa Claus suit (possibly on loan from Colonel Parker, who always kept one handy). To top off the year, Elvis had starred in a hit TV special that had produced a best-selling album and single. The New Year's Eve party was switched to the Thunderbird Lounge for the first time, and entertainers for the evening included the popular B.J. Thomas and the then-unknown Ronnie Milsap. Milsap's country-blues singing style appealed particularly to Elvis, and he was asked to join Elvis' recording sessions scheduled for January. This year, unlike past years, Elvis and Priscilla stayed at the party until the wee hours. It was clear to all that Elvis was having a ball. His life was on the comeback trail.

Now that the TV special was a certified success, it was time for Elvis to focus again on his recording career. For a complete change of scenery, Elvis looked no farther than his beloved Memphis. The second week in January, he began a marathon four-night recording session at American Studios, hidden atop a run-down two-story building in Memphis' low-income ghetto. This was the first time that Elvis had recorded in his hometown since he left Sun Records in 1955, and instead of hiring the usual set of musicians from Nashville or Los Angeles, he

Far East LPs

Pictured here are only three of the many Elvis albums of dubious origin available in the Far East, including Vietnam, the Philipines, and Thailand, during the 1960s. Each of these albums has a cheap photo insert inside a loose plastic liner. Note that Harum Holiday *(which is the title used in many parts of the world where "scarum" is a meaningless word) has the word "Elvis" upside down.*

Value: $100 to $250 each

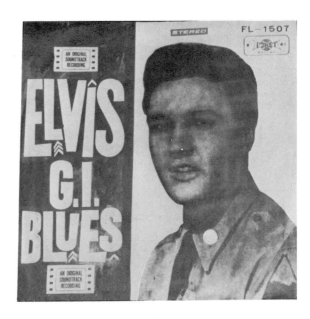

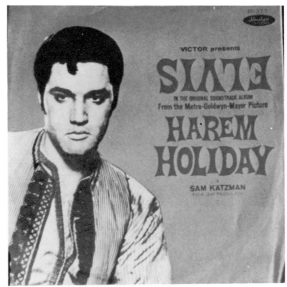

relied on the studio's house band, which had successfully backed many of the soul singers from Memphis' Stax Records. The sessions started each evening at eight and ran straight through until five the next morning. The next week, following another brief bout with tonsillitis, Elvis returned to American for another four nights. In total, he recorded over twenty songs, including such classics as "In the Ghetto," "Suspicious Minds," and "Don't Cry, Daddy," which, when coupled with "If I Can Dream" and "Memories" from the December TV special, announced that the "new" Elvis was indeed back and would be a musical force of demonstrable power.

After the stimulating sessions, Elvis and his family retreated to a private lodge hidden among the mountains of Aspen for a few weeks to celebrate not only the successful recording date but also Lisa Marie's first birthday. In mid-February Elvis returned to American Studios for a week and cut another dozen tunes. Combined with the January sessions, these recordings would be responsible for two gold albums and three singles that each sold over a million copies.

While Elvis was working to rejuvenate his flagging recording career, Colonel Parker had not been idle. In response to the positive reception to the TV special, he had been shopping around for a suitable location to put Elvis back onstage. The movie contracts signed in the early 1960s were coming to an end, and of all the venues open to Elvis at this time, only the salaries paid to top-name entertainers by the resort hotels in Las Vegas rivaled the money Elvis could earn making movies. Both Elvis and the Colonel had always enjoyed spending time in Vegas. It was a town made for and by show business, in much the same way Hollywood had risen to serve the

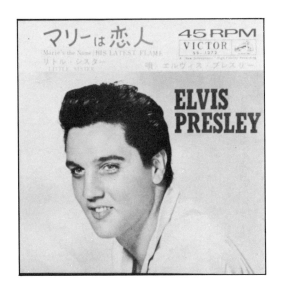

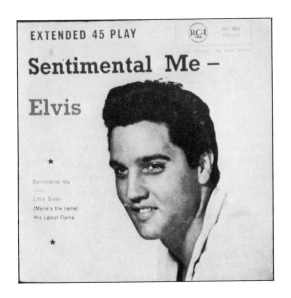

movie community thirty years earlier. So it was decided that if Elvis was ever to make a return to the limelight, now was the time and Vegas was the place. But which hotel? In Colonel Parker's mind, only the biggest was good enough for his boy. And, as it happened, there was a gigantic new hotel being built just off the Vegas Strip. Upon its completion in 1969, the International Hotel would have the biggest showroom in all of Nevada. The owners of the International wanted Elvis to be the inaugural entertainer in the room, but Colonel Parker was too shrewd to allow Elvis to suffer through the break-in period for a new stage setting. Let someone else put up with microphones that didn't work and waiters who were not practiced at serving dinner in the new room. The result: Elvis was booked into the showroom starting on July 31, following Barbra Streisand's month-long opening.

Elvis returned to Los Angeles to begin the last of his contracted movies. Since 1960 he had made three pictures a year. *Change of Habit* would be the end of the string, and, fittingly, the picture also represented a change for Elvis' character. Instead of the womanizing rogue with a heart of gold who sang songs to anything that moved, Elvis played a doctor, "John Carpenter," who fell in love with an out-of-uniform nun portrayed by Mary Tyler Moore. Elvis thought so much of the part that for years he used "John Carpenter" as an alias when flying on commercial airlines or booking hotel rooms. The movie was filmed during March and April on the back lots at Universal Studios, with a few exterior shots in and around Los Angeles.

Charro was released in March, to bitter reviews. Excising the violence had left the movie rather limp, and

Foreign EPs and singles

The three records pictured here are but a small selection of Elvis' singles and extended plays available around the world since 1956. Of special interest here is the Japanese picture sleeve for "His Latest Flame" that has been subtly tinted to give Elvis a more Oriental appearance. The extended play from Girls! Girls! Girls! has no identifying country of origin and may be a foreign bootleg. The Sentimental Me EP is from South Africa.

Value: $75 to $150 each

1969 souvenir photo

Available for only a dollar at the Elvis souvenir stand in the International Hotel during Elvis' August 1969 engagement, this color 8" × 10" uses the same photo that was included free in Elvis' then-current album, From Elvis in Memphis But the message on the back, which is printed in color, has been changed.

Value: $15

The '68 Comeback Vol. 1 and 2 bootleg albums

The importance of Elvis' 1968 television special, officially known as "Singer Presents Elvis," but more popularly referred to as the " '68 Comeback Show," was not lost on Elvis, Colonel Parker, NBC Television, or RCA Victor Records. The complicated nature of the special, combining two separate types of "live" performance and a number of set pieces, required hours of videotape to produce enough material to fill the hour-long show. Copies of much of this videotape were obtained by an interested collector, who, in turn, issued the bootleg album '68 Comeback in 1976. This became the biggest selling Elvis bootleg album ever and spawned '68 Comeback, Vol. 2.

Value: $50 each

1969 International Hotel postcard

Every table in the International Showroom had these standard-sized postcards. The front is a color shot of Elvis taken during his 1968 TV special, and the back has a message that the special will be repeated on the NBC television network on August 17, 1969.

Value: $12

critics were eager to pounce on its lack of drama. "A tedious role that would have driven any serious actor up the wall," said *Variety.* RCA Victor released the beautifully haunting "Memories," another original song from the TV special, and even though it did not sell particularly well, it received lots of airplay on the new "adult contemporary" radio stations. "In the Ghetto" soon followed "Memories," and it was clearly one of the most important songs Elvis had ever recorded. "In the Ghetto" became his first record to crack the top ten music charts since "Crying in the Chapel" in 1965. The record did as much to change the public's attitude toward Elvis' image as the TV special did. Here was "good ole Elvis," country rock 'n' roller, singing about life and death on a ghetto street. And what singing! Elvis' voice fully conveyed the emotions of the lyrics with a potent mixture of hurt and hope.

In early May, finally finished with *Change of Habit,* Elvis and Priscilla returned to Hawaii for a second honeymoon, leaving Lisa Marie with Priscilla's parents. While in Honolulu, they renewed their acquaintance with Tom Jones. Backstage in Jones' dressing room after his show and later in his hotel suite, they shared many easy hours together.

In the middle of May *The Trouble with Girls* started to hit the theaters. M-G-M was so uncertain about this film that there was no national release in the usual sense. It was certainly no surprise that the critics wrote it off as a bore. "The picture has little to offer," said *Variety.* The *Hollywood Reporter* wrote, "Should Presley loyalists be willing to settle for no more than the assurance that their idol is alive and living in Hollywood, the picture will be graced by purpose." Elvis and the Colonel couldn't care less at this point. Their sights were on the stage.

After returning to Memphis, Elvis negotiated the sale of his Flying Circle G Ranch to a Mississippi gun club. Owning the ranch had started as a lark in 1966, and for a time he spent most of his vacations there. But in three short years, the fun times at the ranch were over, and it became another discarded toy. Elvis and Priscilla's personal horses were moved back to the stables at Graceland, and the crowds at the "music gate" were estimated to run as high as three thousand as they gathered to see the happy couple taking daily rides across the grounds.

Elvis flew to Las Vegas in June to inspect the finishing construction touches that were being given to the International Hotel. From there he traveled on to Los Angeles to be fitted for his new stage wardrobe, designed by Bill Belew. Elvis spent the early part of July rehearsing with a handpicked rock 'n' roll band consisting of some of the finest studio musicians available: James Burton (lead guitar), Jerry Scheff (bass), John Wilkerson (rhythm guitar), Larry Muhoberac (piano), Ronnie Tutt (drums), and longtime friend Charlie Hodge (acoustic guitar). He also asked the Jordanaires to come along as his backing vocal group, but they were in such demand in Nashville's studios that their schedule would not allow them to take an entire month off. The Imperials, an equally fine gospel quartet with whom Elvis had worked on the *How Great Thou Art* LP, were chosen in their stead. Elvis also hired the Sweet Inspirations, a female quartet that had made an impression as Aretha Franklin's backing group. The hotel's regular orchestra would be used, and Bobby Morris would conduct.

Elvis, the new band, and an entourage of buddies and relatives arrived in Las Vegas during Barbra Streisand's final two weeks in the new showroom, taking over a floor in the hotel. Rehearsals continued every afternoon with the band, the vocalists, and the orchestra. Colonel Parker's decision to place Elvis second in the showroom was paying off. Streisand had not been able to fill the two-thousand-plus seats twice a night even though she was one of the biggest stars of the time. This left Elvis an open field. Also, the bugs in the new stage equipment had been cleared up, and the restaurant staff had the serving of the dinner show honed to a science. Elvis attended the final Barbra Streisand performance on July 30. As soon as she was offstage, Colonel Parker's crew swarmed throughout the hotel tacking "Elvis" placards to every available inch of wall space. The marquee in front of the International needed only one word to announce the show: "ELVIS." All along the Strip, the excitement was tangible. The king was coming back!

On July 31, Elvis stepped onstage in the Showroom Internationale and made entertainment history once again. His month-long, fifty-seven-show engagement was sold out, and by closing night, August 28, Elvis had set every record for attendance in Las Vegas. Over a hundred thousand fans had attended the shows, and a million and a half dollars had been taken in in receipts. And each performance was phenomenal. The first hour of the show consisted of a few numbers by the Imperials, a typical Vegas routine from comedian Sammy Shore, and some hot soul from the Sweet Inspirations before a brief intermission. The fans were understandably restless. Not knowing exactly what to expect, the audience rippled with anticipatory whispers. Then the lights dimmed. Elvis' band started to rock with a hot opening riff, the hotel orchestra tried to keep up, and, with little fanfare, Elvis sauntered onstage. He was dressed in a black outfit fashioned after the style of a karate *gi,* loose in the arms and legs but hugging his lean torso. He strode all the way across the stage, taking complete command of the showroom while fans screamed and clapped, cried and cheered. He took his sunburst-top guitar from Charlie Hodge. The whole orchestra was wailing; the entire audience was jumping. Everyone was standing, applauding, screaming. Elvis walked quickly up to the microphone at center stage with the same authority he had possessed in the 1950s. And he sang. Oh my, how he sang! He rocked and rolled on "C. C.

Elvis as Recorded at Madison Square Garden LP and promo LP

One of the most collectible of all Elvis' 1970s albums is this promotional copy of Elvis as Recorded at Madison Square Garden *that was sent to radio stations and newspaper reviewers. The record differs from the commercial copies of the album in that each song is "banded." A banded album is one which has a groove to separate each song track. Deejays need this in order to isolate specific tracks for airplay. The promo is a double album because of the space required for banding, but it contains no extra music beyond that on the regular release.*

Value of promo copy: $200
Value of regular release: $15

Rider" and "That's All Right." He mesmerized the fans with older ballads like "Are You Lonesome Tonight?" and "Love Me Tender." And he stunned the crowd each night with his version of "Suspicious Minds," a new song that often ran ten minutes or more. The press from the music trades ate it up. NBC-TV scheduled a rerun of the "comeback" TV special in mid-August. Newsmagazines devoted precious space to his return to live entertaining. The return of Elvis had become a national event. RCA was also on hand, taping several of the shows for release in albums that would spotlight Elvis' concert performances. Without doubt, he proved that he was worth every cent of the $125,000 a week he was being paid by the hotel.

On the night after he closed, Elvis and his entourage were ringside for Nancy Sinatra's opening at the International and then he attended the after-show party hosted by her father, Frank. The next day he and Priscilla and the group left Las Vegas in triumph and traveled to their home in Palm Springs to wind down. RCA rushed out a single of "Suspicious Minds," and it bounded up the charts to become Elvis' first number one pop record since 1962's "Good Luck Charm." Alas, it was also to be his last.

Both *Change of Habit* and Elvis' acting received passable reviews when the picture was released in October, but the movie barely dented the consciousness of

July 12, 1969 issue of Rolling Stone magazine

Yes, Elvis made the cover of **Rolling Stone.** *It took a while, over three years to be exact. But the fact that* **Rolling Stone** *would do a cover story on Elvis at all is a credit to the tremendous changes that had taken place in Elvis' career during the preceding year.*

Value: $15

1970 International Hotel postcard

Along with the menu, each table in the International's showroom during Elvis' 1970 summer festival had several of these 5″ × 7″ postcards for the fans to take home.

Value: $10

the public. By this time, it is doubtful if anyone in the Elvis camp even noticed. It was clear to all that the concert stage had again become the focus of Elvis' career. In November RCA released a double album containing one record of songs from the Memphis sessions and parts of Elvis' Las Vegas act on the other. To no one's surprise, it immediately turned gold.

In mid-December Elvis and his small family returned to Memphis for the holidays, celebrating New Year's Eve with a party at T.J.'s, a club run by Alan Fortas, who had left the entourage after the ranch was sold. It had been an auspicious year, and the king had returned to his throne.

Three days into the new year, Elvis returned to Los Angeles for rehearsals before starting his second month-long stand at the International Hotel. As before, Elvis and his band were in Vegas for afternoon rehearsals at the Showroom Internationale two weeks before opening night. Following the "invitation only" opening-night show on January 24, attended by the celebrities along the Strip, the remainder of the month featured shows at 8:00 P.M. and midnight. Some had advised against this Vegas engagement, saying it was the off-season and too soon after his last appearance. But Elvis proved them wrong. He sold out the run. RCA Victor was again on hand to tape several shows, portions of which would be released as a new album, *On Stage—February 1970.* Elvis closed

We Call on Him song folio

In late 1968, Hill And Range Songs issued this 12-song collection of gospel numbers recorded by Elvis. The cover photo was from 1962's "It Happened at the World's Fair."

Value: $18

"A Little Less Conversation" sheet music

The photo on the cover of the sheet music for "A Little Less Conversation" was taken behind the scenes on the set of Live a Little, Love a Little.

Value: $12

"In the Ghetto" sheet music

This is the second version of the sheet music for "In the Ghetto," and it shows Elvis on stage at the International Hotel in early 1970.

Value: $12

"You Don't Have to Say You Love Me" sheet music

Featuring a shot taken from the rehearsals filmed for That's the Way It Is, *the sheet music for "You Don't Have to Say You Love Me" also informs us that the original title of the song was "Io Che Non Vivo (Senza Te)."*

Value: $10

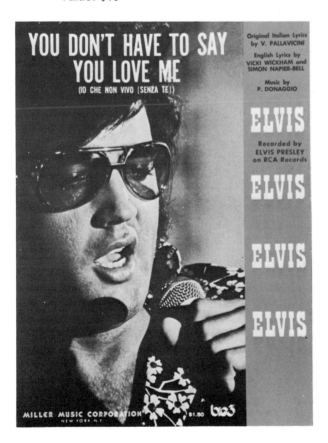

out the month on February 23, but his performing for the month wasn't finished yet.

Colonel Parker, always looking for new ways to show off his charge, had scheduled Elvis for three days at the Houston Astrodome during the Texas Livestock Show. Two shows a day were booked for February 27 and 28 and March 1. Elvis entered the Astrodome riding in an open jeep as thousands of flashbulbs lit the inside of the stadium like lightning in a Texas thunderstorm. Elvis was given an enormous welcome, confirming that his popularity was substantial in locations besides Las Vegas. The total attendance in Houston was 207,494—double the number that had seen him during an entire month at the International.

Elvis and Priscilla retired to the West Coast for a few quiet months away from public scrutiny. They divided their time between Los Angeles and Palm Springs, but returned to Las Vegas for Tom Jones' opening in May. By May 21, the vigilant Elvis watchers outside the gates at Graceland reported, the couple had returned to Memphis in time to celebrate her twenty-fifth birthday.

On June 4 Elvis was in Nashville's RCA studio for yet another massive recording effort. Over five nights he completed thirty-four songs, enough to fill three albums, with a couple of tunes held back for single release. *On Stage—February 1970* hit the stores in June and sold very well, considering that it was the second live album from Elvis in six months.

Las Vegas menus

Starting with Elvis' July–August 1969 engagement at the Las Vegas International, and continuing with all the casino shows in both Las Vegas and Lake Tahoe through 1976, special menus and other table cards were printed. Each person attending could then have a nice, free souvenir of an Elvis show. The style and size varied for every engagement, but the most prized, obviously, are the earlier menus. In 1976, Elvis stopped performing dinner shows, so there were no menus.

July–August 1969 International Hotel menu value: $60
1970 International Hotel menu value: $30
1970 International Hotel menu value: $20
January–February 1971 International Hotel menu value: large, $12; small, $10
July–August 1971 Sahara Tahoe Hotel menu value: $18
August–September 1971 Hilton International Hotel menu value: $18
Value of January–February 1972 Hilton International Hotel menu issued with either a gold or maroon background: $15
August–September 1972 Hilton Hotel menu value: $12
January–February 1973 Hilton Hotel menu value: $10
May 1973 Sahara Tahoe Hotel menu value: $20
August–September 1973 Hilton Hotel menu value: $10
January–February 1974 Hilton Hotel menu value: $15
May 1974 Sahara Tahoe Hotel menu value: $15
August–September 1974 Hilton Hotel menu value: $15
March–April 1975 Hilton Hotel menu value: $15
August 1975 Hilton Hotel menu value: $12
December 1975 Hilton Hotel menu value: $20

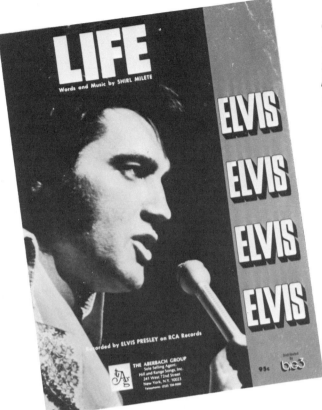

"Life" sheet music

The sheet music for "Life" clearly shows Elvis' dramatic stage presence.

Value: $10

"Burning Love" sheet music

This was the first piece of Elvis' sheet music that did not feature a photo of him. Instead, the fan gets this "cute" cartoon with no mouth.

Value: $8

"Until It's Time for You to Go" sheet music

The color photo on the cover of the sheet music for "Until It's Time for You to Go" was taken from the excised bordello scene in Elvis' 1968 TV special, making it more collectible than others issued at this time.

Value: $18

"It's a Matter of Time" sheet music

"It's a Matter of Time" was issued by Elvis during the 1970s. It did not dent the pop charts, but did peak at a respectable #36 on the country and western sales chart.

Value: $8

"Separate Ways" sheet music

The sheet music for "Separate Ways" uses a mirrored image to reflect the song's title.

Value: $8

One evening in early July, Elvis and a close family friend from Tupelo, Janelle McComb, were walking in the Meditation Garden near Graceland. "It was all lit up, and I don't think I had ever seen it prettier. I had brought him a recent picture of his birthplace. I said, 'Elvis, if we ever were to do anything in your honor or memory, what would you like?' He took that picture and walked back to the house, into the foyer. He said, 'What I would like is a chapel, a place like the Meditation Gardens where my fans could pray.' " McComb kept that conversation as a cherished memory, and after Elvis died the chapel, through her efforts, became a reality.

Meanwhile, Colonel Parker had another movie deal up his sleeve: a documentary about Elvis' upcoming summer appearance at the International Hotel. Camera crews from M-G-M were on hand on July 5 as Elvis arrived on the back lots of Culver City's Goldwyn Studios to rehearse with his band. For the next month Elvis worked on new material, while the M-G-M unit dogged his every move. Opening night at the International Hotel on August 10 found the cameras ready to capture him both onstage and off. The biggest change in the music found Joe Guercio taking over the helm as conductor of the orchestra, a job he would hold for the next seven years. This also was the first of the "Elvis Summer Festival" promotions staged by Colonel Parker at the International. Everywhere one looked, signs celebrated the season; employees were required to wear straw hats, sleeve garters, and photo buttons emblazoned with Elvis' picture and the Colonel's catch phrase. RCA again taped several of the performances for an album to accompany the movie, which would be titled *That's the Way It Is*.

During this engagement Elvis received his first serious death threat in years. On August 26 a security guard was notified that Elvis would be kidnapped that night. Nothing happened, but the next day Colonel Parker's office in the hotel received a similar call. On the twenty-eighth Joe Esposito's wife in Los Angeles was told by a telephone caller that Elvis would be shot in the middle of that night's show. Although nothing came from any of these threats, armed bodyguards stood in the wings during each show with their eyes nervously scanning the audience for any sign of trouble.

After the final night's show, Elvis flew to Phoenix to kick off six nights on the road in the first tour he had undertaken since 1957. M-G-M's movie crews continued to follow Elvis, planning to add footage from the tour to what had already been shot on the studio's back lots and at the International. Elvis' September 9 opening in Phoenix was quickly followed by concerts in St. Louis, Detroit, Miami, Tampa, and Mobile.

It had been a wearing two months, and Elvis looked forward to returning to Graceland for a much-needed week's rest before he had to report to RCA's Nashville studio for a late-September recording session. One of the annual events that he most looked forward to, the Gospel Quartet Convention, was held in Memphis in mid-October. Elvis did not perform, of course, but he attended many of the shows, staying quietly backstage, where he could enjoy the entertainers. It wasn't long before he returned to Los Angeles to warm up his band for his second short tour of the year, which began on November 10 in Oakland and continued on the West Coast before swinging east to play Oklahoma City and Denver.

In December, the film and album of *That's the Way It Is* were both released. Fans who could not attend the Las Vegas shows or see Elvis on tour were finally given a close-up glimpse of their idol. The review in the *Los Angeles Examiner* was generous when it said, "He is super and he survives. He is a brilliant performer, a mammoth figure in pop music history. His timing is superb, his sense of line and form in his movement is superb." However, the newspaper continued, "It is a shame that an opportunity has been missed to make more than just a film for the fans." The newspaper's conclusion: "One day someone will actually put Elvis into a good movie, but they better do it quick before it's too late."

As 1970 came to a close, Elvis was also the subject of a paternity suit filed in Los Angeles by Patricia Parker. She claimed that the son born to her the previous October 19 had been fathered by Elvis during his January stay at the International. Working through his lawyer, Elvis hired a private detective to check out Parker's story. His finding: the woman did indeed have a fixation about Elvis—but not his child. Elvis filed a cross-complaint against Parker and ten unnamed individuals on December 16, claiming attempted extortion. Blood tests were ordered in January 1971; it would take another year for Elvis to be completely exonerated.

On December 19, without a word to anyone, Elvis booked himself aboard a commercial airline flight from Memphis to Washington, D.C., where he stayed long enough to check briefly into the Washington Hotel before continuing on to Los Angeles. Once there, he picked up

Elvis promo photo

This black-and-white, 8″ × 10″ photo had a color advertisement for Elvis' box set Worldwide Gold Award Hits, Volume 1 *on the back.*

Value: $20

Elvis Presley hound dogs

The hound dogs pictured here were given to opening night guests at Elvis' Las Vegas engagements in the early 1970s. The one on the right has a white ribbon with Elvis' name in red. The smaller dog also has a white ribbon with Elvis' name in gold. Similar hound dogs were sold at the souvenir stands.

Value: $50 each

Postcards

Elvis was an "easy sell" in the postcard market. Just about any likeness from his concerts to his movies was certain to find a waiting customer.

Value: $1 to $5, depending on age

one of his buddies, Jerry Schilling, and returned to D.C. He and Schilling took a taxi from the airport to the White House, where Elvis left a handwritten note with a gate guard requesting a visit with President Nixon. Through the efforts of California senator George Murphy, Elvis was accorded a private tour of the Justice Department headquarters and a visit with the deputy director in charge of narcotics investigations, John Finlator. Elvis expounded on his one-man fight against drug abuse and asked Finlator to present him with the badge of a federal narcotics officer. Finlator politely refused.

Later that afternoon, Elvis, accompanied by Schilling and Sonny West, who had arrived from Memphis, was received at the White House for a brief chat with the President. Elvis was dressed in a purple crushed-velvet suit and cape with a large gold belt buckle. His sartorial splendor brought a friendly jib from Nixon. "Mr. President," said Elvis, "you've got your show to run and I've got mine." Elvis brought up the matter of the narcotics officer's badge; Nixon was caught off guard. But not for long: the President ordered his top law-enforcement staff member, Egil "Bud" Krogh, to have Finlator drop everything and come to Nixon's office with the badge. Elvis was so happy that he gave the President a bear hug. The "king" also pulled out the beautifully boxed and engraved .45-caliber World War I comemmorative pistol that he was carrying, and presented it to the President. That night, elated by his coup over the badge, he returned to Memphis.

While out Christmas shopping, Elvis purchased seven Mercedes-Benz cars. One was given to Sonny West as a wedding present (Elvis was the best man). On Christmas Eve, another went to Bill Morris, the former sheriff of Shelby County, Tennessee (Elvis had been a deputy sheriff of his home country since 1964). On the thirtieth Elvis invited Morris to accompany him on a flight back to Washington for a private tour of FBI headquarters. They returned in time for the New Year's Eve party at T.J.'s which again featured country-blues singer Ronnie Milsap.

Colonel Parker's office acted early in the new year to quash rumors currently circulating in Europe that Elvis would be performing in Paris in 1972. In fact, Elvis never did make an overseas tour. Elvis had first been asked to play outside the United States in May 1956, when "Heartbreak Hotel" was issued in England. At that time, agents tried to set up a 1957 engagement at the London Palladium. Elvis' only performances outside the United States were the few times he briefly crossed over the Canadian border to play Toronto, Ottawa, and Vancouver in 1957. Speculation over why the Colonel never took advantage of Elvis' international following—fans would wait forever in England, Europe, Japan, and Australia—has centered on Colonel Parker's past. For decades the Colonel maintained that he was born in 1909 in West Virginia, that his parents were part of a traveling troupe of carnival performers, and that his birth certificate had been lost. Some investigators believe that the Colonel is actually Dutch by birth, that his real name is Andre van Kuyk or Andreas Cornelius van Kuijk, and that he entered America as a teenager, without the benefit of immigration proceedings. These investigators conclude that the Colonel is in fact an illegal allien. Without proof of origin, he couldn't obtain a passport; this was the reason the Colonel never visited Elvis during his eighteen months in Germany. The Colonel always said that Elvis didn't play overseas because of the problems that Elvis' security

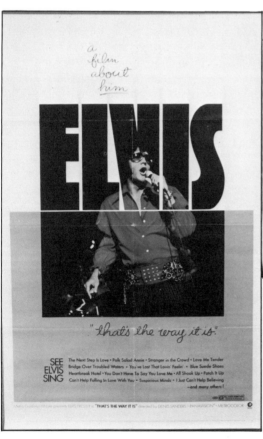

That's the Way It Is ads

Although generally referred to as "Elvis-That's the Way It Is," the original movie title did not use Elvis' name. Fans' reactions to the movie were so strong that the ads for **That's the Way It Is** *command a higher price than those for the movies just preceding it.*

27" × 41" one-sheet value: $30
11" × 14" lobby card value: $10

Elvis Presley wrist watch

One of the first jewelry items that Elvis had custom designed was a man's wrist watch, which he gave away to friends and acquaintances. In January 1971, while hosting a cocktail party at Graceland for the nine other recipients of the Jaycees' Top Ten Young Men of the Year award, Elvis presented each man with a watch as he came through the front door. There was a slight mixup at the door, and according to Frank Taylor who was in charge of the festivities, an assistant transportation chairman for the event accidently received a watch from Elvis, which left one of the honorees out. When notified of the mistake, Elvis said, "I can get another watch. Don't worry about that. But I'm not going to ask him for it back."

Value: $500

Bedroom suite

This furniture came from Elvis' Hillcrest house in Beverly Hills. The headboard was handcarved from rare European wood found by decorator Tom Lane. Even the mattress was specially made for Elvis. The gold cherub lamps provided his bedside light; the brass and marble tables originally sat by the pool.

Value: $100,000+

The Hillbilly Cat "Live" bootleg album

This bootleg album is one of the earliest of the privately pressed albums issued during Elvis' career. It is a two-record set featuring a complete Las Vegas show taped from the audience in August 1970. There are also six "bonus" songs, in the tradition of RCA Victor, taken from the same engagement. If the listener pays close attention, which is a must given the poor quality of the recording, Elvis' charismatic qualities shine through.

Value: $250

men would have in a foreign land. A likelier reason might be the Colonel's reluctance to give up an enormous portion of the gate receipts to outside entrepreneurs and local taxes. Colonel Parker was able to hide his past from most prying eyes until several years after Elvis' death, when he was sued on behalf of Elvis' estate.

Early in January, Elvis was notified that he had been voted one of the country's "Ten Outstanding Young Men of the Nation" for 1970 by the national Junior Chamber of Commerce. He hurried back to Memphis from Los Angeles, where he was rehearsing for his upcoming Vegas stand, and on January 15 Elvis and Priscilla joined the other nine honorees for a three-day affair that included a morning prayer breakfast followed by a question-and-answer session with the press. That first afternoon, Elvis hosted a cocktail party at Graceland for the Jaycees, and later he picked up the tab for the group's dinner at one of Memphis' finest restaurants.

The awards were presented the next evening. Frank Taylor, general chairman in charge of the event, remembers vividly Elvis' stage fright as he waited behind the auditorium curtain to accept his award: "We saved him till last, of course, to build the drama." According to Taylor, Elvis was sitting nervously, leaning with his head back, spread-eagled. Then he'd pitch forward with his head in his hands. "The perspiration was just coming off him. I said, 'What in hell is wrong with him?' Elvis said, 'I'm scared to death. I'm not used to making a speech.' I

1970s Elvis scarf

The tradition of tossing scarves out to the fans in the audience started as soon as Elvis began appearing in concert in Las Vegas in 1969. By the early 1970s, what started as a sweat-soaked scarf or two per concert became dozens and dozens each show. In addition, scarves were sold at the concession and souvenir booths for those not lucky enough to receive one directly from Elvis.

Value: $25

1968 radio and TV specials promo booklet

This is a fine piece of promotion used to announce Elvis' December 3, 1968, TV special as well as his half-hour Christmas radio show that would be broadcast across the nation two days earlier. This 32-page, 4″ × 9″ booklet lists every station carrying either show.

Value: $30

said, 'You've performed in front of ten times as many people.' Elvis said, 'Yeah, but I've never done anything like this.' I guess we talked for about twenty or thirty minutes. He was just wet."

Elvis had planned a much longer speech, but when presented with his award he said simply:

". . . I was the hero of the comic book.

"I saw movies and I was the hero of the movies.

"So every dream I ever dreamed has come true a hundred times. . . .

"I learned very early in life that without a song, the day would never end.

"Without a song, a man ain't got a friend. Without a song the road would never bend. Without a song.

"So I keep singing the song."

It was the first and last time that he ever attended such a function. After the ceremony, Elvis and the other honorees relaxed in a suite of rooms that Elvis had rented at the Rivermont Holiday Inn. Taylor again: "I've talked to a number of people, because it was the only time that I have ever seen him close to living in the real world. He was absolutely mesmerized by the nine other guys, he had so much respect for them. He looked upon these people as really, really outstanding young people. And he had never really associated with that type of person before. And the more he got to talking with them, the more he became one of them rather than just Elvis Presley. We just sort of sat around, and everybody was having a nice time—talking, everybody was relaxed. Elvis felt good because people were talking to him as an individual and not as a star. And then, all of a sudden, somebody almost liked snapped their fingers, and it was back to the make-believe situation. All the bodyguards and Memphis Mafia and the policemen jumped up, and out they went, and the entourage went back into that world of his he had left forty-eight hours ago."

Following more rehearsals in Los Angeles, it was back to Las Vegas in late January to prepare for his January 26 opening at the International. During the month, Elvis was plagued with a variety of problems, including a recurring bout of the flu that had been with

Elvis on Tour ads

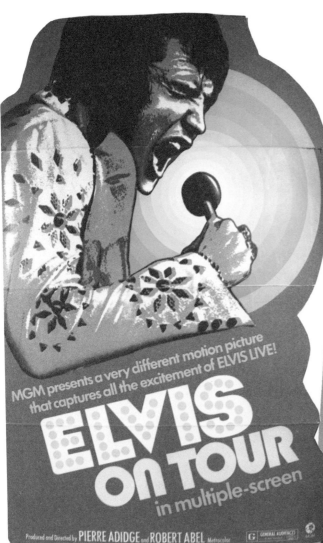

The dramatic drawing of Elvis is used on both the one-sheet and the heavy cardboard stand-up used in the theater's lobby. There was also a one-sheet that used a photo of Elvis instead of the drawing. The movie was issued in what M-G-M referred to as "multiple-screen," which was somewhat misleading. The film was shown on a regular screen, but there were several images shown at one time.

27" × 41" one-sheet value: $30
48" × 30" cardboard stand-up value: $100

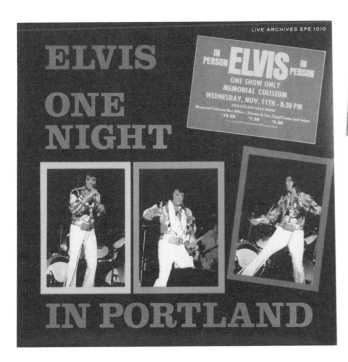

One Night In Portland bootleg album

This 1970 concert show in Portland was called "electrifying" by a local reviewer. It certainly is that and more. Elvis rocks and rolls his way through 51 minutes of sure-fire material, and his energy level sounds fantastic. So does this 1986 European bootleg.

Value: $25

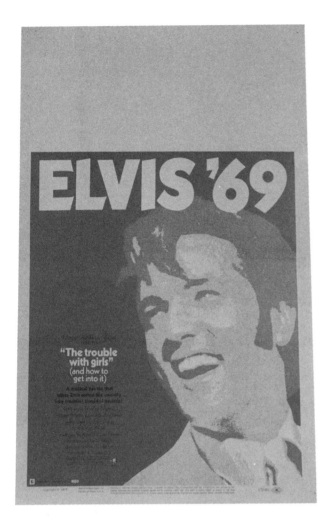

The Trouble with Girls ad

The Trouble with Girls (and how to get into it) *was almost a throwaway in Elvis' movie career, and the poster offers no clue about what to expect from the movie. What the M-G-M advertising people thought a Day-Glo painting of "Elvis '69" had to do with a turn-of-the-century troupe of entertainers is anybody's guess.*

14″ × 22″ window card value: $15

Memphis Memories bootleg album

RCA Victor released two albums taken from Elvis' January-February 1969 sessions. Now a bootlegger has come up with the acetates of different takes, and the fans can have another look at one of the turning points in Elvis' career. Familiar songs such as "Kentucky Rain," "Mama Liked the Roses," and "After Loving You" come alive again on this 1986 bootleg.

Value: $25

A Dinner Date with Elvis bootleg album

This 1986 bootleg from Europe was taped during the same Vegas engagement that gave us the movie That's The Way It Is. *The midnight show on August 20, 1970, was secretly recorded by a fan, with surprisingly clear results.*

Value: $25

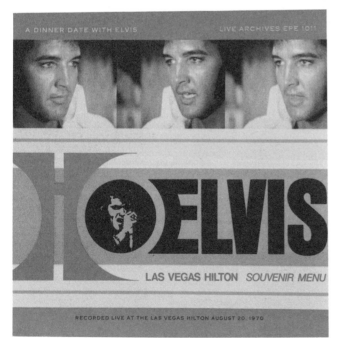

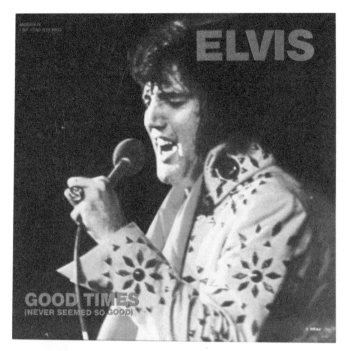

Good Times (Never Seemed So Good) bootleg album

The midnight show on August 26, 1971, was above average for Elvis' month-long Vegas dates. Fortunately for Elvis fans, someone sneaked a tape recorder into the showroom, and this 1986 European bootleg is the result.

Value: $30

Change of Habit ad

Change of Habit *featured the last of Elvis' 31 acting roles. The one-sheet seen here shows drawings of scenes from the movie and is generally a cut above the movie ads from the last half-dozen of his pictures.*

27″ × 41″ one-sheet value: $25

Rough Cut Diamonds bootleg album

This is another in the series of European bootleg albums that offer outtakes of Elvis' songs from unedited session tapes and acetates. The material comes from the summer of 1970 when Elvis was recording songs for the upcoming Elvis Country *LP. This bootleg has very fine sound quality.*

Value: $30

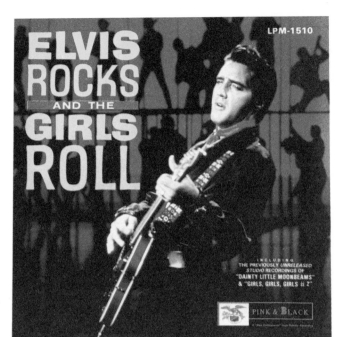

Elvis Rocks and the Girls Roll
bootleg album

Before Elvis recorded the first song for his 1968 TV special, there were weeks of rehearsals. This album re-releases a long, informal session taped backstage at the Burbank Studios where Elvis videotaped his special. The original release of this session came in 1984 on the bootleg Play It Hot, but this 1986 European album has much better fidelity. The flip side contains outtakes from "Girls! Girls! Girls!"

Value: $25

Concert photo folios

Along with the latest menu featuring Elvis' photo, the other item that casino patrons looked forward to seeing every year was the new Elvis photo folio. In 1970 when Elvis took to the road once again, the Colonel packed in a large supply of these popular booklets for those attending the shows across the nation.

Value of Special Photo Folio, Concert Edition (available in two sizes): $15 each

Value of Souvenir Folio, Concert Edition: $15
Value of Special Photo Concert Edition: $15
Value of Special Photo Folio, Concert Edition with blue background: $15
Value of Special Photo Folio, Concert Edition, Volume 5 with red background: $15
Value of Souvenir Folio, Concert Edition, Volume 6: $15
Value of Souvenir Folio, Concert Edition, Volume 7: $15

him since December. Then, during the dinner show on February 19, one of the overly excited females in the audience broke through security and reached the stage, and in the ensuing scuffle Elvis smacked himself in the mouth with the microphone, cracking a tooth and prompting an early exit so that he could be treated by a dentist before the midnight performance. The remainder of his engagement was uneventful, and he closed out the month-long string of twice-a-night appearances on February 23. As usual, he and Priscilla stayed over to attend the next star's opening night. This time it was Ann-Margret; considering the romantic rumors that had circulated during the 1963 filming of *Viva Las Vegas,* the backstage visit was pleasantly low-key. Both stars were now married, and time had smoothed Priscilla's suspicions.

Elvis' next recording session in Nashville was scheduled for March 15. Only four songs were completed on this date before Elvis, complaining of an eye infection, called it quits to seek medical aid at Nashville's Baptist Hospital. The eye problem was severe enough to warrant a three-day stay, and tests determined that he was suffering from secondary glaucoma in his left eye. Elvis was soon home in Memphis, sporting a black patch to cover the eye. The glaucoma was the result of irritation caused by the bright lights when he performed, and the only cure would have been to give up the stage, something that Elvis found impossible to consider. He was fitted for tinted glasses, which he often wore, but the problem would be bothersome for the rest of his life. He took a

World's Largest Stuffed Teddy Bear

Donated to the Youth Hotel
by
ELVIS and the Colonel

Hear Elvis on RCA Records

Small Elvis painting poster

A smaller 7" × 12" version of the poster that accompanied the Worldwide Gold Award Hits, Volume 2-The Other Sides box set was sold at the souvenir stands during Elvis' August 1971 stay. The back of the poster promoted one of Colonel Parker's famous stunts, the world's largest stuffed teddy bear.

Value: $10

much-needed rest later in the month, flying to Hawaii with Priscilla and several friends, and staying until early April.

Upon returning to his home in the hills above Los Angeles, Elvis placed an order with a Beverly Hills jeweler for more of the solid-gold necklaces sporting the initials "T C B" and a lightning bolt. The letters symbolized the phrase coined by soul singers, "takin' care of business." The lightning bolt was added by Elvis to signify "right now!" He presented these necklaces to the closest members of his inner circle. For the wives and other women in his organization, he had "T L C" necklaces, which stood for "tender loving care."

Elvis was featured on the May 4 cover of *Look* magazine, which was running the first of two parts of an excerpt of Jerry Hopkins' favorable biography, *Elvis*. Amazingly, this was the first time that Elvis made the cover of a news or features magazine during his lifetime. He never did make the cover of *Life, Time,* or *Newsweek.* In mid-May Elvis returned to Nashville to complete the recording session that had been aborted in March because of the eye inflammation. He worked every night for a week, completing thirty songs, enough to fill a new Christmas album and help fill out three more LPs.

The awards for Elvis in 1971 continued throughout the year. On January 22 he received a plaque from Great Britain's guide dog foundation, which honored him for sending personal items for auction by English Elvis fan clubs to raise money for the foundation. In May, Elvis'

Complimentary plastic bags

After 1970, hotel guests at the Las Vegas Hilton International on Elvis' opening nights were treated to a special gift from the Colonel. These colorful shopping bags always featured Elvis' current album on one side and usually another release on the other. Inside might be a pocket calendar for the current year, an RCA Victor catalog of Elvis' current releases, a photo or two of Elvis, a "personal" letter from the Colonel, and maybe a copy of the latest Elvis album.

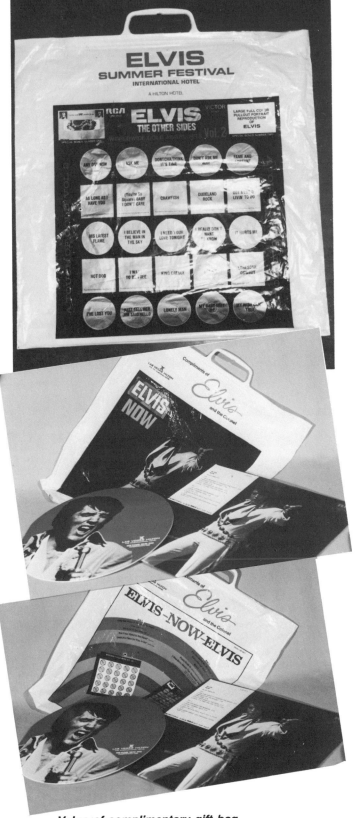

*Value of complimentary gift bag
   (empty): $15
Value with promo copy of album: $60*

adopted hometown of Memphis honored its favorite son during the first Memphis Music Awards ceremonies. He was named a recipient of the Founder's Award, and "Suspicious Minds" was named the outstanding single recorded in Memphis during 1969. But Elvis never attended any musical awards shows, not even the one in Memphis. In June, his birthplace in Tupelo was opened to the public after having been thoroughly restored by the East Tupelo Garden Club. The small house stood next door to the Elvis Presley Center recreational building and swimming pool, a complex financed largely by his 1957 Tupelo concert and subsequent Christmas donations. During 1971 the Memphis City Commissioners finally found a suitable way to permanently honor Elvis, renaming a twelve-mile portion of state highway "Elvis Presley Boulevard." When the new signs were installed, in January 1972, it immediately became apparent that no signpost on earth could keep an Elvis Presley Boulevard sign from becoming the cherished booty of a determined fan. Consequently, the only signs left today those that hang twenty feet in the air over the various main intersections. Finally, on August 28, between shows in Las Vegas, Elvis received the Bing Crosby Award (soon renamed the Lifetime Achievement Award) from the National Academy of Recording Arts and Sciences, in recognition of his artistic creativity and influence in the music field.

In early June Elvis returned to Nashville to finish recording songs for a new religious album, *He Touched Me,* before flying to Los Angeles to rehearse for his first engagement on the shores of Lake Tahoe, Nevada. His booking at the Sahara Tahoe Hotel, opening on July 20, easily broke the attendance record for casinos at the lake during his two-week engagement. The day after he finished, he was in Las Vegas preparing for his regular month-long summer festival at the newly renamed Hilton International Hotel. To accommodate the overwhelming demand, several extra weekend performances were added at 3:00 A.M.

Over the Labor Day weekend, ninety radio stations throughout the country aired the twelve-part *Elvis Presley Story,* marketed by Watermark, Inc. This was the first multipart radio program devoted to the life and music of a single artist, and the response was outstanding. As the month at the Hilton International came to a close on September 6, it was announced that Elvis had broken his own two-show record for showroom attendance, with 4,428. This new record would stand for years. Fire codes were ignored to allow the overflow crowd into a space designed to hold no more than 2,000 per show.

Returning to Los Angeles, Elvis took delivery of the very first Stutz Blackhawk Coupe automobile manufactured. Appropriately enough, the second Blackhawk was sold to Frank Sinatra. The cost was $35,000, at a time when a Cadillac was going for about $10,000. This would be Elvis' favorite Hollywood car, relegating his customized Rolls-Royce to second-banana status. Now feeling the need for a special Memphis car, he purchased a customized Mercedes-Benz for $90,000.

In October Elvis was notified that the Imperials would no longer be able to work as his backing singers. As with the Jordanaires before them, their studio jobs were too lucrative for them to give up half the year for casino engagements and tours. Elvis decided to call on his old friend from the days when he was a star-struck kid attending all-night gospel sings at the Memphis auditorium. In those days, J. D. Sumner had been with the Blackwood Brothers Quartet, and he had one of the lowest bass voices known to man. Now the leader of the Stamps Quartet, he was more than willing to drop everything to work with Elvis. The next tour would also see the first use of comedian Jackie Kahane, who was replacing a series of comedians (including Sammy Shore and Nipsy Russell) who had previously filled that thankless spot on the bill. Both Kahane and the Stamps would remain with Elvis for all the remaining tours.

The November tour was longer than usual, running twelve days with fourteen shows, starting in Minneapolis and swinging through Ohio to Boston before turning south to Texas and Alabama, then west to Salt Lake City. During the tour, Elvis rented an F-28 customized jet that had previously seen service in 1968 with Richard Nixon's campaign for President. In Baltimore, Elvis barely escaped the postconcert crush of the crowd when he found the backstage doors locked. He made it to the waiting limousine just one step in front of hundreds of rabid fans. It was standard procedure for him to be out of the auditorium or coliseum before the orchestra played its last note; then one of the Stamps would walk to the microphone and announce, "Elvis has left the building."

That year's Thanksgiving was not the happiest for Elvis. His record sales had been slipping most of the year, and he now had no records on any of the charts. His latest albums—the new Christmas release, *The Wonderful World of Christmas,* and a budget LP, *I Got Lucky*—were not destined to be big sellers. After the last tour, the glaucoma in his left eye was again troublesome, and a doctor told Elvis to put on his eye patch for a few days. All of this paled, however, in the face of Priscilla's infidelity.

The marriage was in its fourth year, but after the birth of Lisa Marie in February 1968, things had never been quite the same. The return to live entertaining meant that the couple spent weeks separated while Elvis and his buddies stayed in Vegas or Tahoe, or made mini-tours across the country. Elvis had a standing rule that no wives were allowed to accompany the tours, the only possible exception being a few days at the beginning and end of the longer hotel stays. Although they tried to ignore the facts, it was common knowledge among those

Charro ad

Charro *was to be a new start for Elvis' movie career, and the one-sheet plugged this angle: "a different kind of role . . . a different kind of man." In the end, it was more like a 1960s spaghetti western with little of the violence that made the Italian films so popular and little of the comedy and romance that made Elvis' recent films at least passable. In 1972, the Starcine Winchester magazine in France published an excellent 48-page feature on the film, which had a total of 281 separate "clips." The captions and dialogue are all in French.*

27" × 41" one-sheet value: $25

"Elvis Country" album and bonus photo

Elvis tried something different with this album release. After the success other rock artists had experienced with "concept" albums, Elvis attempted his own version in "Elvis Country." Between each number were spliced portions of the song "I Was Born about Ten Thousand Years Ago." The songs are a nice mix of contemporary country hits like "Snowbird," classic country such as "Little Cabin on the Hill," and early rock 'n' roll as in "Whole Lotta Shakin' Goin' On." There are even a couple of pieces that Elvis sunk his teeth into: "I Washed My Hands in Muddy Water" and "It's Your Baby, You Rock It." Two of Elvis' current hits, "Until It's Time for You to Go" and "There Goes My Everything," are included to round out the collection. A bonus included a 5" × 7" card featuring a tinted photo of Elvis as a two-year-old waif on one side and a black-and-white shot from the movie Elvis-That's the Way It Is *on the other.*

Value of album: $20
Value of photo: $10

Starcine Winchester *magazine*
value: $30

wives left in Memphis that everyone, Elvis included, took advantage of the many available women who flocked to their appearances. Frustrated by the long separations and the lack of attention on Elvis' part, Priscilla had initiated an affair with Mike Stone, whom she and Elvis had met in Hawaii in 1968 and who had subsequently become her karate instructor. Elvis was so preoccupied that he hardly seemed to notice. Then again, maybe Priscilla had become just another of his discarded toys. At any rate, by December it was apparent that the marriage was falling apart. Priscilla stayed with Elvis through the Christmas holidays; then she took Lisa Marie and returned to Los Angeles, setting up housekeeping in an oceanside apartment and leaving the Bel-Air and Palm Springs houses to Elvis.

As Priscilla's separation from Elvis became common knowledge in January 1972 , life around the superstar continued as usual. On January 26 Elvis was booked in Las Vegas for his annual winter stay at the Hilton International. In a typical move, Colonel Parker blanketed southern Nevada with 145 billboards to announce Elvis' engagement, setting another record of sorts. Whether Elvis was affected by Priscilla's departure or whether it was just the first sign that Elvis was wearying of the regimen of two shows every night for a month, most of his performances were kept to a contract-satisfying limit of forty-five minutes, with Elvis singing one number after the next and having little interaction with the audience.

RCA taped four straight dinner shows for an upcoming album, *Standing Room Only*. The project was ultimately scrapped, and no legitimate album was re-

The Palm Springs estate

Elvis and Priscilla bought this house in April 1970 from Marjorie McDonald, one of the founders of the McDonald's hamburger chain. Elvis retained ownership of the estate as part of his divorce settlement and kept it until his death in 1977. The 5,000-square-foot home on 2 acres of land is now being restored to Elvis' original design, and is available for rental.

He Touched Me album and promo

Pictured are the promotional and the commercial copies of Elvis' third religious album, He Touched Me. *The only difference between the two is the title sticker on the promo copy—and the collector's value.*

Value of commercial copy: $20
Value of LP with sticker: $60

Elvis Sings the Wonderful World of Christmas album and bonus photo

The first Elvis Christmas album was released to a mighty furor in November 1957. His second album devoted to Christmas songs, released 14 years later, found Elvis a respected member of the show business community. The new album had little of the fire that made such songs as "Santa, Bring My Baby Back to Me" and "Blue Christmas" immediate rock 'n' roll classics. It also didn't have the legendary book-style cover with the eight album-sized pages of color portraits; instead it had a 5" × 7" color postcard.

leased using this title. In the late 1970s an enterprising and knowledgeable bootlegger did commandeer the title for a pair of releases, *Standing Room Only* "volumes 2 and 3," cleverly playing on RCA's reluctance to issue the original album. Many of the songs taped by RCA during this time popped up on various bootleg albums in the late 1970s. (RCA ultimately only released three of the songs.) Inexplicably, RCA Victor never released a complete Las Vegas show during Elvis' life. The month at the Hilton International came to a close on February 23. Instead of lingering to catch the other entertainer's shows, Elvis immediately rounded up his buddies for the trip to Los Angeles and his empty house.

In February, during televised ceremonies that he did not attend, Elvis was awarded his second Grammy in the religious category for *He Touched Me*.

Meanwhile, Colonel Parker had convinced M-G-M to support another film documentary focusing on Elvis' life on the road. Production started in late March, as Elvis was rehearsing at RCA's new Los Angeles studios on Sunset Boulevard. During the practice sessions, Elvis cut one of his finest 1970s rock numbers, "Burning Love," produced by Felton Jarvis. Elvis was aware that Jarvis was suffering from kidney disease; later, through Elvis' efforts, a kidney donor was found, the operation was performed, and all the medical expenses were completely covered. This was typical of Elvis' loyalty and generosity where his friends were concerned.

Value of album: $20
Value of photo: $10

In Las Vegas during the spring, a story circulated that Elvis was about to switch hotels, from the Hilton International to the yet-to-be-built M-G-M Grand. According to one report, Elvis and the Colonel were helping to finance the new hotel by putting in $6 million of their own money. Whether or not the part about the financial arrangement was true, Elvis remained at the Hilton.

Still, M-G-M was very much a part of their lives as the April tour unfolded in Buffalo. The filming of the documentary was scheduled to catch Elvis in mid-tour, after he had performed in Detroit, Dayton, and Knoxville. The first show thoroughly covered by the M-G-M crew was in Hampton Roads, Virginia; it was followed by shows in Richmond and Roanoke. The cameras caught Elvis both onstage and off in every situation surrounding the tour. The cameras, which never lie, also showed that his weight was beginning to be a problem. At thirty-seven, his always handsome face sported the beginnings of a double chin. The tour continued with performances from Ohio to Texas. In San Antonio, Elvis met with eight-year-old Denise Sanchez just before going onstage. Denise was terminally ill with cancer, and Elvis was the light of her life. He autographed a poster for her and made certain that she and her family had good seats for the show. During the concert, he even dedicated the emo-

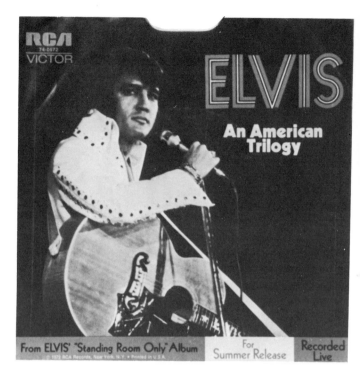

"An American Trilogy" picture sleeve

Along the bottom of this picture sleeve for "An American Trilogy" is a banner promoting Elvis' mystery album, Standing Room Only, **to be released during the summer of 1972. The album never appeared, for reasons that are still unclear.**

Value: $25

Worldwide Gold Award Hits, Vol. 2, The Other Sides record and poster

The second RCA Victor boxed set from Elvis included the other sides of his hit singles as well as a number of extended play tracks. It also came with two freebies. A triple-fold poster of a full-length painting of Elvis and a swatch of cloth cut from Elvis' personal wardrobe.

**Value of complete package: $75
Value of bonus poster: $15
Value of envelope with cloth: $10**

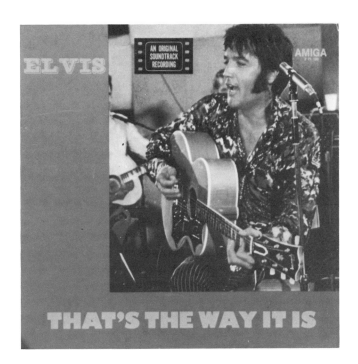

That's the Way It Is, The King: From the Dark, to the Light! and King of Las Vegas Live bootleg albums

In 1970 RCA Victor issued an album that from all superficial appearances looks like the soundtrack from **Elvis-That's the Way It Is,** *except that only two songs on the album were actually taken from the soundtrack of the movie. It was left to the bootlegger to bring the actual soundtrack to the fans. These three American bootlegs,* **That's the Way It Is, The King: From the Dark to the Light!** *and* **King of Las Vegas Live,** *all went to actual copies of the film for their material and came up with slightly different versions of that soundtrack. The best, from the standpoint of presenting all the songs in the movie, is the 1978 release* **That's the Way It Is.** *On the other hand, 1974s* **The King: From the Dark to the Light!** *does include one side of songs from Elvis' other documentary,* **Elvis on Tour. King of Las Vegas Live,** *also from 1974, concentrates solely on the last half, or concert portion, of the movie.*

That's the Way It Is *bootleg album value: $50*
The King: From the Dark to the Light! *bootleg album value: $75*
King of Las Vegas Live *bootleg album value: $75*

tional "Lord, You Gave Me a Mountain" to her. While the meeting and the subsequent press coverage bore the heavy hand of a Colonel Parker publicity stunt, it was a genuine gesture on Elvis' part. He realized that it was just such dedication on the part of his fans that had kept his popularity alive through the years.

Elvis had never given a concert in New York City (if one does not count his television appearances in 1956 and 1957), and the Big Apple was impatiently waiting. When tickets for his four June performances at Madison Square Garden went on sale on May 8, all eighty thousand were snapped up in less than twelve hours. Fans had come from hundreds of miles away to stand in line. Elvis, meanwhile, was resting in Hawaii, to which he had invited Priscilla and Lisa Marie in an ultimately futile attempt to resolve the separation. After two weeks of plying her with gifts and promises of devotion, he threw in the towel and returned to the mainland.

The Madison Square Garden appearances were the talk of New York City, and Elvis was forced to hold one of his few major press conferences. As with most of Elvis' media chats, he offered little of any import. When asked why he had outlasted all of the other entertainers from the 1950s, he flippantly said, "I take vitamin E!" The only time he approached seriousness was on the subject of his show business image. "The image is one thing," Elvis said, "and the human being is another. It's very hard to live up to an image." He refused to answer questions about antiwar demonstrators: "I'd just as soon keep my own personal views about that to myself." He showed off his gold-plated belt, a 1969 gift from the International Hotel for his record-breaking performances, and then Colonel Parker put an end to the circus and Elvis went back to rehearsals. So, with little to quote, only snips of the interview made the evening's TV news and the following morning's papers. During the next three days Elvis set a new mark for attendence, as he was the first solo performer to sell out the Garden for four straight shows. RCA Victor captured two of the shows on tape, and in a record-breaking nine days released one of them on the album *Elvis as Recorded Live at Madison Square Garden*. Elvis' concerts brought out a bevy of celebrities, including such contemporary rock stars as Bob Dylan, George Harrison, John Lennon, David Bowie, and Art Garfunkel. The performances at Madison Square Garden were the beginning of another two-week tour, which ran from Ohio through Texas before an exhausted Elvis returned home to Graceland.

By this time, rumors of an impending divorce between Elvis and Priscilla filled all the movie magazines and tabloids. Despondent over photos and reports that relished showing Priscilla and Mike Stone "on the town" in Los Angeles, he was often melancholy. He frequently spent long periods in his bedroom quietly watching television or reading either the Bible or another of the

The Legend Lives On bootleg album

This American bootleg album from 1978 begins with a monologue by Elvis taken from an August 1969 Vegas show and then skips to February 1972 for another Vegas concert. Several songs issued here differ markedly from those issued by RCA Victor, including "Hey Jude" with the "Yesterday" intro. Others are live recordings of songs that had not been issued by RCA Victor in 1978. Considering that the material was surreptitiously taped by a fan seated in the audience, the sound quality is surprisingly good.

Value: $50

many religious books from his library. Elvis was searching for some meaning in the shambles of his personal life. Soon the call went out for Larry Geller, the Hollywood hairdresser, who would return as Elvis' religious instructor and counselor. With no further interference from Colonel Parker, Geller would remain with Elvis until the end. Down, but not out for long, Elvis was soon spotted attending midnight movies in Memphis with actress Cybill Shepherd.

The offers for Elvis to perform outside the United States reached new heights when an Australian promoter told Colonel Parker that he would pay Elvis $900,000 for three appearances. The Colonel, as usual, dismissed the idea outright. "Elvis is booked solid for the foreseeable future" was his pat answer to such queries. Another rumor, which (on the face of it) looked even more unrealistic, was announced by the local Memphis newspapers in July. The papers stated that plans were afoot for Elvis to perform on a worldwide television hookup from Honolulu in October. On this subject, Colonel Parker remained uncharacteristically silent.

Elvis' longtime pal George Klein had been on the lookout for a suitable woman to be a permanent replacement for Priscilla, and when he brought a former Miss Tennessee to the midnight movie sessions at the Memphian Theater on July 5, there was immediate electricity between Elvis and Linda Thompson. Within days, she was spending most of her spare time with him. But Elvis, as usual, had wandering eyes. The next week, while Linda was away on a brief vacation, Elvis entertained a

World's largest hound dog poster

Colonel Parker was so proud of his "world's largest stuffed hound dog," which he used to attract customers to the souvenir booth at the Las Vegas Hilton, that he had posters made up showing the display. The back of the first poster shows a map of Elvis' sold-out tour dates, along with a plug for the Hilton Hotel chain. It's important to note that the Colonel donated all the souvenir stand's receipts to a local hospital or other charity.

Value: $15
Value of Elvis with the hound dog display poster: $15

showgirl from Las Vegas, Sandra Zancan. After she returned to Vegas, Priscilla paid a brief visit. The stopover by Priscilla, it turned out, was to tell Elvis personally that she was making legal moves to file for a separation. By the end of July, as Elvis was in Las Vegas preparing for his next month-long engagement, the country's newspapers were carrying the story, tempered with the news that the couple was trying for a reconciliation. But both of them knew now that it was too late to go back. The marriage was finished.

The usual "Elvis Summer Festival" started a month before Labor Day at the Hilton (which had finally dropped the "International" name altogether). Fans were quick to note that most of Elvis' karate kicks had been eliminated from the show. His singing voice was said to be strong, but there was little interplay between Elvis and the audience. Linda Thompson was invited to spend the first and last weeks of the engagement with Elvis; the middle two weeks Elvis saw both Sandra Zancan and Cybill Shepherd. He closed his stay at the Hilton on the fourth, and the next day he hosted a press conference at the Hilton to announce that there would indeed be a worldwide television broadcast of a Honolulu concert. The show would be telecast the next January via satellite, and would be shown live in the Far East, including Japan, Hong Kong, and Australia. Later that day, a tape of the show would be seen all over Europe. The United States would have to wait until April to see *Elvis: Aloha from Hawaii*. It was predicted that the program would reach the largest audience in the history of television, and RCA reported that it would market an album of the show worldwide.

Nineteen seventy-two saw Elvis' record sales fluctuate wildly. One of the most-requested songs from his live shows, "An American Trilogy," was released as a single in April, and it sold fewer copies than any of Elvis' previous regular single releases. One reason may lie in the fact that the same song had been released by its composer, Mickey Newbury, only six months earlier. "Burning Love" was rushed out to recoup his audience, and it quickly became Elvis' last big-selling pop single, reaching the number two spot on the pop music charts in October. As mentioned previously, Elvis was now considered more of a country performer than a pop singer. Most of his songs were now styled after the country music of the day. As a matter of comparison, "Burning Love," a hot pumping rock song, didn't even chart in the country field. On the other hand, Elvis' singles bearing a more country flavor would regularly reach into the top ten in country music while failing to dent the top twenty in the pop field.

In November *Elvis on Tour* opened across the United States to positive reviews and strong box office receipts. It was one of the first commercially produced movies using multiple images, showing up to three different

Promo disks

Inside the casinos, Elvis' name was visible wherever a customer looked. These large, heavy, plastic or cardboard promotional disks were hung out of reach of all but the most avid fan. Each evening, after Elvis' show had closed, the Colonel's staff would replace those disks that had become part of some fan's collection.

Cardboard promo disk value: $30
Heavy plastic promo disk value: $50

Summer festival pennants

A regular item at the Elvis souvenir stands in the casinos each summer were these colorful pennants. The ones shown here are from the early 1970s and were used for the International Hotel (which changed its name to the Hilton International in 1971 and finally just the Hilton by August 1972). There were also pennants for the Sahara Tahoe Hotel. The pennants were available in a wide variety of background and printing colors.

Value: $20

Six-door Mercedes

This six-door Mercedes is the most valuable car Elvis ever owned. It is a 1969 original with solid copper floors. This model was made in very limited numbers, primarily for royalty. Elvis can be seen riding in this car in his last movies.

Value: $500,000

shots at the same time. The movie was directed by Martin Scorsese, who went on to direct such award-winning films as *Taxi Driver, Raging Bull,* and *The Color of Money. Elvis on Tour* was called by *Variety* "a bright, entertaining pop music documentary," and it won the Golden Globe award for best documentary. But Vincent Canby of the *New York Times* saw something in the Elvis on-screen that was disturbing: "Underneath the storybook myth is a private person who is indistinguishable from the public one." Elvis had said during his June press conference in New York that it was hard to live up to an image. What the public never grasped was that Elvis was now desperately trying to be "Elvis Presley" both on and off the stage. He was starting to see himself as others saw him. He was beginning to believe in the image. It was the fatal flaw in his personality.

Elvis and Linda Thompson were in Los Angeles at this time, preparing for another tour. Elvis was using his karate training in an attempt to keep his weight under control. He was visiting the Santa Monica studio of Ed Parker, a Hawaiian whom he had met in 1968, when he was introduced to Dave Hebler, another karate expert, who owned a school in Glendora. Hebler was soon asked to join Parker as one of Elvis' bodyguards on tour. On Hebler's first visit to Elvis' Bel-Air home, he was given a $10,000 Mercedes 450SL that belonged to Charlie Hodge. Before the sun rose the next morning, Charlie had a new Mercedes as a replacement. Such was the initiation into the inner world of Elvis Presley.

The next round of appearances started on November 8 in Lubbock and zigzagged west toward its conclusion in Long Beach. Elvis immediately flew to Honolulu for a

Nativity scene outside Graceland.

five-day visit that included two concerts and a press conference with more news about the upcoming TV spectacular. Elvis announced that the show was going to be a benefit for the Kui Lee Cancer Fund, and Elvis and the Colonel kicked off the fundraising by paying $1,000 each for their own tickets to the show. Kui Lee was one of Hawaii's most beloved composers and a cancer victim. Lee's best-known composition, "I'll Remember You," was a personal favorite of Elvis'.

On his return to Memphis, Elvis was looking forward to the holidays. With four-year-old Lisa Marie around for the festivities, Graceland took on a special glow. Elvis was in a better mood than in the previous year, and he was seriously working to keep his weight under control so that he would present his best appearance during the Hawaiian TV special. He lavished fine gifts on everyone, including a fur for each of the wives of his entourage. For Linda Thompson, only the most spectacular floor-length mink was fine enough, and he was delighted when she made a grand entrance down the center stairs at Grace-land wearing the coat.

the Final Curtain

In the early days of January 1973, preparations intensified for Elvis' TV spectacular in Honolulu. In keeping with the desires of the Kui Lee family, tickets were available for a donation to the cancer fund, with no minimum set. After two weeks of mail orders, the tickets went on sale over the counter in Honolulu; by the end of the first day fewer than one hundred seats remained. Colonel Parker came up with the idea of selling tickets for the dress rehearsal, and the clamor started all over again.

The mayor of Honolulu proclaimed "Elvis Presley Week" on January 8; the next day Elvis arrived at Honolulu International Airport. He was ferried via helicopter to the grounds of the Hilton Hawaiian Village Hotel, where his landing was videotaped for the TV show's opening segment. In a rare move, Elvis had allowed all of the wives to join their husbands during the group's stay in Hawaii. Left to themselves, everyone enjoyed each other's company as they played games on the beach and toured the island's attractions, including the memorial to the USS *Arizona* that Elvis' 1961 concert had helped to build. Elvis remained secluded in his penthouse suite for the next two days, leaving only to attend rehearsals at the International Center Arena. These practices were always well attended by the wives, several of whom had never seen Elvis perform, and who added to the excitement. On January 12 Elvis performed a full dress rehearsal in front of a sellout audience.

Elvis: Aloha from Hawaii was beamed via Globecom satellite at thirty minutes after midnight on January 14. Most of the countries in the Far East saw the telecast live, including Australia, Japan, South Korea, Thailand, the Philippines, and South Vietnam. Viewers in Communist China picked up the broadcast from Hong Kong. Ratings for the show were among the highest ever recorded in the region: Elvis was seen on 70 percent of all the television sets in use at the time. The show was seen later that day in thirty countries around the rest of the world, with the notable exception of the United States, which would have to wait until April for a special version of the show. The total estimated number of viewers worldwide was over a billion, making it the largest audience to date for

Concert pennant

Similar to the "Summer Festival" pennants sold at the casinos, these were sold during the tour concerts. All Star Shows vendors would ply the audience before the show, during intermission, and often after the concert in the parking lot.

Value: $15

Ticket stubs

Every fan who ever saw Elvis perform live cherishes the ticket stub. The value of individual stubs varies depending on age, design, and whether or not they have been torn or otherwise mutilated.

Value of 1954–55 stubs: $35
Value of 1956–61 stubs: $25
Value of 1969–77 stubs: $10–$15

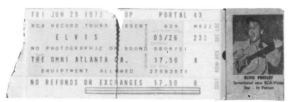

any televised entertainment special. It was also the most expensive, with the cost topping $2.5 million. With the addition of the dress rehearsal, the total amount netted for the Kui Lee Cancer Foundation was $75,000, triple the original estimate of $25,000. Elvis and the Colonel had covered all operating expenses and had made certain that none of the ticket money went anywhere except to the cancer foundation. The concert itself was a carbon copy of the usual Las Vegas routine, with Elvis again barely acknowledging the audience. But the exercise and dieting of the past two months had paid off. Elvis was in top physical form and even threw in a few karate moves, which had been missing from recent performances. And his voice could not have been stronger. But, in the canon of his television appearances, *Elvis: Aloha from Hawaii* would pale next to the explosiveness of his 1956 appearances for Ed Sullivan, Milton Berle, or *Stage Show,* or his redemption in 1968. After the show, in appreciation of his entourage's support, Elvis bought diamond and emerald rings for the wives. The hotel's jewelry shop rang up a sale of over $10,000.

As soon as the concert was finished, it was time to pack and leave the islands. There was no time to linger—Elvis was scheduled to open at the Las Vegas Hilton on January 26. A few days into the month-long stand, Elvis complained of a throat ailment, something common to singers in the arid air of Las Vegas. Both shows were canceled, and he spent that night in the local hospital. The next night he struggled through the dinner show, but was unable to go back onstage at midnight. There was a recurrence of the throat problem two weeks later, delaying the show thirty minutes, and for two nights thereafter it was apparent to those at the dinner show that he had a bad case of laryngitis, and the midnight performances were again canceled. Because the shows were instant sellouts, tickets could not be exchanged for performances on succeeding nights. Fans—some of whom had traveled from Japan and Europe and who had saved money and waited months for this chance to see Elvis—were just out of luck.

Security badges

Backstage security was an ongoing concern whenever Elvis performed live. Beginning in 1956 and continuing through the 1970s, "Elvis" badges were issued to identify authorized personnel. Every tour had its own distinctive badge shape, and each night required a specific color.

Value of 1970s security badges: $25

Peace ring

The peace sign on this ring is created from diamonds on a black enamel background. Elvis wore it in the late 1960s and ultimately gave it to Linda Thompson.

Value: $6,000

Separate Ways album and bonus photo

RCA Victor felt that they had done so well with their experiment of issuing the hit "Burning Love" on a budget album that they put the single "Separate Ways" and its B side, "Always on My Mind," on another Camden subsidiary release. They were coupled with a hodge-podge of songs from Elvis' movies and his heyday in the 1950s. To help push the album's sales, another bonus photo was included, this time barely more than a postcard of Elvis live onstage.

Value of album: $12
Value of photo: $8

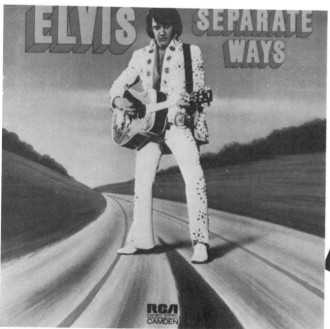

In the midst of his running bout with the sore throat, he was doing the midnight show on February 18 when four men leaped up onstage in a threatening manner. The first to arrive was subdued by Red West, who had immediately entered from the wings to protect the star. The remaining men were met by three more bodyguards, as well as Vernon Presley and Tom Diskin of Colonel Parker's office. In the melee that followed, Elvis pitched one of the men off the stage and onto the ringside tables. After order was finally restored, Elvis told the crowd, "I'm sorry, ladies and gentlemen . . . I'm sorry I didn't break his goddamned neck is what I'm sorry about! If he wants to shake my hand, that's fine. If he wants to get tough, I'll whoop his ass!" The crowd roared its approval through a seven-minute standing ovation. The four men were arrested on charges of public intoxication, but Elvis refused to press charges of assault. He did obtain copies of three of the men's police "rap sheets," which he kept on file for several years and frequently produced when recounting the incident. Excepting overexcited fans who meant no harm, it was the first time that he had been attacked onstage. The incident left him more than a little shook up.

Back in his penthouse after the show, Elvis was still in a macho mood, and he decided that something had to be done about Priscilla's boyfriend, Mike Stone. His wrath was apparently rooted in Priscilla's refusal to allow Lisa Marie to travel to Las Vegas to see Elvis during the last week of his engagement. Elvis was so furious with Stone, whom he saw as the instigator of this change in custom, that he had to be sedated. His rage lasted several days. The month in Las Vegas concluded on February 23 without further incident.

After the fight made local headlines, Elvis became acquainted with boxer Muhammad Ali, who was in town training for a March 31 heavyweight title fight against Ken Norton. In a gesture of friendship, Elvis gave Ali a fancy robe to wear into the ring. Alas, Norton creamed Ali and broke his jaw; the robe was immediately discarded as having brought bad luck. The friendship was maintained, however, and Ali gave Elvis a pair of golden boxing gloves inscribed "You are the Greatest."

The Sun Years bootleg album

In the mid-1960s, Sun Records was sold by Sam Phillips to Shelby Singleton and the operation was moved to Nashville. Immediately after Elvis' death, Singleton tried to cash in on Elvis' association with Sun Records. He announced that he would release the tapes from the Million Dollar Quartet session of December 1956, but lawsuits from RCA Victor, the Elvis estate, and Johnny Cash prevented further action. So he decided on a documentary approach. The resulting album, which was successfully kept off the market, is a mess. The bits and pieces of Elvis' recordings were actually lifted from RCA Victor's "stereo-ized" versions, not from original Sun recordings. From the collector's standpoint, only one version of this shoddy album is worthwhile. This version has a light yellow cover, and the record label is a facsimile of the ones used in the 1950s by Sun.

Value of regular version: $10
Value of old label version: $50

Promised Land promo

This 18″ × 24″ hanging promotional item advertised Elvis' latest album, Promised Land, on one side and three of his other recent albums on the back side (pictured here).

Value: $40

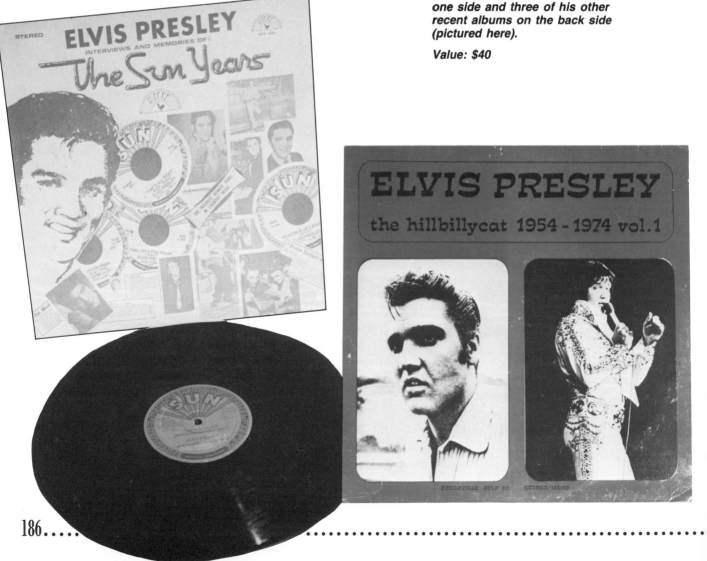

Big Boss Man bootleg album

This opening night show from Elvis' August 1974 stand at the Las Vegas Hilton was unusual, featuring several numbers new to his casino repertoire. Applause was polite, but certainly not overwhelming, and the next night it was back to the regular show, which he didn't tamper with again. This 1987 bootleg from Switzerland (by way of Italy) captures all the opening show, but has below-average fidelity even for a pirated release.

Value: $20

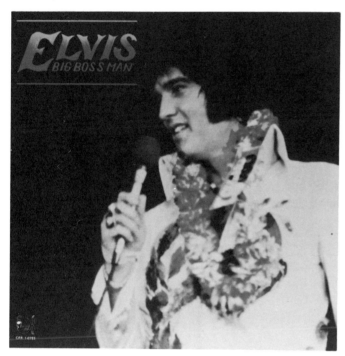

Hillbilly Cat 1954–1974, Vol. I

tleg album

s early European bootleg arently set out to contrast 'is' style from 1954 to 1974. at resulted is a strange mix of gs from Elvis' first two Ed llivan TV shows in 1956 and gs released by RCA Victor from 6 to 1971. Fortunately, there ver was a volume II!

ue: $50

Offers continued to reach Colonel Parker's office. One of the most appealing called for Elvis to perform six concerts at Earl's Court Stadium in London for $500,000. The promoter had arranged for the concerts to be carried on closed-circuit television to most of England. The Colonel, upon hearing that Earl's Court was a sports stadium, dismissed the request, saying "Elvis doesn't need to sing in baseball fields anymore."

The Colonel was meanwhile preoccupied with renegotiating Elvis' contract with RCA, even though his current contract had well over a year to run. The new seven-year deal proved particularly sweet for the Colonel. Aside from the usual royalties to be paid on future record sales, RCA Records also agreed to pay All Star Tours (Colonel Parker) $675,000 over the course of the contract, with RCA Tours matching that amount. Colonel Parker would also get 10 percent of RCA Tours' profits. There were other perks, such as offices and staffing, most of which lined only the Colonel's pockets. But the key item of interest called for RCA to pay $5 million, split equally between Elvis and the Colonel, for the royalty rights to Elvis' entire catalogue of recordings up to 1973. The net result, not counting the royalties from future record sales, was to provide Elvis with $2.5 million; the Colonel would take home at least twice that amount over the course of the contract. After taxes (and Elvis had always paid his full share of taxes, without seeking any financial shelters), Elvis would receive $1.25 million in lieu of any further royalties on his older records, which continue to be steady sellers for RCA. The Colonel had loaded the contract with apparently self-serving clauses, and would spend years in court battling the Elvis Presley Estate after Elvis' death.

On April 4 the United States finally got a chance to see *Elvis: Aloha from Hawaii.* The NBC-TV broadcast contained an additional twenty minutes of songs that were not part of the original concert. Ratings were high, with over half the country's sets tuned to Elvis. A double album from the special had been rushed out by RCA in February; following the hoopla surrounding the U.S. broadcast, the LP went on to become the final number one pop record of Elvis' career.

In early April, Elvis and a dozen followers traveled to San Francisco to attend the California Karate Championship. Advance publicity had erroneously reported that Elvis would perform a karate demonstration, but his contract with the Sahara Tahoe Hotel precluded any "personal appearances" in a radius of three hundred miles of Lake Tahoe within thirty days of an engagement at the hotel. Colonel Parker had gotten word of the "appearance," and made certain that Elvis remained a spectator.

The first tour of 1973 started on April 22 in Phoenix. The tour stopped in Anaheim for two days before winding through California and the Pacific Northwest, finally closing in Denver. On May 4 Elvis opened at the High Sierra Theater at the Sahara Tahoe Hotel. His shows had been badly overbooked, and a near riot followed as hundreds of fans who had been promised seats were not admitted. As a result, extra performances were added to satisfy as many fans as possible. With that exception, everything went smoothly until the sixteenth, when Elvis abruptly canceled the last three days of his engagement following the midnight show. By dawn of the seventeenth, he was in Los Angeles recuperating from what was reported to be a case of the flu and chest congestion.

After a month of rest in the California sun, Elvis was feeling well enough to begin another tour in Mobile on June 20. He hopscotched from Atlanta to New York State, and played such diverse cities as Pittsburgh and Oklahoma City. Elvis' concert appearances, which had heretofore been much wilder and more spontaneous than the casino shows, were now falling into a similar rut, with Elvis seeming to rush through his portion of the show. One song followed the next with monotonous regularity. It was a rare event when he'd add to the repertoire—like "Flip, Flop and Fly" in Uniondale, New York—or make small talk to the audience.

A few weeks of vacation at Graceland were followed by a scheduled four-day recording session at the studios of Stax Records in Memphis. Two nights into the session, several of the musicians from Elvis' backing band had other commitments and were replaced by Stax's regular house band. Elvis was openly disgruntled and worked on only one song that night before calling it quits. He didn't even show up for the next night's session; the band laid down several instrumental tracks to which vocals were later added.

The big news as Elvis was preparing to open at the Las Vegas Hilton on August 6 was the rumor that Elvis and Colonel Parker were calling it quits. Although relations were obviously strained, the presumed misunderstanding was quickly resolved, though tensions seemed to linger. An unrelated incident occurred one night during a party in Elvis' penthouse suite. Elvis was demonstrating how to break a wrestling hold, and he allowed a fan, Beverly Albreco, to get a full nelson on him. Showing off, Elvis crashed down hard with his foot and broke her ankle. It took her two years, but she finally filed a lawsuit against him.

By now the monotony of the Vegas shows was getting to Elvis, and one reviewer speculated that Elvis might be sleepwalking through them. Nevertheless, the month's shows all sold out. Feeling more at ease, Elvis remained in Las Vegas for a week following his closing performance, attending several shows, including that of Tom Jones. Before leaving Vegas, he suffered a minor fracture of his wrist while practicing karate in his hotel suite. Returning to Los Angeles with Linda Thompson, he

Record/card from Poland

The exact date of release of this 7" record/card from Poland is uncertain, though it appears to have been the early 1970s. This is one of the first "official" records by Elvis issued behind the Iron Curtain. The two songs, "Can't Help Falling in Love" and "Return to Sender," are on one side of the cardboard card, with the other side carrying recording information.

Value: $100

Elvis promo card

Though postcard sized, the ad on the back of this 1973 card left no room for a message. It was given away in record stores.

Value: $15

1970's Elvis photos

Remember the ads that screamed "48 photos for only $1.00"? Well, here they are. Each sheet is 5" × 7".

Value: $5 each

HERE IS ELVIS' GREAT LP CATALOG 1973 EDITION

FROM
RCA RECORDS
RCA RECORD TOURS
RCA RECORD DISTRIBUTORS
RADIO STATION PERSONNEL
RECORD DEALERS
RACK JOBBERS
ONE STOP OPERATORS
COIN MACHINE OPERATORS

AND MANY THANKS ALSO, FROM ELVIS

cedes 600

ls purchased this 1969 rcedes 600 limousine for istmas that year. He kept it il 1974 when he gave it to mie Velvet.

ue: $250,000

celebrated the completion of the Vegas engagement by buying several new cars and a bagful of jewelry.

By mid-September he was resting at his Chino Canyon home in Palm Springs. During his stay an event occurred that received a lot of press coverage when it was first revealed in 1977. A teenager who had been picked up by a member of the entourage during the Las Vegas stay was invited to join the guys in Palm Springs. One night she nearly overdosed on Hydocan cough syrup and had to be rushed to the hospital, where she nearly died. At least one eyewitness reported later that Elvis was not even in the same room when the girl was gulping down the cough syrup. In fact, according to this firsthand account, the men who later chose to capitalize on this story were asleep during most of the incident.

While Elvis was in Palm Springs, a recording session was attempted at his home to overdub the uncompleted instrumental tapes from the Stax sessions in July. Elvis was aided by Voice, a vocal group from Nashville that he admired, which featured the fine tenor of Sherrill Nielsen. At this time, Elvis was also nurturing an idea for a new film: a kung fu/adventure movie in which he would star. His interest in the project ran hot and cold for the next two years, but never really got off the ground.

In late September Colonel Parker signed a contract for two more years of shows at the Las Vegas Hilton. Elvis' boredom with the casino routine was apparent in a major revision of the normal month-long format started in

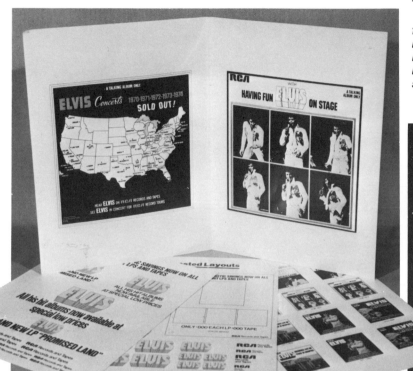

RCA promotional folder

This fold-open promotional folder from RCA Victor was sent to record stores to promote Elvis' latest album, Promised Land. Included with the folder were suggested advertising layouts.

Value: $35

1969. From now on, he would perform only two weeks at a stand. The issue of singing twice a night and the overbooked showrooms would have to wait a year, until the Colonel devised a method by which tickets were issued for all of Elvis' future performances.

The divorce from Priscilla was finalized on October 9. Originally, she had agreed to settle with Elvis for a lump-sum payment of $100,000, a few cars, and some jewelery. She changed her mind at the insistence of her lawyer, and the final settlement gave her $725,000 in cash plus a monthly stipend of $14,200. Priscilla was granted custody of Lisa Marie, although the girl would continue to visit her father on a regular basis at Grace-land and in Las Vegas. Elvis appeared at the Santa Monica courtroom proceedings wearing a jogging suit; after kissing Priscilla farewell, he drove away in the customized Blackhawk. He immediately flew back to Memphis, where on October 15 he was rushed to Baptist Memorial Hospital for "recurring pneumonia." In addition, he was diagnosed as having an enlarged colon and toxic hepatitis. He remained hospitalized for two weeks.

Elvis started a second week-long series of recording sessions at Stax on December 10. This time, his regular band remained on hand for the entire time and there was no confusion. It was Elvis' most productive recording session in over two years, and resulted in eighteen completed songs. However, Elvis' depressed state of mind

1973 Sahara Tahoe taxi ad

When Elvis played either Las Vegas or Lake Tahoe, the Colonel's advertising campaign was not limited to just the marquee and the inside of the casino. This large, heavy plastic banner was mounted atop a taxi cruising the streets around the Sahara Tahoe Hotel in May 1973.

Value: $75

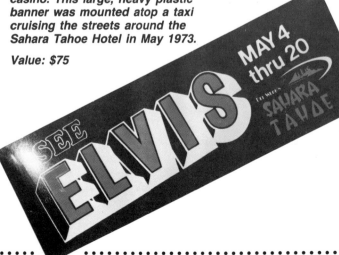

Elvis souvenir tour photo

This cardboard 8″ × 10″ color photo of Elvis was sold both on his tours and during his engagements at Las Vegas and Lake Tahoe. The back of the photo shows a map of the United States with every city that Elvis played from 1970 to 1973 highlighted with a star.

Value: $10

following his divorce and illness was reflected in a tearful set of songs that included "Help Me," "It's Midnight," "My Boy," and "There's a Honky Tonk Angel." He did rip into one rock 'n' roll number during the session, which, in a sense, told his own story—Chuck Berry's "Promised Land," a classic rocker about a boy who loses sight of his life's purpose while crisscrossing the country, only to find that his "promised land" was back home all along.

True to the spirit of the divorce settlement, five-year-old Lisa Marie arrived to spend the holidays with her daddy, and although his mood seemed to pick up considerably whenever she was around, he also appeared to be overly preoccupied once Christmas had passed. A week later, after Lisa Marie had returned to Los Angeles, numerous presents from friends and fans remained wrapped and under the tree.

As Elvis celebrated his thirty-ninth birthday, Georgia governor Jimmy Carter proclaimed "Elvis Presley Day" following Elvis' five sold-out performances at the Omni in Atlanta during 1973. The shows had brought in $800,000 in ticket sales as eighty-five thousand fans converged on the city. The total revenue gained by the city from hotel rooms, restaurants, parking fees, and other odds and ends was estimated to have exceeded $2 million. In Memphis there was a parade down Elvis Presley Boulevard, led by the mayors of Memphis and Tupelo. The solitary figure of Elvis could be seen standing on the porch of Graceland as the Humes High marching band strutted by playing "Happy Birthday."

Elvis 1975 Hilton postcard

The Hilton Hotel issued its own postcard promoting Elvis' Summer Festival in 1975. The words "Elvis Now" are superimposed on the side of the hotel complex.

Value: $5

Dec. 2, 1975 special gift bag

Only 2,000 special guests received this promotional gift bag filled with gifts from Elvis and the Colonel. Those not invited to opening night could purchase a similar bag, without any baubles, from the souvenir stand for $3 during the regular run of the show.

Value of December 2, 1975
gift bag (filled): $60
Souvenir shop bag value: $10

Four days after his birthday, he was aboard his personal plane, heading for Los Angeles to prepare for the upcoming winter stint at the Hilton on the twenty-sixth. This was the first of the shortened, two-week engagements. Voice, the vocal group that had helped overdub the songs at Elvis' Palm Springs retreat in September, was now a permanent part of the company. This cost an additional $10,000 a month in salaries, which came out of Elvis' pocket, but he was convinced that they would add a new dimension to his already overblown stage sound. Sherrill Nielsen, the group's tenor, was spotlighted during each concert in an emotional duet of "Softly, As I Leave You" with Elvis. It was also during this engagement that a devilish Elvis took a little target practice with his .22-caliber pistol, aiming at a light switch on the wall of his hotel room. The bullet passed through the wall and narrowly missed Linda Thompson, in the dressing room on the other side. Although frightened, Linda was otherwise unharmed. She remained Elvis' steady during this period, but he also found time to squeeze in a week with actress Sheila Ryan while Linda was off tending to other matters. Fidelity was never Elvis' long suit.

The Vegas stands had become moribund. The shows seemed set in concrete, and Elvis was patently bored most of the time. His daily schedule at the Hilton seldom varied. He would receive a wake-up call at 4:00 P.M., followed by a light breakfast. The remaining hours

"Moody Blue" sheet music

Appropriately, the photo on the sheet music for "Moody Blue" is tinted blue. The picture comes from the opening number of Elvis: Aloha from Hawaii television special in January 1973.

Value: $8

Aloha from Hawaii Via Satellite
LP and EP

Elvis' fantastic Hawaiian television satellite special generated mountains of much-needed praise and publicity. RCA Victor was ready to ship the album even before the show was aired. This was Elvis' first quadraphonic release (VPSX 6089), but the album was also issued through RCA Victor's record club in a stereo version (R 213736) not available in stores. RCA also produced a compact 7" stereo disk for the jukebox trade.

Value of quadradisc LP: $50
Value of record club stereo issue: $40
Value of 7" compact disk: $80

before going downstairs to prepare for the first show were taken up with television. His favorite programs were game shows, TV evangelism, and football. He would leave the penthouse at 7:30 P.M. to descend to the dressing room located a floor below the main stage. Following the introductory performances by the Sweet Inspirations, Jackie Kahane, and the Stamps, Elvis would take the stage at about 9:00 P.M. for a concert that lasted forty-five minutes to an hour. He then returned to his suite to repeat the ritual while waiting for the midnight show, after which there was usually a party in Elvis' suite if the performances had gone without any major flaws. Elvis would retire at daylight; at four in the afternoon, the routine would begin again. It's little wonder that he took occasional potshots at light switches, chandeliers, and TV sets.

When it came to football, Elvis' favorite professional team was always the Cleveland Browns. "The thing I keep up with most is professional football. I know all the players. I know all their numbers, who they play for. I've had people quiz me on it. I like a game when we have nothing to do. I watch all the games that I can. I get the films from the teams themselves if I can. Next to entertainment and music, [football] would be the biggest thing."

The two weeks in Vegas closed on February 9 without further incident, and he remained on the West Coast until the start of the year's first series of concerts on March 1. This tour was the longest since he had returned to live performing in 1969, running twenty days with a total of twenty-five shows, and routed southward from Tulsa through Texas, Louisiana, and Alabama before turning up the East Coast and curling back into Tennessee. The overwhelming demand for tickets meant that several cities originally scheduled for a single concert had a second show added; in some cases, the tour looped back upon itself, playing the same city two separate times within a week. In Houston Elvis set a one-day record at the Astrodome with two shows attracting over eighty-eight thousand fans, just barely eclipsing the number who had attended his Astrodome performances in February–March 1970. The final show of the tour was held on March 20 in Memphis' Mid-South Coliseum, the same venue that had been almost named for Elvis in the 1960s when the Memphis city fathers were hunting for a suitable way to honor their favorite son. This show was taped by RCA for release on the album *Elvis as Recorded Live on Stage in Memphis*. This was the most up-tempo show released by RCA from Elvis' days on the road. Of the twenty songs he brought home to Memphis, over half were old-fashioned rock 'n' roll, including such rarely performed numbers as "My Baby Left Me," "Lawdy, Miss Clawdy," "Long Tall Sally," and "Blueberry Hill." In contrast to the short shows in Las Vegas, Elvis was onstage in Memphis for an hour and a half in front of a boisterous and supportive hometown crowd. If just for a night, he was the king of rock 'n' roll once again.

In early April, an Australian promoter upped the ante for Elvis to perform overseas. "I'd like to offer you a million dollars for a single show by Elvis." Once again, the Colonel refused to take the bait, noting that "a million is plenty for me, but now, what about Elvis?"

Elvis rested for six weeks before hitting the boards for four days in California beginning on May 10. He opened a ten-day run at the Sahara Tahoe Hotel on the sixteenth, missing two midweek shows because of the flu. On May 20, something happened that would plague the entourage for years. A real estate developer from California alleged that he was invited to a late-night party in Elvis' suite. When he arrived at the penthouse, he claimed, he was beaten by Elvis and his bodyguards David Stanley, Sonny West, and Dick Grob. The man filed a lawsuit in October 1974. Although Elvis and company were finally exonerated, the bodyguards were left with a reputation for being fast with their fists.

The third tour of 1974 started on June 15 in Fort Worth. It ran seventeen days and played twenty-five shows in fifteen cities. The tour hopscotched around most of the United States, reaching as far north as Niagara Falls, as far south as Baton Rouge, and as far west as Salt Lake City. The distances involved meant that Elvis and the rest of the company spent most of their time on board one of their four airplanes, traveling between shows. They'd catch a few hours' sleep when they could, and considered themselves lucky if there was a hotel room waiting at the end of the flight. It was grueling and disorienting for everyone, especially the star. His life became a series of nameless stages, each offering the deafening roar of approving audiences, followed by long midnight flights aboard the cramped private plane. As a singer, he knew that the first thing that would go from a lack of sleep was his voice. Laryngitis is almost epidemic among touring companies. But Elvis appreciated the efforts that his fans had made to see him, and would try not to disappoint them with a mediocre performance. For several years he had relied on sleeping pills to squeeze out a few extra hours of rest on these tours. Now, when he was groggy upon awakening, he required a stimulant to start his "day." Many musicians with such habits relied on "uppers" and "downers" from street sources. Elvis had seen several close friends, including Johnny Cash and Carl Perkins, hooked on "pep pills." That was why he hired Dr. Nichopoulos to travel with the tours. Elvis wanted to make absolutely certain that any drugs were dispensed by a physician.

Back in Memphis, Elvis took part in a July 4 karate demonstration put on by Red West's Tennessee Karate Institute. The ninety-minute show was held at the outdoor

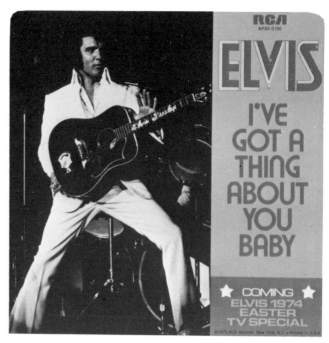

"I've Got a Thing about You Baby" picture sleeve

In January 1974, when "I've Got a Thing about You Baby" was issued as a single, plans were afoot for Elvis to star in his second TV special during the Easter season. The special never came about, but the picture sleeve seen here features the ad.

Value: $12

Having Fun with Elvis on Stage
Boxcar LP

In August 1974, Elvis and the Colonel signed an agreement setting up Boxcar Enterprises to issue certain mutually acceptable items. Their first venture was Having Fun with Elvis on Stage. It was sold at souvenir stands in Las Vegas and Lake Tahoe for about a year. The album then reverted to RCA Victor, which issued it as a regular release.

Value of Boxcar issue: $150
Value of RCA Victor issue: $20

Aug. 19, 1974, invitation and menu

Each person in the opening night audience received a special invitation from Elvis and the Colonel, and the show featured a complimentary dinner and free cocktails for all. As you might imagine, the invitations to these shows were eagerly sought after. As a result, the invitation itself is very collectible.

Value: $25

Overton Park Shell, and starred Elvis' part-time body-guard and Hawaiian friend Ed Parker. A week later Elvis attended the opening game of the Memphis Southmen of the new (and short-lived) World Football League. He sat in the owner's box, where he was introduced to the crowd by the announcer. Soon thereafter, he and a group of friends slipped away to Honolulu. Before the end of two quiet weeks, his presence was discovered, which forced an early return to Memphis.

Rehearsals for the next Las Vegas gig started in Los Angeles in early August. On the fifteenth Elvis signed a new agreement with Colonel Parker that transferred all of his commercial rights to Boxcar Enterprises, a company jointly owned by Elvis, the Colonel, and the Colonel's right-hand man, Tom Diskin. Their first joint venture would be a special album issued by Boxcar Records, titled *Having Fun with Elvis on Stage*. The Colonel was well aware that RCA owned only Elvis' *singing* voice. Elvis' speaking voice was something else again, and the Colonel smelled a little extra profit. This album may be the strangest legitimate release ever to bear Elvis' name; it featured only Elvis' spoken monologues and ramblings clipped from tapes made while he was in front of live audiences. An interesting concept, perhaps, but whole sections of the record were devoted to listening to Elvis laugh at an unknown joke or stage high jinks. To the Colonel's credit, a large number of the albums were donated to the various charities that ran the "Elvis" concession booths during their engagements in Las Vegas

Elvis' declining record sales during the last few years of his career is reflected in the scarcity of picture sleeves for several of his last singles. The picture sleeves for "If You Talk in Your Sleep," "Hurt," and "Moody Blue" are almost as rare as those from 20 years earlier.

Value of "If You Talk in Your Sleep" sleeve: $20
Value of "Hurt" sleeve: $18
Value of "Moody Blue" sleeve: $16

and Lake Tahoe. The album became an immediate collector's item, fetching double the seven-dollar sales price in collectors' record stores.

Las Vegas in August was another quick two weeks, highlighted by Elvis' receiving his eighth-degree black belt in karate onstage during a performance. He also found time to meet privately with Barbra Streisand, who was looking for a co-star for her update of the classic 1937 and 1954 movies *A Star Is Born*. Elvis' role would have been that of an aging rock 'n' roller, and he seemed genuinely interested in the project. The idea was immediately nixed when word filtered down to Colonel Parker, not because of the role's possible detriment to Elvis' career, but because Elvis would be receiving second billing to Streisand. The movie was released in 1976 with country singer Kris Kristofferson playing the part.

After closing in Las Vegas on September 2, Elvis returned to Graceland, where he tried to work on his karate, but the sport no longer held his attention. Having earned his eighth-degree black belt, he realized that further advancement was beyond his grasp. Karate, just like slot cars, speedboats, ranching, and matrimony, had been a passing phase. To combat his boredom, he went on a shopping spree. He bought the entire stock of Lincoln Mark IVs from the local Lincoln-Mercury dealer for $60,000, then went down the street and purchased five new Cadillacs. Needing a few new personal toys, he

Today album and quadradisc

The idea of quadraphonic sound was dying when RCA Victor released Elvis' Today album. Only a few copies were available in quad, with most produced in regular stereo.

Value of stereo LP: $15
Value of quadradisc: $100

kept two of the cars for himself. The rest were distributed to relatives and members of the entourage, including Linda, his uncle Vester, and Red West. Then he began eating.

By the late-September start of the fourth 1974 tour, Elvis looked terrible, although his appearance gradually improved over the next few weeks. The roadshow commenced in Maryland and zigzagged through the middle of the country, playing Michigan, Ohio, Indiana, Kansas, and Texas until October 9. Two days later he opened a four-day stand at Lake Tahoe; it was the first of his "in concert" casino shows, with presold tickets for two cocktail shows each evening, and no dinner show. Tickets were unheard of in the free-and-easy nightlife of Nevada, but the Colonel was firm. The previous overbooking at the Sahara Tahoe had upset him immensely, and he realized better than the hotel management that the fans must be kept happy. The idea worked so well in Lake Tahoe that he moved to initiate the same system in Las Vegas.

After closing at Lake Tahoe, Elvis divided his time between Los Angeles, Palm Springs, and Memphis until mid-December. Published reports said that Elvis was sending expensive gifts to Priscilla in an attempt to woo her back, but if they were true, he was unsuccessful. It was another blue Christmas in Memphis. For the first time in memory, the annual New Year's Eve celebration was canceled.

Elvis' excessive spending was the subject of one report, which noted that while he had earned over $7 million during 1974, he had spent even more than that on "expenses" of a business (over $4 million) and personal (over $3 million) nature. Significantly, $6 million had come just from his concert appearances in Las Vegas and Lake Tahoe and on tour. Following the 1973 contract with RCA that sold the rights to his early record catalogue, and after a year of otherwise dismal releases, the money that Elvis earned from record sales, movie rentals, and publishing rights had slowed to a trickle.

Elvis turned forty on January 8. He approached this watershed birthday with great trepidation. Having lived the past twenty years as one of the most powerful sex symbols in America, and indeed throughout the world, the idea of gracefully growing old was not easy to accept. National magazines had taken a close look at him during recent months, and their headlines stung: "Is there life for Elvis after 40?" He was rumored to be so depressed that he spent most of the week locked in his room with Linda Thompson, and turned away queries from even his most trusted aides.

The January Las Vegas engagement was canceled, and the local Memphis newspapers quickly announced that the reason was so that Elvis could diet. The Hilton in Las Vegas quickly responded that the real grounds be-

Sold Out Volume 2 bootleg album

In 1974, a Canadian record pirate issued Sold Out, *a bootleg containing various songs from Elvis' concerts around the country. In 1986, a European bootlegger decided to see if lightning would strike twice.* Sold Out Volume 2 *contains 15 live songs from 1969 through 1975. They come primarily from Vegas shows, and the sound quality is above average. Reportedly, this album was limited to only 500 copies, making it extremely rare.*

Value: $50

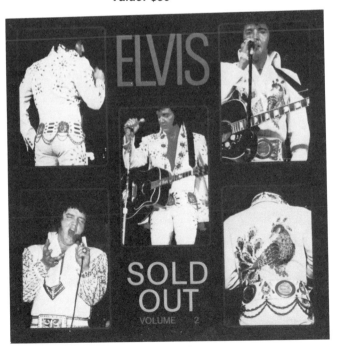

hind the change were solely the hotel's desire to have Elvis open its new $20 million addition, scheduled for an April 1 ribbon-cutting.

In fact, Elvis' weight had been a source of serious concern ever since the Hawaiian TV special in January 1973. With the separation from Priscilla and their subsequent divorce, it was apparent that any previous check on his appetite was now gone. He had always been a voracious eater, consuming small mountains of extra-fried bacon at breakfast, platefuls of cheeseburgers for lunch, and piles of rich southern-fried cooking for dinner. Snacks filled the hours in between. At age forty, his years of overeating had caught up with him with a vengeance. He suffered from a painful twisted and enlarged colon, a condition greatly aggravated by his diet. And his frequent attempts to control his weight through the use of prescribed diet pills did little more than elevate his already high blood pressure.

In a dark blue funk, he did what he had always done—bought cars. On January 17 he started early, and by the end of the day he had bought, and given away to friends, eleven Cadillacs. But that was small change—he also placed a $75,000 bid on a $1.5 million Boeing 707 jetliner that had been impounded after the owner, fugitive financeer Robert L. Vesco, defaulted on payments. (Vesco's ongoing difficulties with the federal government scotched the deal, and Elvis' opening bid was never returned.) Four months later, on April 17, Elvis finally found a plane suitable for touring, buying a 1958 Delta Convair 880 for $225,000. It was promptly renamed the

Magazines: General interest

One remarkable fact concerning Elvis' career is that, until May 4, 1971, Elvis had never appeared on the cover of any magazine not directly related to show business. Even the week of his death, with the nation feeling the loss, Elvis did not make the cover of any of the three national news magazines, Time, Newsweek, or U.S. News & World Report. The 1971 Look cover celebrated the publication of the first of a two-part condensation of Jerry Hopkins' fine book, Elvis. After 1971, the cover stories came sparingly. In February 1977, Preview magazine, aware that three of Elvis' bodyguards were writing an expose, offered another cover with a more lurid twist.

May 4, 1971 Look *magazine value: $20*

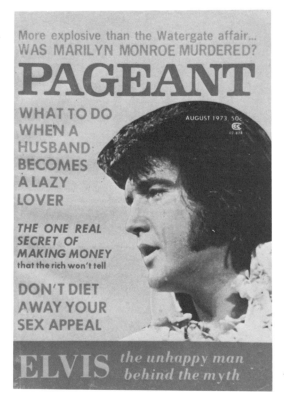

August 1973 Pageant *magazine value: $8*

March 1974 Pageant *magazine value: $8*

November 1975 Country Music *magazine value: $8*

January 13, 1975 People *magazine value: $6*

February 1977 review *magazine value: $8*

Lisa Marie. The plane was ferried to Fort Worth for extensive interior remodeling that by October would bring the total tab for the *Lisa Marie* to $983,075. Whenever possible, sometimes as often as twice a week, Elvis would make a late-night flight to Fort Worth to inspect the remodeling.

On January 29 Elvis was admitted to Baptist Memorial Hospital for a "general medical workup." Later, hospital spokesman explained that Elvis suffered from an impacted colon and hypertension.

During Elvis' stay in the hospital, his father suffered a heart attack and was admitted to the same facility. Throughout Elvis' career, Vernon had tried to keep the family on an even keel. He was a frugal man and a born hard worker, but his toughest task proved to be organizing Elvis' private financial affairs in a businesslike manner. It was Vernon who handled the family checkbook, and so it was Vernon who was constantly at odds with Elvis' insatiable attraction to ranches, cars, jewelry, and now airplanes. Vernon never fully recovered from the effects of his heart attack, and one side effect was that Elvis had lost one of his last restraints.

Elvis remained in the hospital for two weeks, after which he retired to Graceland for more rest. During this time, he was frequently spotted riding one of his new horses. Encouraged by Dr. Nichopoulos, Elvis also took up racquetball. And, as always, he and Linda and a group of friends spent many postmidnight hours at the Memphian Theater.

No matter what the press said about Elvis' poor health, offers for overseas appearances continued to come into the Colonel's office. In March he received a firm offer from a boxing promoter for a show at Earl's Court in London. The Colonel objected that ticket prices (starting at twenty pounds apiece) would be too high for the average fan. Another promoter offered two million pounds for a single performance at London's Wembly Stadium. Again, the Colonel declined with his old excuse: "Thanks, but we're all booked for the foreseeable future."

Elvis received his third and final Grammy from the National Academy of Recording Arts and Sciences during a March 1 TV awards show. This Grammy, like the other two, was presented in the religious category; specifically, for the inclusion of the song "How Great Thou Art" on the Memphis live concert LP. Elvis, as always, did not pick up the award in person.

After more than a year away from the recording studio, a three-day session was scheduled at RCA's Los Angeles headquarters, starting on March 10, but only three or four songs were recorded each night. This may have been enough for a new album, but it was hardly a sign of artistic commitment and vigor. Then it was time to return to Las Vegas.

The new addition to the Hilton was a 30-story, 620-room tower that rose above a new convention center to make it the largest resort hotel in the world. Elvis' performances starting on March 18 were ticketed for the first time, just as at Lake Tahoe the previous October. After three months of rest, Elvis looked healthy, though he was still carrying more weight than usual. The shows ran smoothly through the final performance on April 1, when the early show was an invitation-only event celebrating the opening of the new wing. Considering that this was April Fool's Day, Elvis performed in a very straightforward manner. The midnight show, by contrast, was full of water pistols, pranks, and high jinks, including Colonel Parker's entrance onstage dressed in his Santa Claus suit. It was even rumored that between the 8:00 P.M. show and the midnight performance, Elvis strolled through the lobby of the hotel dressed in a turban and a long flowing robe.

There was little time to rest in Memphis before the first tour of 1975, and during the next two weeks Elvis was seen to look tired and overweight. Opening night was in Macon, Georgia, followed in quick succession by a swing through Florida and then on to Tennessee, Georgia, Louisiana, and Mississippi. Nine cities, eighteen shows, fourteen days. This would now be standard operating procedure: two weeks on the road, the same amount of time at home. Las Vegas and Lake Tahoe would be squeezed in, just like another tour.

The next tour started on May 30 in Huntsville, Alabama. Eight cities, seventeen shows, and twelve days

Elvis magazine

In 1975, Ideal Publishing Company issued the first of a proposed series of magazines on Elvis, but only two issues were sold before Elvis' untimely death.

1975 Elvis: Yesterday . . . Today magazine value: $20
1976 Elvis: The Hollywood Years magazine value: $20

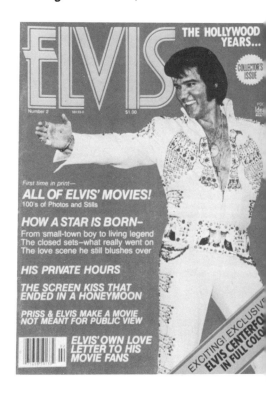

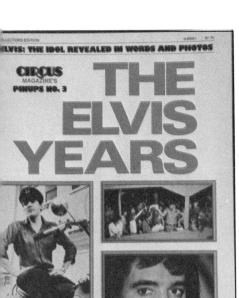

The Elvis Years magazine

In the mid-1970s, one of the magazines that gave Rolling Stone a run for its money was the monthly Circus. "The Elvis Years" from 1975 is their third "pinup" special, and it features a fine text by rock 'n' roll historian Nik Cohn. There are lots of wonderful, obscure photos, including a few in blazing color.

Value: $15

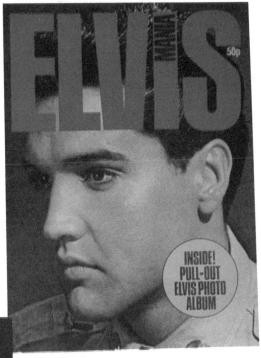

Elvis Mania magazine

Published in England in 1975, Elvis Mania magazine features a pull-out, 32-page photo album along with reviews of Elvis' records and information about books, fan clubs, magazines, and collectibles.

Value: $15

ecember 20, 1975, issue of Faces agazine

aces was a short-lived takeoff on e Life magazine size and format. e second issue featured Elvis the cover story, something the ore prestigious Life never did! e accompanying article, "The ing' Comes Back," by Charles ke offers readers a brief, e-page overview of Elvis at the d of 1975.

alue: $20

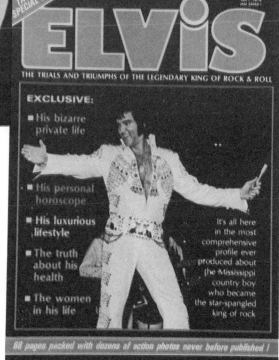

Elvis, The Trials and Triumphs of the Legendary King of Rock & Roll magazine.

Tattler was one of many supermarket gossip magazines that sprang up in the 1970s. In May 1976, they issued a special on Elvis that offered nothing new for the fans and was printed on cheap newsprint paper.

Value: $10

Blue jumpsuit

Elvis was to wear this jumpsuit on his last tour, but when he tried it on, it was too tight and a larger version had to be rushed to completion. Elvis died before he could perform in either suit.

Value: $10,000

Moody Blue album

Issued only a month before Elvis died, the album Moody Blue was scheduled to be pressed on blue wax only during its first run. In August, just a week before Elvis died, the black vinyl pressings were begun. Immediately after his death, however, RCA Victor decided to return to the blue pressings, but not before the press reported their supposed rarity. This misconception continues today, with many people certain that the blue copies are worth a fortune. To compound the problem, Moody Blue is now back on black wax, but the identification number has been changed. The rare ones are AFL1-2428 just like the blue copies.

Value of black (AFL1-2428): $200
Value of blue pressing: $10

Reader's Digest boxed LPs

In 1975, Reader's Digest in England issued one of the finest ever boxed sets of Elvis albums, Elvis Presley's Greatest Hits. The set had six LPs, with a total of 95 songs. Each album came with a special cover, which, when pieced together, made a 2' × 3' mosaic of Elvis in concert. Included was an eight-page booklet, "The Elvis Story." In 1983, Reader's Digest in the United States issued their own Elvis boxed set, Elvis! His Greatest Hits, a seven-record compendium with 84 songs. A 12-page booklet discussed each song, but didn't have special sleeves.

Value of Reader's Digest (England) boxed set, Elvis Presley's Greatest Hits: $250
Value of Reader's Digest (U.S.) set, Elvis! His Greatest Hits: $50

Thunderbird cape and belt

At the June 30, 1973, show at the Omni in Atlanta Elvis heard that a woman in the audience had brought her seven-year-old son dressed as an Elvis-lookalike. Elvis had the houselights turned on so that everyone could see the boy and then presented him with this belt and cape. This was one of Elvis' most valuable costumes, studded with real turquoise and coral.

Value: $75,000

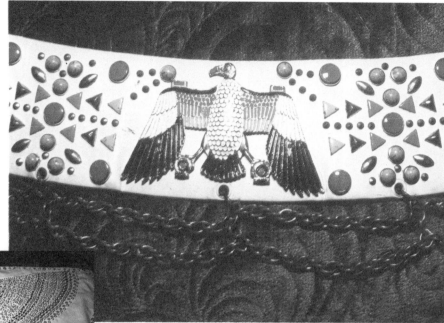

Lapis ring

Another favorite piece of jewelry was the lapis and gold ring worn by Elvis in the 1970s.

Value: $7,500

Lion ring

This lion ring was one of Elvis' most unusual pieces of jewelry. It was made of 18-carat gold and featured a ruby mouth and emerald eyes. Elvis gave this ring to Linda Thompson's cousin when she visited Linda and Elvis at the Atlanta Hilton in 1973.

Value: $20,000

Black opal ring

The stone in this ring would be of considerable value even if Elvis had never worn it. Black opals are extremely rare and this one is especially large. Elvis had jewelers all over the world searching for a stone like this, and when it was found in 1971, he had it flown to Hawaii where it was set in this 14-carat gold ring.

Value: $50,000

Bedroom suite, "coat of arms," RCA television

The bedroom suite pictured here belonged to Elvis' parents and was part of the furnishings of their home on Lauderdale Courts. The "coat of arms" hanging over the bed was hand-knit by a fan in the 1970s and features a karate insignia. The RCA television in the lower right corner of the picture is the set from the famous shooting incident. After firing off the shot at Robert Goulet's image, Elvis had the set smuggled out of the house so that Lisa Marie would not know what had happened. It was stored in a trailer on the grounds for about a year and then repaired and given to Earl Pritchett.

Bedroom suite value: $15,000
Coat of arms value: $2,500
RCA television value: $15,000

Elvis Commemorative Album

The most successful Elvis album ever released was not sold in stores, but hawked over television beginning in August 1973. It is believed that the original Elvis TV two-record package of hits sold more than 25 million copies before it was repackaged in September 1978 as the Elvis Commemorative Album and pressed on gold wax. Maybe that's why the commemorative LP sold so poorly.

Value: $80

later, Elvis stumbled home to Graceland. The pace was already too much for him. On June 16 Elvis was back in the hospital, this time in Memphis' Mid-South Hospital, where he underwent two days of eye tests to check the glaucoma that had plagued him for several years. There were unconfirmed reports that Elvis actually spent this time having a face lift. If so, the cosmetic surgery must have been slight, as none of the entourage back at Graceland noticed anything out of the ordinary.

In late June, it was reported that Elvis had purchased a $1.2 million twin-prop airplane for Colonel Parker as an early Christmas present. The Colonel politely refused this extravagant gift, thereby avoiding a hefty gift tax and the expense of maintaining and staffing the craft. Instead, he told Elvis that he'd just as soon keep on using the singer's Jetstar (and have Elvis foot the bill).

Tour number three started on July 8 and wandered from the middle of the country through the Northeast and upper South, playing twenty-two shows in seventeen days. Back in Memphis, Elvis fought off the dog days of summer by buying nine Lincolns, but he returned them the next day after one of the guys mentioned that the dealer had neglected to give him a courtesy discount for quantity. He immediately turned around and bought fourteen Cadillacs from another dealer. One of these new cars made national news when it was given away, on the spur of the moment, to local bank teller Minnie Person. The circumstances: she had seen Elvis drive into the lot and had stopped to admire his customized Caddy.

In late July, while Linda was away on business, Elvis courted another local belle, Melissa Blackwood, a former Queen of the Memphis Southman football team. In lieu of flowers, he bought her a new Pontiac convertible; then they flew to Fort Worth in his Jetstar to check on the renovation of the *Lisa Marie*. But as soon as Linda was back in town, Blackwood was history.

Still feeling especially generous, Elvis made a personal loan to Dr. Nichopoulos of $200,000 in late July. Nichopoulos received the money free of any interest after offering his home in the Eastwood Manor section of Memphis as collateral. It was not uncommon for Elvis to make such loans to members of his entourage, and he financed several of their homes. At one time he even wanted to split up ownership of the Flying Circle G Ranch and start a commune!

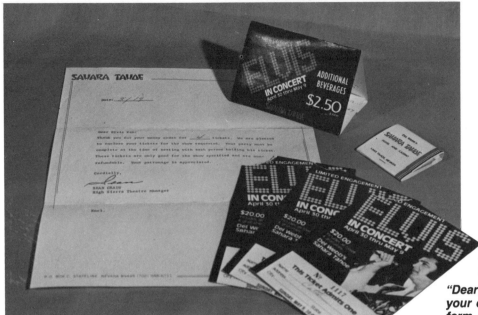

The oddest request of all to cross the Colonel's desk came in August. A New York City promoter offered $2.5 million for Elvis to appear in *Ciao Rudy,* a musical tribute to the late silent-film star Rudolph Valentino that would be opening at Radio City Music Hall the next January. The Colonel quietly declined.

If Elvis needed any indication of just where his life style was heading, and whom it was influencing, he got a clear sign on August 7, when his stepbrother Rick Stanley was arrested at Memphis' Methodist Hospital trying to pass a forged prescription for Demerol, a powerful sedative. Rick acknowledges that he had a serious drug habit at the time, although it was apparently news to Elvis. On this evening, Elvis did more harm than good when he pulled some strings down at the Shelby County sheriff's office to spring Rick by morning. Rick wasn't the only one having problems with clinics. Elvis' pet dog, Get-Lo, a chow, came down with a kidney ailment. The dog was flown to Boston in Elvis' small jet, and after two days in an exclusive hotel, Get-Lo was admitted to a central Massachusetts veterinary clinic. The dog recovered and returned to Memphis in November, trailing a vet bill in the thousands of dollars.

Elvis opened another two-week Las Vegas engagement on August 18. The omens were not good. En route to Vegas aboard his new Jetstar *Hound Dog I,* Elvis had taken some medication that brought on shortness of breath, and the plane was forced to land in Dallas so that he could seek a doctor's attention. In a few hours he was well enough to continue. Once the concerts started, all went well until the midnight show of the twentieth, which was marked by almost continuous pranks with water pistols that had been passed to him from two girls in the front row. The next morning, at six, Elvis was whisked out of the hotel for a rush flight back to Memphis, accompanied by Dr. Nichopoulos. By midmorning, all traces that Elvis had been performing at the hotel were gone. Up in a whiff of smoke went the placards, streamers,

Elvis in Concert album and bonus flyer

The Colonel insisted that the tradition of including bonus flyers and photos with the record albums continue even though Elvis was no longer alive. The first RCA LP to be released following Elvis' death was the two-record soundtrack to the TV special Elvis in Concert. *Inside was a full-color, four-page flyer "autographed" from "Elvis, Vernon Presley, and the Colonel."*

Value of album: $15
Value of insert: $5

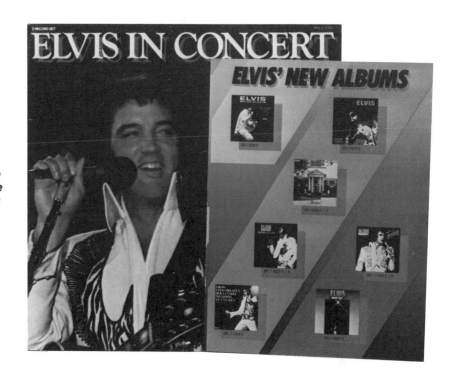

Memphis, Tennessee bootleg album

Featuring outtakes from sessions in 1964 and 1969, this bootleg album was issued in Europe in 1985. The material is taken from studio acetate test pressings used by Elvis and others in his crew to decide which take of a song to include on an album. The sound quality is acceptable if one ignores the frequent "pop" and "click" inherent in soft plastic acetate.

Value: $30

banners, the souvenir booth, and the front marquee proclaiming "ELVIS." In thier place were small cards in the lobby announcing, "The remainder of Elvis' engagement has been cancelled due to illness." The hotel issued a statement saying that Elvis was suffering from fatigue. In Memphis, he was admitted to Baptist Hospital for "tests." In a few days he was well enough to leave the hospital for a few hours each day. Dr. Nichopoulos issued a statement saying that the tests showed Elvis to be suffering from exhaustion but that there was no "serious medical problem," and he predicted that Elvis would be back on the road within five months. All tours for the next few months were canceled.

Following his return home from the hospital on September 5, two full-time nurses were retained. Their hours were usually nocturnal, from 11:00 P.M. until 2:00 the next afternoon. Elvis kept his nursing staff until January 1976.

The next few uneventful months were highlighted by the first flight of the *Lisa Marie* on November 27. The remodeling had added a bed, a conference table with large upholstered chairs, and a long blue crushed-velvet couch. The maiden voyage was to—where else?—Las Vegas, where Elvis was scheduled to make up the canceled August shows starting on December 2. In the interim, the Colonel had again changed the format of the shows. No more two shows a night; now, except on weekends, there was a single show at 10:15 P.M. The new regimen seemed to agree with the star, and throughout the two weeks he appeared to be in high spirits. He took requests and performed many songs that were not part of his regular Vegas act. Elvis was further cheered when

Lisa Marie was allowed to come to Las Vegas for a visit. After the show closed, Elvis hurried back to Memphis to enjoy the holiday season at Graceland. After starting on a sour note, the year had finished on an upbeat one.

There was one more concert left for 1975, and on December 31 Elvis flew to Pontiac, Michigan, where he performed a special New Year's Eve show at the Silverdome in front of 62,500 fans, setting a new record for attendance at a single show.

The first week in January, Elvis, Linda Thompson, and enough associates to fill three houses traveled to Vail for a repeat of their winter vacation of 1974. For Elvis, nothing could beat the excitement of riding snowmobiles at night through the woods with the lights switched off and the throttle wide open. During the day, Elvis went house hunting, wearing a jumpsuit and ski mask to keep from being recognized. The mask gave him such a severe facial rash that he required a doctor's attention. As always, there was time to buy more cars. The entourage traveled down the mountain to Denver, where Elvis bought five Lincoln Continentals that were presented to members of Denver's police department, which acted as his security guard in Vail. The doctor who treated the rash also got a Lincoln; so did one of the police officers' wives. In all, the cost for the new cars topped $70,000. As news of the car-buying spree leaked out, a Denver broadcaster complained over the air about the gifts to police officers; Elvis responded by sending him a new Cadillac. It was late in the month before Elvis and the group returned to Memphis.

The "jungle room" at Graceland was set up as a recording studio by RCA for a session that started in early February. For the next week, each night was devoted to recording material that would later appear on an album to be titled *From Elvis Presley Boulevard*. When he was finished, Elvis gathered his friends for a return trip to Vail, where they frolicked (without buying any more cars) until early March.

Back on the concert circuit for the first time since July, Elvis opened a short tour in Johnson City, Tennessee, with three shows in three days, starting March 17. Then he took the troupe through North Carolina, Ohio, and Missouri before returning to Memphis. At home, he played racquetball daily in the new court that he had had constructed in its own building behind Graceland. He was also spotted riding his three-wheel motorcycle through Memphis and attending midnight movies. The more things changed, the more things seemed to stay the same.

Phony wedding bells were rung throughout the year. First there was a widow in Athens, Alabama, who announced to the press that Elvis was going to marry her on April 7. No matter how improbable it sounded, hundreds of fans gathered up at the church. On July 12 a secretary

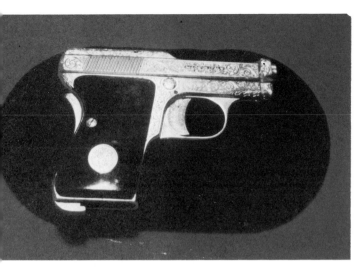

Gold Baretta

This gold-engraved Baretta was originally owned by Blake Edwards. Elvis was very keen to have this gun in his collection, but Edwards was equally reluctant to sell. Elvis went to extremes to achieve his end. In 1972 he purchased Edwards' entire home; the gun was part of the deal.

Value: $100,000

"My Way" sheet music

The sheet music for "My Way" was issued twice using Elvis' photo. The first time came in 1973, after "My Way" was issued as part of the Elvis: Aloha from Hawaii album. The photo included eighteen other singers who recorded the number. After the single "My Way" was released in November 1977, another piece of sheet music was issued showing only Elvis in concert from the 1970 film That's the Way It Is.

Value: $10 each

in Las Vegas waited in vain (along with many fans and the lunatic fringe of the press corps) at one of the many wedding chapels that dot the neon landscape. She was certain, she said, that the gentleman who had proposed to her was Elvis. Colonel Parker's office at M-G-M in Culver City was swamped with calls both times from reporters trying to get the story verified. There were also frantic calls from some of the more devoted of Elvis' female fans, who were worried that, if the rumors were true, they had again lost their chance to wear his ring around their neck.

On April 12 Elvis made his first business venture outside the realm of show business and without Colonel Parker's constant advice, as he, Dr. Nichopoulos, Joe Esposito, and a fourth man set up a business as Elvis Presley Center Courts, Inc. Dr. Nick was an amateur racquetball champion in Memphis, and had brought Elvis to the sport when his interest in karate waned. What was more, both Dr. Nick and Esposito saw this as a chance to make some personal money. The group's primary intent was to raise capital to build a series of racquetball courts in Memphis, but the project folded within a year.

The third week in April, Elvis started his second short tour of the year. Seven cities and eight shows later he was en route to Lake Tahoe for an April 30 opening night at the Sahara Tahoe Hotel. It was "Elvis in Concert" again, with only one show a day for ten days. The closing night, which fell on Mother's Day, Elvis gave an electrifying and crowd-pleasing performance. He rocked his way through two straight hours of music, a far cry from the usual forty-five-minute casino shows. And although he was visibly overweight, he more resembled a burly truck driver than the potato mountain depicted in the gossip magazines. Certainly, the Mother's Day show left no doubt about his stamina.

After presenting Linda with a new Lincoln Continental, Elvis was off on another series of one-nighters in late May, with shows in Indiana, Iowa, Oklahoma, and Texas concluding with three days of concerts in Atlanta. There was a brief nineteen-day respite in Memphis, with Elvis spending most of his time in his bedroom at Graceland before the fourth tour of the year, which started in Buffalo on June 25. That tour swung down the eastern seaboard before looping back along the Gulf Coast to Texas and finally closing in Memphis.

After the last tour, Elvis escaped to his Palm Springs home. It fell to Vernon to notify bodyguards Red and Sonny West and Dave Hebler that they were being discharged. This was not the spur-of-the-moment "firings" that had occurred throughout the years. This was permanent. Red had been with Elvis since he had defended him during their days at Humes High School. Sonny, Red's cousin, had joined the payroll in the 1960s, and

Hebler had worked for Elvis as a karate instructor and bodyguard since 1972. The reason for Vernon's action centered around the lawsuits being brought against Elvis by people who claimed to have been roughed up by the trio in their excessive zeal to shield Elvis. As with most of the disagreeable decisions in his life, Elvis let somebody else play the heavy. Three months later, in a rambling phone call to Red West, Elvis tried to offer an explanation for the manner in which the incident had been handled. By then, the trio had contacted a publisher and were hard at work turning out a manuscript detailing their years with Elvis, and the call fell on deaf ears.

On July 23, with less than three weeks' rest, Elvis was back on the entertainment circuit, his fifth of 1976: from Kentucky up to New York and back down the East Coast in fourteen days, playing fifteen shows in ten cities before returning to Memphis for three weeks and the start of tour number six on August 27—Texas, Alabama, Florida, Georgia, Mississippi, and Arkansas; thirteen more concerts in twelve cities. It was in Mobile that Elvis was first informed about the book that was being written by his former bodyguards. Elvis was in shock at the thought that anyone who had been a member of his inner circle would betray intimate knowledge about him. He hired a detective to see if he could prevent the book from coming out.

September was spent in Memphis and Palm Springs before the seventh tour of the year, which opened on October 14 in Chicago and hopscotched across the upper Midwest for fourteen days. Elvis was barely home before RCA trucked a ton of equipment out to Graceland for a three-day recording date starting on October 29. Only three songs were recorded during the first eleven-hour session, as Elvis spent most of his time singing gospel songs with the backup vocalists. Elvis remained upstairs for most of the second night, and the band spent its time laying down the tracks on two songs that remained uncompleted. After the last night's work was over, Elvis had a Lincoln delivered to Graceland, which he presented to J. D. Sumner, leader of the Stamps Quartet, in appreciation for his help with the session.

Early in November, following the lead of all of the other permanent ladies in Elvis' life, Linda Thompson called it quits. She wrote a "Dear John" letter expressing her feelings, and then ran up a $30,000 bill on Elvis' credit cards. Over the course of their four-year affair Elvis had showered Linda with an estimated $250,000 in jewelry, as well as any number of expensive cars and a home near Graceland. There had also been gifts of houses for her parents and for her brother, who remained on Elvis' payroll as a bodyguard.

Elvis didn't wait long to replace Linda. Elvis met twenty-year-old Ginger Alden and was immediately smitten with her striking resemblance to the young Priscilla.

Magazines: Elvis' love life

Over the years, Elvis has been linked romantically with dozens of women, from his movie co-stars and Las Vegas showgirls to TV personalities and hometown sweethearts. After he married Priscilla in 1967, most of this type of coverage ceased, but when his marriage broke up in 1972, the movie magazines started up again even stronger. Only one of these magazines deals exclusively with Elvis.

The next night he invited her to fly to Las Vegas for the evening. They returned to Graceland just in time for another event that made national news. In the wee hours of November 23, rock 'n' roller Jerry Lee Lewis was arrested at the front gates of Graceland after being refused admittance to the grounds. Lewis claimed to have been invited to come out to Graceland by Elvis, but the gatekeeper refused to let him in, and a call to the house found Elvis asleep. The police were called after Lewis started yelling and leaning on his car horn. Lewis was booked for starting a disturbance and carrying a concealed pistol. Later, when Elvis was notified, he refused to press any charges. After all, in spite of the years, Jerry Lee, like Elvis, remained a rocker.

The night after Jerry Lee came calling, Elvis started his eighth tour of 1976 with a show in Reno. This time he concentrated on the Pacific Northwest before playing San Francisco, where he was joined by Ginger Alden, and closing in Anaheim. He flew from there to Las Vegas to open a ten-day stand at the Hilton on December 2. Everyone noticed that Elvis was in high spirits. Even Priscilla came out to share opening night. Elvis' companion for the engagement was still Ginger, and he even brought her parents to Vegas during the second week's stay. It was his first Hilton appearance in a year; it would also be his last.

For Christmas, Elvis presented Lisa Marie with an electric golf cart that she merrily rode around Graceland's grounds. Elvis thought this was a terrific idea, so he ordered another half dozen. He presented Vernon with a touching poem that he had asked his good friend Janelle McComb to write for the occasion. The past year had been a good one in light of the problems of 1975, but Elvis' holiday spirit was curtailed by his ninth and final tour of the year, a four-day event that opened in Wichita on December 27 and wound through Dallas, Birmingham, and Atlanta before ending on New Year's Eve in Pittsburgh. Throughout December, critics commonly remarked that his weight seemed to be finally under control. Much of each concert was tailored to feature the power that he had developed in his voice. Songs such as "Hurt" and "How Great Thou Art" were given bombastic treatments; during particularly upbeat shows, they were sung twice in a row.

As Elvis and Ginger were returning to Graceland following the New Year's Eve show in Pittsburgh, her grandfather passed away. They attended the funeral in Harrison, Arkansas, on January 3, flying there with fifteen members of his "security staff." But that was not all. Elvis had Lamar Fike drive his Lincoln Continental from Memphis to Harrison, a distance of two hundred and fifty miles, much of it without the benefit of freeways, so that he and Ginger could travel in luxury from their motel to the airport. For Elvis, such luxury had become an everyday necessity.

Changing Pants! bootleg album

In 1975, Elvis broke the existing record for attendance for a single performance with his New Year's Eve concert at the Silverdome in Pontiac, Michigan. Over 62,500 fans got even more than they bargained for when, during the middle of "Polk Salad Annie," Elvis split his pants. It's too bad RCA Victor didn't see fit to release this concert, which is one of the last really great shows given by Elvis. This 1986 European bootleg suffers from very muffled recording quality.

Value: $30

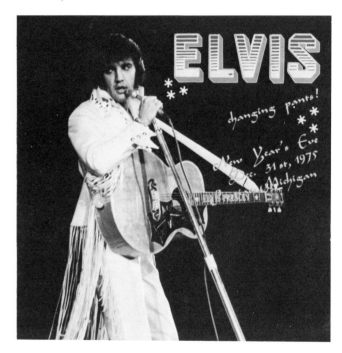

On the morning of January 20 Elvis, accompanied by Ginger, traveled to Nashville for a recording session. Elvis was scheduled to attend a 9:00 A.M. session at Creative Workshop Studios, but chose instead to remain secluded at the motel where he had booked the entire top floor. With his producer, Felton Jarvis, he listened to demo tapes for hours while the musicians at the studio laid down rhythm tracks. During his three days in Nashville, Elvis never once went to the studio.

From Nashville Elvis and Ginger flew to Los Angeles, where on January 26 he presented her with a $70,000 diamond ring whose center stone weighed eleven and a half carats. Ginger felt certain that the ring was Elvis' way of asking her to marry him, but other members of Elvis' family and entourage were not so certain. Most of those closest to Elvis knew that he could never keep a secret, no matter how small, and he never once mentioned the subject of marriage to his closest associates at this time, Vernon or his first cousin Billy Smith. Her repeated claims would be dealt with harshly after Elvis died.

By early February, RCA was desperate to have Elvis record studio material for immediate release. Again a mobile recording studio was dispatched to Graceland; this time it was set up in the racquetball court. After keeping the musicians waiting in a motel for three days, Elvis complained of a sore throat and the session was canceled. This would be the last attempt to record Elvis in a studio situation. It was a sad end to his remarkable recording career.

Diamond cross

Elvis wore this 14-carat gold and diamond cross in the 1970s.

Value: $4,000

Burning Love and Hits from His Movies, Vol. 2 album and bonus photo

RCA Victor chose not to release "Burning Love," Elvis' biggest hit in three years, on a regular album. Instead, the song was the leadoff number on a budget album marketed through RCA's subsidiary, Camden Records. The remaining eight tunes that comprise the album are little more than rehashed renditions from such almost-flops as Spinout, Kissin' Cousins, *and* Double Trouble. *As a pacifier, RCA wisely issued a color 8" × 10" bonus photo taken from one of Elvis' recent stage appearances. Remarkably, the album stayed on the best-seller charts for half a year.*

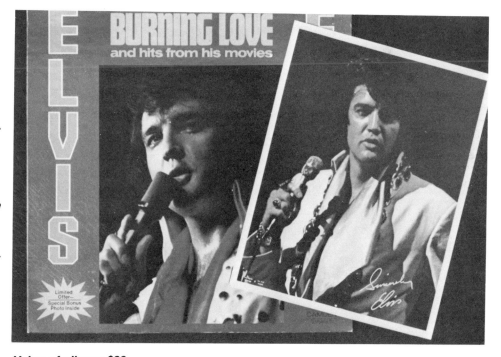

Value of album: $20
Value of photo: $15

The first tour of 1977 was booked to begin on February 12 in Hollywood, Florida. Elvis inched his way up Florida day by day before swinging through Alabama, Georgia, the Carolinas, and Tennessee, playing in nine cities in ten days. Panic spread through the entourage as Elvis was warned of a serious threat to his life before his St. Valentine's Day performance in St. Petersburg. As usual, the fans showered Elvis with gifts on this day set aside for lovers, and security was especially tight following repeated threats that one of the gifts would be booby-trapped. The tension was nerveracking. Picking a home-made Valentine off the stage, Elvis' bodyguards didn't know whether it would blow up in their faces. But, like all of the previous threats, it was a false alarm, and the show went off without a hitch.

On March 3 Elvis signed his last will and testament, a document that many feel was drawn up at Vernon's insistence, as Elvis always hated to read legal papers. That same day, Elvis made another loan to Dr. Nichopoulos, this time for $50,000, with a generous twenty-five years for repayment. Later, he left Memphis in the *Lisa Marie* with a planeful of family and friends for a ten-day vacation in Hawaii. A house was rented in Kailua, on the west side of Oahu. It was a much-needed break, even if the trip did cost Elvis over $100,000.

On March 23 Elvis was back on another twelve-day tour, winding through the southwestern part of the country before heading east to Louisiana, then on to Mobile, Macon, and Jacksonville.

On the twenty-eighth, in Austin, Eddie Fadal saw him perform for the last time. Backstage, it was obvious that Elvis was in very bad health. Fadal recalls their last conversation: "I asked him, 'What's going on? Elvis, you look terrible. Do something for yourself.' Elvis replied, 'Aw, what's the use?' 'What's the use' . . . that was his answer. So I surmised from that—I had to surmise, since that's all he said—I felt like he'd reached every pinnacle of success there was. There were no more mountains to climb. I think he'd just lost interest. He'd had the satellite show from Hawaii that went all over the world. How you gonna top that? The big Madison Square Garden concert was a phenomenal success. How you gonna top that? The big Astrodome thing in Houston. You can't top that! The Jaycees 'Man of the Year.' How you gonna top that? All of these big tremendous successes and tremendous acknowledgments and recognition. I think he began to believe that there were no more mountains to climb. He just didn't care anymore."

A week into the tour, in Baton Rouge, during the intermission following the first part of the show, the crowd was stunned as the announcer reported that Elvis' part of the show had been canceled. His fragile health had taken another downturn. He refused to get out of bed and go onstage. He was placed aboard the *Lisa Marie* and

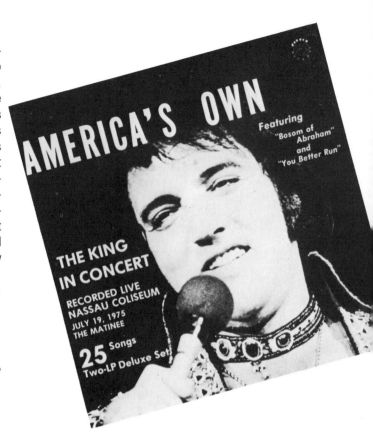

"The Fool" album

Although officially titled Elvis, *this album was soon nicknamed "The Fool album" after its opening song. Whether it was due to poor sales or, as legend has it, to Elvis temper-tantrum over the fans' nickname, the album was quickly withdrawn from circulation. It has never been reissued in this country.*

Value of Elvis *album including "Fool": $30*

America's Own bootleg album

In 1975, on the backside of his career, Elvis could still wow a crowd like few other performers. In fact, that may well have been the last year for the truly ecstatic Elvis concert. America's Own, recorded on July 19, 1975, documents just such an event. There is the added treat of Elvis and Charlie Hodge singing a duet of "You Better Run," a gospel number that Elvis never recorded officially. Although taped from the audience, the sound quality is above average for a bootleg.

Value: $150

flown to Memphis under the care of Dr. Nichopoulos. As soon as the plane touched down, he was admitted to Baptist Memorial Hospital for intestinal flu and fatigue.

Less than a week later, Elvis walked out of the hospital, discharging himself against Dr. Nichopoulos' wishes and leaving behind all of his clothes and personal belongings. Priscilla and Lisa Marie arrived soon after for a brief visit. Rarely were she and Elvis with their child at the same time. Since the divorce, Lisa Marie had traveled with either a nurse or a member of the Graceland staff when she went to Memphis or Las Vegas to spend time with her father.

Elvis was soon pronounced well enough to tour again, so the company dutifully trouped from North Carolina to Chicago in thirteen days. While he was playing Milwaukee, rumors that Elvis was about to split with Colonel Parker surfaced again, based on a story in a Nashville newspaper. According to the report, Colonel Parker was in poor health and needed money to cover gambling losses, estimated to have run as high as a million dollars during Elvis' two-week engagement at the Hilton the previous December. The bottom line, according to the article, was that Elvis' contract was up for sale. The Colonel called the newspaper and offered a complete denial. It was well known that Colonel Parker enjoyed the gaming tables in Las Vegas, and it was a common sight to see him holding down his favorite chair at the roulette wheel. But, as the Colonel said, "So what if I do lose large amounts? I win almost as often." By nature, he was a high-stakes player, and he had plenty of money to cover his bets. After expenses, Elvis' two-week tours in 1977 were bringing in an estimated $800,000.

When Elvis returned to Memphis he was met with a lawsuit from Dr. Nichopoulos and Joe Esposito, who were unhappy over his withdrawal of support for the Presley Center Courts racquetball project. Elvis had originally thought that he would be required to give only his consent to the use of his name in the venture; now it looked as though he was going to be called upon to finance the business, with $1.3 million out of his own pocket for starters. Vernon also was in the courts, being sued for divorce from Dee, his wife of almost seventeen years. Their divorce was granted in November by a judge in the Dominican Republic. Before the dust could settle, Elvis was back on tour with a May 21 performance in Knoxville, followed by one-nighters from Maryland to Maine. These shows were followed by appearances in Baton Rouge, Jacksonville, Macon, and Mobile to make up for the canceled shows in March and April.

On a celestial whim, Elvis decided to buy jewelry featuring everyone's birthstone, even though the bill came to over $60,000. Elvis believed that his personal birthstone, as determined by numerology, was a black sapphire, and he wore several pieces with that stone onstage. Unlike other artists who use "stage jewelry," which glitters but is not gold, Elvis insisted on wearing the real McCoy. One risk in this indulgent habit, however, was that some of the more exuberant females at stageside were always trying to slip off a ring or two while Elvis was bestowing a kiss. After the loss of a $3,000 black diamond ring, he was forced to wear bandages around his knuckles so that the rings were nearly impossible to remove. Elvis put up with this inconvenience because he wanted his fans to see where their money went. This was not idle boasting, but just another way to please his devoted audience.

Two weeks later, it was back on the road—for the last time. Colonel Parker had struck a deal with CBS to have camera crews cover the June tour for a one-hour special to be televised in the fall. June 17 saw his opening concert in Missouri, followed in quick succession by shows throughout the middle of the country.

Bizarre incidents were now an everyday occurrence. After midnight in Madison, Wisconsin, as Elvis was being driven from the *Lisa Marie* to his hotel room, he saw two youths ganging up on a service station attendent. Elvis had the limousine stop, and he jumped out, assumed a karate stance, and warned the youths that he would take them both on. A fight was, fortunately, averted, and Elvis posed for pictures with the assailants before signing autographs for those at ringside. The next night, in Cincinnati, Elvis complained that the air conditioning in his hotel room was not cold enough. He grabbed a bodyguard and marched down the street to another hotel and booked two rooms. Incidents such as these were occurring with dizzying frequency. His weight was now totally out of control. He appeared bloated in the face and belly from a combination of the twisted colon and the medication he was taking to control his high blood pressure. Glaucoma made his eyes puffy, and tears streamed down his face from the pain when he looked into the bright spotlights. But even with all of his medical problems, his voice never failed him. It was full-blown and powerful, and certain to hit the exact note. He sounded reborn, but he looked near death. The final performance of his long career was given in Indianapolis. It was an unspectacular show, ordinary by the standards he had set in earlier shows, but the sold-out house still stood and cheered into the night even after the anouncer told them, "Elvis has left the building."

Returning to Memphis for a much-needed vacation, he rented Libertyland park in the evenings to amuse the visiting Lisa Marie, or organized private midnight movie parties. But during much of July he stayed locked in his bedroom and would see only a few friends. He was openly despondent over the imminent publication of the book by Red and Sonny West and Dave Hebler. He had been shown portions of it, and he knew it was going to

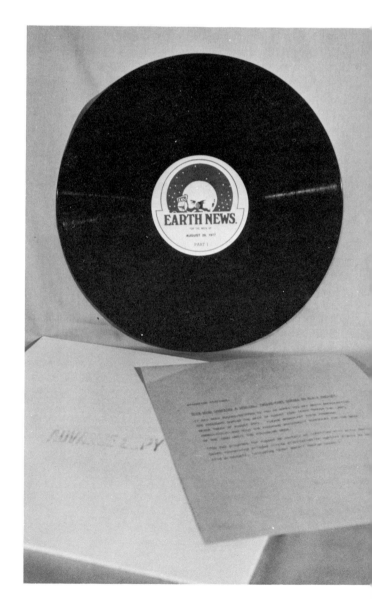

damage his public image. He even wondered whether the revelations in the book might destroy his career.

He was watching his diet now that he was back home, but he still weighed in at close to 230 pounds, and the next tour loomed, as always, just a few days away. There never seemed to be enough time to wind down before the next series of shows. On August 15, in preparation for the next tour, Dr. Nichopoulos wrote prescriptions for a larger than usual series of medications, including several powerful sleeping potions. That afternoon, Elvis and Ginger rode motorcycles through the Memphis suburbs with his cousin Billy Smith and Billy's wife, Jo. Late in the evening, Elvis visited his dentist, and he returned to Graceland about twelve-thirty in the morning. It was the sixteenth of August.

He loosened up with a little racquetball on his private court from 4:30 to 6:30 A.M., and then relaxed by playing "Unchained Melody" and "Blue Eyes Crying in the Rain" at the piano. After retiring to his upstairs bedroom with Ginger, he complained that he was restless and ordered some medication to make him drowsy. About 9:00 A.M., still unable to fall asleep, he retired to his dressing room—bathroom just off the bedroom. He carried a religious book on the Shroud of Turin.

Ginger awoke at two that afternoon, alone in bed. She found Elvis, in his pajamas, slumped over on the red-carpeted dressing-room floor. He wasn't breathing. She called aide Al Strada on the house intercom. As soon as he reached Elvis' sleeping quarters, Strada summoned Joe Esposito, who had just arrived at Graceland. Esposito immediately tried to resuscitate Elvis. Lisa Marie and Vernon, anguished at the scene unfolding in front of their eyes, had to be restrained. An emergency call was made to the firehouse a short distance away on Elvis Presley Boulevard. Dr. Nichopoulos was quickly notified, but he arrived at Graceland in only enough time to hop into the ambulance for the seemingly endless ride to Baptist Memorial Hospital. There was never any hope of reviving Elvis. He had died quietly in his beloved Graceland.

Earth News, August 29, 1977

Caught off guard when Elvis died, Earth News, a syndicated radio program, had to rush-release a 12-part special to be aired during the week of August 22, even though the labels on the record read August 29, 1977. The record came in a plain white sleeve marked "Advance Copy" and was accompanied by a letter printed on brown paper explaining the situation to station program directors.

Value of Earth News record for August 29, 1977: $160

the King Lives On

It was pandemonium inside and outside Graceland from the moment Elvis' death was announced. Stunned relatives and close friends rushed to the mansion to share their grief. The *Lisa Marie* and its crew were pressed into service to fly to Los Angeles so that Priscilla, Linda Thompson, Jerry Schilling, and other West Coast friends of Elvis could return to Memphis without delay.

The front gates of Graceland became a rallying point for an estimated 100,000 devoted fans from around the country who converged on Memphis during the next two days. To add to this confusion, the Shriners were holding their annual convention in Memphis, and all hotels within a radius of one hundred miles were immediately filled. The weather also worked against such a large, outdoor gathering as the temperature climbed above 100 degrees. Dozens of medical teams were called to Graceland to treat those who collapsed, and the front grounds of the mansion resembled a battlefield as medics tried to comfort those who had fainted. In Tupelo telephone circuits in the phone company's central office became overloaded.

The morning after he died, Elvis' body was brought back to Graceland to lie in state in the foyer. Early that afternoon, following a short informal service for the immediate family, an estimated 75,000 distraught fans attempted to file past the open casket for one last, quick glimpse of their fallen king. The actual number who were able to squeeze past the open coffin could not have been more than ten or twenty thousand. The first sight that greeted fans was the seamless brass casket. Then, suddenly, there was Elvis dressed in the white suit that Vernon had given him the previous Christmas. Many fans remarked that he looked at peace, as though the trials of the past few years were past. Later in the evening, soul singer James Brown slipped unnoticed into Graceland to pay his respects. He and Elvis had been friends since 1956, the year they both hit the national scene.

In the early morning hours of August 18, a further tragedy occurred. A car went out of control and plunged into a milling crowd of three hundred mourners just outside Graceland's gates, instantly killing two female fans

Porcelain bust

This 8 ¾"-tall bust was offered by Goebels of West Germany in 1977. It is made from white bisque porcelain and was copyrighted by and licensed through Boxcar.

Original price: $50

News of Elvis' death crowded other news off the front pages of the two Memphis newspapers.

Value of original newspaper: $10
Value of reprint: $1

Bronze sculpture

"Journey to Graceland" is a single sculpture consisting of three distinct figures of Elvis. It was created by noted sculptor Bill Rains and is cast in bronze. Bronze I is limited to 42 castings and is 41″ high; it sells for $25,000. Bronze II is an 18″ bronze in an edition of 142 castings and is $5,000. Bronze III is 12″ in an edition of 1,042 castings and sells for $1,500. Limited and open edition posters are also available. All pieces are sold directly through Bill Rains Productions and a few selected galleries.

Elvis Aron Presley promo LPs

The terrific eight-record boxed set,
Elvis Aron Presley, *spawned two
promotional records. The first,*
Excerpts, *was sent to record
stores and has 38 minutes of snips
and snatches from the entire
collection.* **Selections** *was mailed
to radio stations and contains 12
complete songs.*

Value of Excerpts *promo: $125*
Value of Selections *promo: $175*

Susie Q bootleg album

*The songs on this 1984 European
bootleg are mainly taken from
Elvis' live shows and feature either
items he had not previously
recorded or versions completely
different from those released. The
title song, unfortunately, is heard
only briefly.*

Value: $25

Michelob Presents "Elvis Memories"

*This promotional LP was sent to
Budweiser Beer distributors to
hype the Elvis Memories 3-hour
radio special that aired August 13,
1978, over the ABC radio network.
The album contains highlights
from the broadcast sponsored by
Michelob.*

Value: $200

Pewter figure

This is one of three "strictly limited edition" pewter figures offered by Perth Pewter through a 1977 licensing agreement with Boxcar/Factors. Each figure was approximately 5" tall and weighed 1 pound; all were numbered and signed by the artist, Ron Spicel.

Original price: $50

and injuring a third. It was another strange, morbid twist in the seemingly endless days and nights of sadness.

The funeral was held the afternoon of August 18. Among the celebrities who squeezed into the first floor of the mansion were the ever-faithful Ann-Margret, RCA's Chet Atkins, Caroline Kennedy (who was secretly acting as a reporter for *Rolling Stone* magazine), and Tennessee Governor Ray Blanton. Inspirational music was provided by Kathy Westmoreland and J. D. Sumner and the Stamps, along with some of Elvis' favorite gospel singers Jake Hess and the Statesmen Quartet and James Blackwood of the Blackwood Brothers. Parting remarks were made by TV evangelist Rev. Rex Humbard; Rev. C. W. Bradley, pastor of the Wooddale Church of Christ; and Jackie Kahane, comedian with Elvis' stageshow. Elvis' coffin was sealed, and the funeral caravan of sixteen white Cadillac limousines followed the white hearse slowly up Elvis Presley Boulevard to Forest Hills Cemetery. The 800-pound casket was carried by six pall bearers: Joe Esposito, Dr. George Nichopoulos, Charlie Hodge, Felton Jarvis, Lamar Fike, and Billy Smith; and Elvis was laid to rest in a marble mausoleum just one hundred yards from his mother's grave. The next afternoon, at Vernon's request, the flowers from the 3,166 floral wreaths (valued at more than $100,000) were given away to fans filing quietly past Elvis' tomb.

Sadly, even in death Elvis found no immediate resting place. On August 29, three men were arrested for allegedly plotting to steal Elvis' body. Guards were hired to protect the mausoleum at a cost of $200 per day. One week after the incident, Vernon's lawyer petitioned Memphis City Commissioners to allow him to move Elvis and Gladys to an area of the grounds of Graceland known as the Meditation Garden. The lawyer pleaded that not only was security for Elvis a matter of utmost necessity, but those wanting to use the cemetery were being bothered by the continuous crowds of milling sightseers. The bodies were moved to Graceland on the evening of October 2. Although there had been no announcement, a hundred fans had gathered at the Music Gate when the two white hearses arrived with the bodies.

I Can't Help Falling in Love with You
bootleg 78 rpm

There's no rhyme or reason for this 78 rpm bootleg except possibly to fill the needs of the minuscule market for 78 rpm jukeboxes. Maybe that's why one copy is worth so much. The song "I Can't Help Falling in Love with You" is backed by "Burning Love."

Value: $30

Guitar Man album and flyer

Guitar Man *was another attempt to issue older recordings by Elvis in a manner that would generate new sales. The tapes of the songs on* Guitar Man *were all remastered to eliminate virtually everything except Elvis' vocals; then new musicians were hired to overdub contemporary backings. Sometimes it worked; most of the time it didn't. Included with original issues of* Guitar Man *was an 8½" × 11" promo flyer for the upcoming film,* This Is Elvis.

Album value: $10
Flyer value: $5

On November 27, the Meditation Garden next to Graceland was opened to the public. Thousands of people had waited through the night in a near-freezing downpour to be among the first to see Elvis' gravesite. To foil any further attempts to steal Elvis' body, his 800-pound casket was encased in a 3,000-pound vault covered with a 2,000-pound granite slab and an 800-pound, full-length bronze plague that featured an inscription from Vernon, reading in part, "God saw that He needed some rest and called him home to be with Him."

With the filing of Elvis' will on August 22, 1977, the public learned that he had left his entire estate to his daughter, father, and grandmother. The many close relatives who depended on Elvis were provided for in a general clause that allowed for support for their health, education, comfortable maintenance, and welfare, as long as Vernon Presley remained executor of the estate.

An inventory of Elvis' personal belongings was filed in November. Included were his extensive gun collection, including three machine guns, 32 photo albums filled with stills from his movies, and his many trophies and awards. For transportation he owned eight new luxury cars, seven golf carts, six motorcycles, two Stutz Black Hawks, and a pink 1955 Cadillac, not to mention a jeep, a wrecker, two trucks, a jet airliner (the *Lisa Marie*), and a

Gold record plaque

The figure of Elvis, designed by Mark Freed, has a patina finish and is three dimensional and mounted on a simulated gold record. Manufactured in 1977 by A&A Specialties, this plaque was licensed by Boxcar/Factors.

Original price: $40

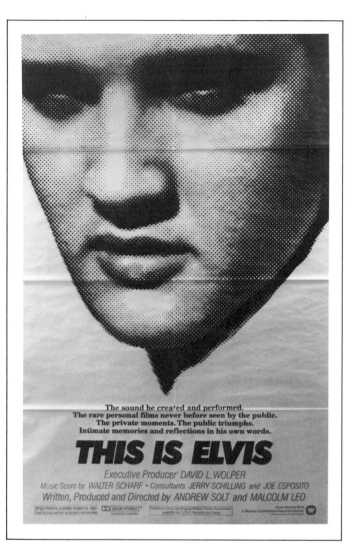

The sound he created and performed.
The rare personal films never before seen by the public.
The private moments. The public triumphs.
Intimate memories and reflections in his own words.

THIS IS ELVIS

Executive Producer DAVID L. WOLPER
Music Score by WALTER SCHARF • Consultants JERRY SCHILLING and JOE ESPOSITO
Written, Produced and Directed by ANDREW SOLT and MALCOLM LEO

This Is Elvis ad

After Elvis' long association with both Paramount and M-G-M, it is interesting that Warner Brothers, one of the few Hollywood film companies that Elvis never worked for, was the company responsible for issuing what will probably stand as the definitive film biography on Elvis. The movie advertising failed to play up any of Elvis' career, private life, or image. All we get is the foreboding stare graphically enhanced through the use of a billboard-sized dot pattern.

27″ × 44″ one-sheet value: $20

smaller commuter jet (the *Hound Dog I*). The stables at Graceland housed four horses and a pony. There were numerous television sets throughout the house including two in the ceiling above his bed. His jewelry included a gold cross inlaid with 236 round diamonds and numerous other stones, and his personal wardrobe filled several large closets. The total estate was valued at $10 million, including an estimated $150 million in royalties owed by RCA.

By the end of the year, a more complete financial picture had emerged: Elvis had left real estate (Graceland and his Palm Springs home) valued at better than $1 million, miscellaneous properties (including a large parcel of land across the street from Graceland) valued at $.5 million, a $1 million checking account, insurance policies totaling $96,000, stocks and bonds worth $26,000, and promissory notes on money that he had loaned various individuals (including the two notes to Dr. Nichopoulos totaling $270,000) in excess of $1.3 million. The funeral expenses had come to $46,464, with another $6,121 paid to the Memphis Police Department for their services in controlling the crowds. The reentombment of Elvis and Gladys at Graceland had cost $10,000, and the cost of maintaining Graceland was $36,000 per month. Elvis' income from August 16, 1977, to the end of the year was $2.1 million.

If Elvis was finally allowed his final rest, those left to oversee his affairs were busy from the day of the funeral. At Colonel Parker's insistence, Vernon Presley signed an agreement with Factors, Inc. making them the exclusive distributor and sole licensee for all non-musical Elvis merchandise. The Colonel had been shocked at the brazenness of the souvenir peddlers outside the walls of Graceland who had hawked tee shirts and bumper stickers to the mourners without bothering to pay royalties on the use of Elvis' name or likeness. Earlier in the year, Factors had proven itself worthy of carrying the Elvis standard in the merchandising wars when the company signed up the *Star Wars, Rocky,* and Farrah Fawcett accounts. Factors had a reputation for licensing quality goods and for quickly bringing lawsuits against the pirates. According to Factors, the deal for rights to Elvis was made to "eliminate the unauthorized and unlicensed merchandising of the Elvis Presley name which is depriving the Presley estate of revenues to which it is rightfully entitled."

Within six weeks it was like a return to the fall of 1956. The Factors' licensees had churned out costume jewelry, buttons, posters, plaques, trash cans, tote bags, decals, tee shirts, and drinking mugs all bearing the logo "The King Lives On." But for every license granted to sell Elvis memorabilia, Factors had to contend with hundreds of "coffin riders" who were making a quick buck off of Elvis' legion of fans. Factors reportedly filed over 400 lawsuits against merchandise bootleggers during the first two years following Elvis' death.

Still some of the earlier efforts, while in questionable taste, appeared to be legal: in Ohio, portions of a 1956 Cadillac once owned by Elvis were melted down and turned into pendants selling for $4.95, and copies of the August tribute editions of the Memphis, Nashville, and Tupelo newspapers were being hawked for $15 a set.

Elvis' death was as much an event for the media as it was a personal tragedy for his millions of fans. The national television news programs combined footage of Elvis' career with scenes of the mourning fans in front of Graceland. The night of August 16, both NBC and ABC television networks ran half-hour specials at 11:30 P.M. hosted by David Brinkley and Geraldo Rivera, respectively.

On radio, Elvis' death had an even greater impact as many stations devoted their entire programming day to his music. Watermark received two-hundred requests for its 12-part radio special, *The Elvis Presley Story,* on August 16 alone.

Elvis' final TV special, *Elvis in Concert,* which had been taped during his last tour in June, aired on October 3 over CBS-TV. The critics were less than kind in their opinions of Elvis' performance. Most agreed with *Variety* that "his famous smirk had become a leer" and he had "lost a good deal of his primitive, gutsy quality." Worst of all, Elvis "walked through thirteen songs, mostly mumbling." *Elvis in Concert* was not the first attempt by television to capitalize on Elvis' death. NBC-TV had shown an abbreviated, one-hour version of *Elvis on Tour* on September 7. That same network signed Ann-Margret to host a three-hour *Memories of Elvis* night on November 20, replaying the 1968 *Elvis* special back to back with 1973's *Elvis: Aloha from Hawaii.*

The rush by fans around the world to buy virtually anything with Elvis' name on it caught everyone by surprise. Hardest hit that first day were record stores as fans stood in long lines holding as many Elvis albums and singles as their arms could carry. Within hours there wasn't an Elvis record to be had in most stores. RCA's main plant in Indianapolis immediately began pressing only Elvis records 24 hours a day and was soon shipping 20 million Elvis records a week. By mid-October, half of the top sixteen places on *Billboard*'s country album chart belonged to Elvis.

And then there was Steve Goldstein, an entrepreneur worthy of comparison with Colonel Tom Parker. Within hours after Elvis died, he purchased a small quantity of an Elvis budget album selling in stores for $2.98 and offered it at $6.98 through a midnight TV ad in New Orleans. The next morning, when he had 150 orders, he expanded his line of records and bought time in more markets. Orders poured in with such ferocity that phone systems in several cities shorted out whenever the ads

Graceland magazine

By far the finest publication from an Elvis fan club is the Graceland *magazine from West Germany, which began publication in 1979. Each 50+-page issue is jammed with articles and rare photos. It is only published in German, which is unfortunate for those fans who do not speak the language.*

Subscriptions to Graceland *magazine available from:*

Elvis Presley Gesellchaft e.v.
Postfach 1264
D-8430 Neumarkt 1
West Germany

Elvis Sings for Children and Grownups Too! album

Elvis always wanted to record an album especially for children. He died before starting such a project, so Colonel Parker gathered songs appropriate for the younger set that Elvis had sung in his movies. Original releases included a greeting card. Interestingly, the album erroneously contained an alternate take of "Big Boots."

Value of album: $10
Value of card: $2

Elvis Presley Plaza

Eric Park's bronze of Elvis now stands overlooking the Mississippi River in Memphis' Elvis Presley Plaza.

aired. Within a few months, he had moved nearly 700,000 LPs for an average price 30 to 60 percent higher than the list price of the same records in stores.

In the publishing industry, anything with Elvis' name on it sold in tremendous quantities. Grosset & Dunlap ordered a 400,000-copy reprint of *The Illustrated Elvis* by W. A. Harbinson, which had sold only 40,000 copies when originally published in 1976. A half million copies of May Mann's pocketbook, *Private Elvis,* were reprinted. The K mart chain of discount stores placed the world's largest book order when they asked for 2 million copies of *Elvis: What Happened?* Other outlets had similar requests and within a month, 3.5 million copies of this latest book about Elvis were on store shelves. Within a month, the number of magazines devoted exclusively to Elvis approached two dozen; by the year's end there were a hundred. The September 12, 1977, issue of the *National Enquirer* that featured on its cover a snapshot secretly taken of Elvis lying in his coffin sold over six million copies—the largest single issue of a newspaper or magazine ever.

Records paying tribute to Elvis were not long in coming. On August 19, acetates of the first song to eulogize Elvis were mailed to radio stations, but the demo disks failed to reveal the name of the singer. "The King Is Gone" had been written by unknown country vocalist Ronnie McDowell the evening following the announcement of Elvis' death, and McDowell said he did not feel it proper to capitalize on the situation. The song, of course, became an immediate hit, selling a million copies the first week of its release, and McDowell capitulated to the siren's call of fame and went on to become a star in country music.

He Walks Beside Me album and booklet

He Walks Beside Me *gathers together several previously released spiritual numbers. Original copies of the album include a 5¾" square miniphoto album containing 14 pages of photos of Elvis in concert and two pages of ads for Elvis' albums.*

Value of album: $10
Value of booklet: $8

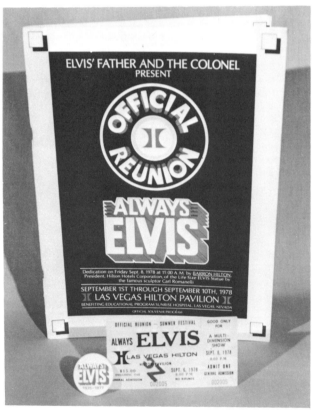

"Always Elvis Festival"

Pictured are the souvenir program, ticket, and button from Colonel Parker's "Always Elvis Festival" at the Las Vegas Hilton.

Original price of program: $1
button: $.25
ticket: $15

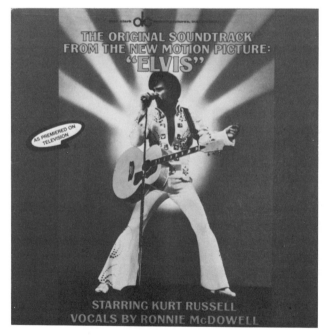

Elvis soundtrack

Although Ronnie McDowell sings Elvis' songs in this made-for-TV production of Elvis, many fans feel that this record is a "must" for their collection. After all, Kurt Russell did give an outstanding performance, one that only Elvis could have topped!

Original price: $8

"Our Memories of Elvis" singles and picture sleeves

The two Our Memories of Elvis *albums from 1979 featured Elvis' vocals without any overdubbing. What the fan heard was the "pure" sound of Elvis accompanied by just a few musicians. Of the two singles released from the albums, "There's a Honky Tonk Angel" is the most interesting. The labels of the first run of this single gave credit to a vocal group and string arrangement when the point of the record was to omit just those types of backups. Later copies corrected this mistake.*

Value of "Are You Sincere" with sleeve: $18
Value of "There's a Honky Tonk Angel," with error,: $25
Value, without error: $18

By the end of August, the number of tribute records of one sort or another had topped a dozen, with a new single being released virtually every day. Within six months there were hundreds of singles and albums out either mourning Elvis' passing or praising his career. Most of the tributes were from unknown singers, with the exception of Merle Haggard's "From Graceland to the Promised Land." There were also tributes from three members of Elvis' troupe: Kathy Westmoreland, Jackie Kahane, and J. D. Sumner and the Stamps.

One man who did not share McDowell's concern over propriety was Nashville's Shelby Singleton, current owner of Sun Records, which he had purchased from Sam Phillips in 1969. On August 26, with much bally-hoo, Sun Records re-released its single version of "That's All Right"/"Blue Moon of Kentucky" without putting the singer's name on the label. Singleton had tried the same ploy in 1972, and those who were familiar with Elvis' voice were not taken in; the singer was Jimmy Ellis, who later billed himself as Orion.

If the new Sun single failed to make much of an impression, Singleton wasn't dismayed. In September 1977, he rush-released an album, *The Sun Years,* consisting of a muddled narration about Elvis' 18 months at Sun Records interspersed with snips of Elvis' songs taken from both RCA and bootlegged records. Singleton was immediately sued jointly by RCA and Vernon Presley for $4 million in damages for what he billed as an "historical document." Two months later, Singleton agreed to pay RCA $45,000 in damages, but he still came out the winner because he was allowed to keep the $600,000 that the album had grossed.

Concert tickets

There was quite a lot of confusion for the promoters of Elvis' last tour when fans decided not to turn in their tickets for a refund. Some fans kept them for souvenirs, and some sold them for as much as twice the face value.

Original price: $15

On December 14, 1977, Singleton announced that he was releasing a five-record album set titled *The Million Dollar Quartet,* consisting of the two hours and twenty minutes of tapes made by Sam Phillips on December 4, 1956, at Sun Studios that featured the impromptu singing of Elvis, Carl Perkins, Jerry Lee Lewis, and Johnny Cash. Singleton had inherited the unreleased tapes when he bought the company. In the same announcement, he also reported that he was releasing a single LP, *1955 Sun Days,* which had studio chit-chat from Elvis, Roy Orbison, Cash, Perkins, and Lewis leading into various outtakes of key songs never before released. According to Singleton, Elvis would be heard imitating Hank Snow on *Face to the Wall,* as well as singing three songs in which he playfully copied Bill Monroe's bluegrass singing style. Once again RCA filed a lawsuit, this time joined by Cash and Perkins, and was successful in immediately stopping the release of both albums. It is noteworthy that a bootleged album of what appears to be the first volume of the *Million Dollar Quartet* did surface in 1978.

RCA wasn't through with Singleton. They filed another lawsuit requesting that all tapes containing Elvis' voice be turned over to them. Singleton said that if RCA did win the rights to the tapes, he would bill them $10 million for storing them since 1955, and RCA would have to send a task force to his studios to listen to every tape in the vault. RCA blinked, and today the tapes remain with Singleton.

Nearly a year later, Shelby Singleton shipped a new release to radio stations. On November 16, 1978, New York's WHN-AM played "Save the Last Dance for Me" that the record label identified as being sung by Jerry Lee Lewis, but which was actually a duet by Lewis and an unknown vocalist who sounded to many like Elvis. There was such a strong reaction at WHN-AM that the record was placed on every-other-hour rotation. Singleton, as was his usual ploy, remained silent except to boast that RCA couldn't touch him this time, and he let the curiosity of the press give his record reams of free advertising. Soon, the truth was out: The record had been doctored to include the second vocalist; upon close examination he turned out to be none other than Singleton's favorite Elvis imitator, Jimmy Ellis.

Within the limits of the law, Singleton's album *The Sun Years,* falls into the category of being a bootleg album since it used material owned by RCA. Others were less public in their dealings than Singleton, and for several years after Elvis died, a growing number of independent entrepreneurs offered a wide assortment of albums and singles culled from Elvis' concerts, television guest appearances, TV specials, and studio session outtakes.

Before Elvis' death created the vast market for this previously unreleased material, a bootlegger would normally limit his pressings to 500 or 1,000 copies offered

Elvis HBO special album

On January 8, 1985, to celebrate what would have been Elvis' fiftieth birthday, Home Box Office (HBO) broadcast a special one-hour show that consisted of Elvis' complete, first sit-down concert from June 1968. Portions of it were to become part of Singer Presents Elvis, the 1968 comeback special. RCA Special Products planned to reissue the 1968 soundtrack from the TV special in 1985 with a tie-in to HBO, but the album was withdrawn before it was shipped to stores. The album comes with a 19" × 24" poster of Elvis dressed in black leather from that sit-down concert.

Value: $100+

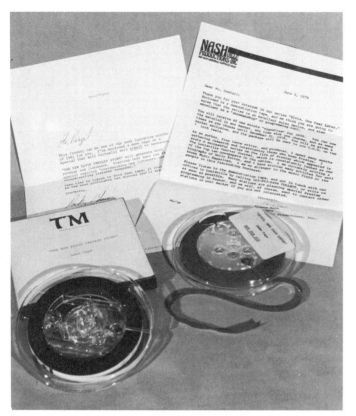

discretely through ads in fan magazines. By the end of 1977, the bootleg albums were being run off in multiples of 10,000 copies each, and ads for them were appearing blatantly in national record collecting publications and music magazines. RCA, the FBI, and the record industry, working through its legal arm the Record Industry Association of America (RIAA), initiated a crackdown on bootleggers that culminated in a number of arrests at the annual Memphis convention in August 1980. In March 1982, a bust of the nation's largest bootleg operation resulted in arrests in Florida, California, and Maryland. President Reagan sealed the fate of future bootlegging in this country on May 24, 1982, when he signed legislation that made record bootlegging a felony offense in the same category as piracy and counterfeiting. With that, the era of Elvis bootlegging in the United States came to a close. By mid-1983, however, European fans started issuing six to eight new bootleg albums a year, currently available in the United States only by mail order.

The growing number of Elvis imitators was another matter entirely. Before Elvis died, there had been a dozen or so singers who looked somewhat like Elvis and sang close enough to be entertaining. After Elvis died, the overwhelming demand for his music, seen first in the enormous sales of his records and then in the growth of

Elvis tribute radio shows

The two 5″ reel-to-reel tapes pictured here are promotional tapes sent to radio stations to advertise upcoming Elvis specials. The tape of 1978's Elvis, One Year Later *was produced by NASHville Productions, and* The New Elvis Presley Story *is a 1981 tape from TM Programming.*

Value of Elvis radio promo tapes: $50 each

Hollywood magazines

Elvis' death was felt deeply in Hollywood where he made 33 movies. Two of the rarest magazines issued after Elvis' death were the Hollywood Studio Magazine *and* Casting Call, *both trade publications in Tinseltown.* Casting Call *only had Elvis' photo on its September 1, 1977, issue, but* Hollywood Studio Magazine *devoted nine pages to a recap of his career.*

Original price: $.50 and $1.00

"Baby Let's Play House" 1984 single

RCA issued a special record that was to be available only during "Elvis Week" in Memphis and Tupelo in August 1984. There were so many records left over, however, that they are still sold in souvenir shops across the street from Graceland. The two songs are taken from Elvis' show in Tupelo on September 26, 1956, and the record is pressed on gold vinyl.

Value of single with picture sleeve: $15

Organizers

Reed Productions manufactures a full line of Elvis "organizers," from spiral notebooks to checkbook covers. Prices range from $2 to $5 depending on the item. Direct mail catalogs are available, but you must send Reed Productions a self-addressed legal-sized envelope with $.39 postage in order to receive one.

Elvis puzzles

There were half a dozen different jigsaw puzzles bearing Elvis' likeness that appeared shortly after his death. None appear to be licensed by Boxcar or Factors.

Original price: $5 each

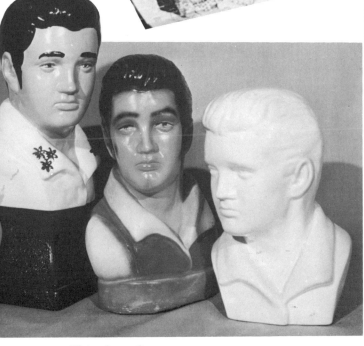

Elvis plaster busts

This is another example of poor workmanship bearing Elvis' likeness. Yet these plaster busts from Mexico used to be found in flea markets from coast to coast.

Original price: $5 each and up

Elvis plaque

This life-sized likeness of Elvis is "molded from durable styrene plastic, bronzed with acrylic lacquer, and molded on an 11 × 17 inch oval of polished simulated black walnut." Read between the lines: The entire item is made from lightweight plastic and licensed in 1977 by Boxcar/Factors.

Original price: $25

the bootlegging industry, was transferred to these imitators, and hundreds popped up with shows immortalizing various aspects of Elvis' career.

A well-received tribute of another type opened in London's Astoria Theater in December 1977. Simply billed as *Elvis,* this stage production covered Elvis' entire career by using three singer/actors, Timothy Whitnall, Shakin' Stevens, and James (P. J.) Proby. The show played to packed houses for several months before Proby was fired for refusing to stick to the script. There were several attempts to bring Elvis' life to the stage in this country, but none were as successful as this London production.

On September 5, 1978, a single of "Tell Me Pretty Baby" was sent out to the nation's radio stations. According to the record's promoters, the song was recorded in 1954 by a then-unknown Elvis Presley in Phoenix, Arizona. The tape of the song remained undiscovered until the summer of 1978 when it fell into the hands of Don Reese of Dallas, a long-time record promoter. Reese claimed to have obtained a voiceprint from the University of Texas in Dallas which verified that it was Elvis on the tape. When Reese played the tape for various people who knew Elvis, including members of the house bands at the *Louisiana Hayride* and the *Big D Jamboree,* all agreed it was genuine. It is unfortunate that the national press services picked up the story and printed it without checking thoroughly because 18,000 copies of "Tell Me Pretty Baby" were shipped with a few weeks.

No one in the press thought to check Elvis' life story and ask themselves what he would have been doing in Phoenix in 1954 in the first place. A little checking also revealed that Audio Recorders, the studio where Reese claimed the song was recorded, did not exist until 1958. It was the biggest outright hoax ever perpetrated surrounding Elvis, either during his life or afterwards.

In October 1978, Vernon Presley and RCA obtained a restraining order against further production or distribution of the record. At a hearing in Dallas a month later, a judge heard depositions from Scotty Moore, Vernon, Sam Phillips, and Michael Conley (the singer whose voice was actually on the record). The judge learned that Conley had been asked by his manager, Hal Freeman, to make the record in June 1978. Conley, who lived in Madison, Maine, said he heard nothing more about the song until it was being promoted as Elvis' first recording. Freeman denied everything, but lost a jury trial in March 1979. RCA was awarded $100,000 in legal fees.

In July 1978, a most touching story about Elvis came to light. *McCall's* magazine ran an excerpt from the book, *To Elvis with Love,* about a ten-year-old girl who was dying in a Swedish institution for the handicapped. The girl—identified only as Karen—had a crush on Elvis, and through her social worker and the book's author, Lena Canada, she was able to get a letter to Elvis. He an-

Sounds of Solid Gold, Vol. 15 boxed set

The U.S. Marine Corps issued its own public service radio shows that stations run for free when time permits. Several of these six-record sets have Elvis songs. This is volume 15, which contains "Hound Dog" as part of program 4.

Value: $50

Elvis belt buckle

This is the first edition "Official Elvis Presley Commemorative" belt buckle (as it says on the back) authorized by Boxcar/Factors in 1977. Later editions look the same, but do not have the first edition marking on the back.

Original price: $20; later editions sold for $7

Elvis plate

This official Elvis Presley commemorative plate bears a lithograph in brown ink by Adler and was produced in 1977 by Limoges of France under a licensing agreement with Boxcar/Factors. The 10" plates were limited to 10,000, each numbered by hand.

Original price, 7 ½" diameter: $25
10" diameter: $50

swered the letter, and for several months, in the late winter and spring of 1962–63, Karen and Elvis carried on a remarkable correspondence. The book was later made into a television movie.

With the massive merchandising of Elvis, it was only logical that some sort of commemoration be held annually in Memphis. The first convention of the fans was in January 1978 and drew 15,000. The Orpheum Theater played Elvis movies continuously for thirty hours, but drew only 800 customers. Factors had a large exhibit and souvenir booth at the Mid-South Fairgrounds, but most people felt the $4 admission was exorbitant. The only souvenirs for sale at the Factors convention were those officially leased since August, and fans soon quickly realized that there was little they hadn't already seen. At Cook Convention Center, a "fans" convention had 65 exhibitors, and the people were having a good time viewing "free" films and browsing at the dealer's tables. At Graceland, thousands braved a chilling snowstorm and stalled traffic to lay flowers at Elvis' gravesite.

The August 1978 gathering of the Elvis faithful was plagued by heavy rains and a police strike that placed Memphis on an 8 P.M. nightly curfew. Nevertheless, every facility within 200 miles was jammed as a crowd estimated as high as 150,000 invaded Memphis. Vester Presley, Elvis' Uncle and longtime gatekeeper at Graceland, reported that 10,000 to 12,000 fans were visiting the gravesite daily starting two weeks before the August 16 anniversary. Fans came from as far away as Australia, Belgium, Canada, China, England, France, Greece, Holland, Japan, Norway, Spain, and the Virgin Islands. Among the memorial events planned were another week-long film festival at the Orpheum Theater and a memorabilia exhibition sponsored by Elvis associates Charlie Hodge and Dick Grob at the Cook Convention Center. The site of the old Sun studios was also opened by the Gray Line Tours company for a look-see by visitors.

"Merry Christmas, Baby" 1985 single

To help promote the re-release of the "almost" original artwork for the Elvis Christmas Album, RCA Victor reissued the single "Merry Christmas, Baby" with a new picture sleeve similar to that on the album. The first pressing of the single was on green wax; subsequent pressings were on black.

Value of green pressing: $10
Value of black pressing: $2

Sun label coasters

This unique idea presents eight of Elvis' Sun Records labels in the form of drink coasters. Made from yellow plastic over a foam backing, each coaster is 3 ¾" in diameter.

Original price: $4 a set

Colonel Parker reported to the press in March 1978 that Jerry Weintraub would produce a film about Elvis. "It will be done first class all the way or it won't be done," said Colonel Parker. "It will probably star a big-name actor or a good actor, but it will definitely not be any of the Presley imitators. Elvis' own voice will be used." By May, the concept had been changed from a movie to a multimedia show starring Elvis that was planned for a tour of theaters and arenas.

A month later, the Colonel announced that there would be an official Elvis convention at the Las Vegas Hilton that September. "Always Elvis" was designated as the convention's title, and dealer's tables went on sale in July for an astounding $2,500 each for the eleven-day run (September 1–10). Ticket prices were also high at $15 per day. The Weintraub multimedia show, which was also named "Always Elvis," had now become a part of the convention.

The Colonel's "Always Elvis" festival opened on schedule to dismal reviews and small crowds. The "convention" was little more than a series of dealers' tables hawking only items approved by Factors Inc.—which had a large display—with a once-a-day presentation of the multimedia show. On September 8, a special dedication of the Hilton's showroom to Elvis and the unveiling of bronze sculpture of Elvis by Carl Romanelli was attended by 1,700 fans who came to ogle Priscilla and Vernon. Elvis' jetliner, *Lisa Marie,* was opened for tours at a nearby airport before leaving for West Germany to be put on display.

On January 15, 1979, Vernon Presley was admitted to the hospital for an "irregular heartbeat." Throughout that spring he suffered a series of heart problems. Although he was said to be resting at home in "stable" condition in May, he was soon readmitted to Baptist Memorial Hospital, and on June 26, 1979, he died of heart failure in the same hospital where his son had been pronounced dead nearly two years earlier. The responsibility for overseeing the Elvis estate passed on to the trio of Priscilla, Elvis and Vernon's certified public accountant, Joseph Hanks, and the National Bank of Commerce in Memphis.

Sun label buttons

There was a knowledgeable California record dealer who sold his car to buy a Sun Records button just like one of these. And he was warned not to. Sun Records in 1954–55 didn't promote Elvis with buttons showing his latest records. No record company did at that time. These pin-buttons are 2 ¼" in diameter, made with a clear plastic cover and a metal back.

Original price: $1 each

Hair care products

"Love Me Tender" shampoo and conditioner are manufactured and marketed by Natural Choice Industries.

Bottle banks

The Elvis Presley bottle banks are available in either blue or amethyst and retail for $15.95. They can be purchased directly from the manufacturer, Vineland Commemorative Bottles.

Elvis, a Dick Clark television production, was broadcast from 8 to 11 P.M., February 11, 1979, over ABC-TV, sweeping the evening's ratings against two formidable movies: *Gone with the Wind* (CBS-TV) and *One Flew Over the Cuckoo's Nest* (NBC-TV). Kurt Russell was nominated for an Emmy for his outstanding portrayal of Elvis. The songs in the made-for-TV movie were sung by Ronnie McDowell, and Elvis' associates Charlie Hodge and Kathy Westmoreland appeared on-screen in several segments playing themselves. Priscilla reportedly received $50,000 to help write the dialogue and check the script for accuracy. The movie broke theater records upon being released in several foreign countries.

A second movie made for television, NBC's *Elvis and the Beauty Queen,* had Linda Thompson as its advisor and an unknown actor Don Johnson, who gained 40 pounds to portray Elvis in his final years. The point of the film seemed to be to portray Elvis as a complete wacko, and the show did poorly in the ratings.

Immediately following Elvis' death, citizens of Tupelo began to raise funds to erect the memorial chapel that Elvis had mentioned to Janelle McComb in 1970. She became the chairwoman of the Elvis Presley Memorial Commission, traveling for a year and a half in an effort to see this dream become a reality. Thousands of fans from all over the world were present on August 17, 1979, for the dedication of the chapel that had been financed entirely by donations from Elvis' fans and associates. The chapel was designed by L. P. McCarty, Jr., son of the man who hired Vernon to drive his vegetable truck in 1946. The centerpiece of the chapel is a stained glass window with the Lord's Prayer as its theme.

After 1978, the August conventions in Memphis became the highlight of the year for many Elvis fans, while the January anniversary of Elvis' birth was a time for quiet reflection. Starting in August 1979, the Memphis State University hosted a day-long "Salute to Memphis Music" festival that included a seminar on Elvis' career, a memorial service, and a banquet honoring Sam Phillips. Entertainment that year was headlined by Ronnie McDowell, the Jordanaires, Brenda Lee, Faron Young, and Chet Atkins. With the death of Vernon only two months passed, the Presley family had originally wanted to keep the grounds of Graceland closed on August 16, but they finally relinquished to the press of the crowd and allowed fans to visit the gravesite.

In 1980, a Nashville promoter booked the Cook Convention Center in Memphis for the week of August 16 for the next ten years. His "convention," billed as "Memphis Music Festival—A Salute to Elvis," was intertwined with that of the now-annual Memphis State University "Salute to Memphis Music."

More than any other aspect of Elvis' passing, the controversy over his alledged misuse of prescription drugs and their link to his death continues to linger. In

September 1979, after two years of stories about Elvis'
long-time dependency on sleeping pills and a fifteen-
month audit of Memphis pharmacies, the five-man Tennessee Board of Medical Examiners accused Dr. George
Nichopoulos of "indiscriminately prescribing" in the case
of Elvis Presley.

Friends close to both Elvis and the doctor quickly
came to his defense. Marty Lacker, a member of the
entourage, stated that many of Elvis' pills were actually
placebos (or sugar pills). Ginger Alden told the Medical
Board that many of the shots given to Elvis that he was
told were sleeping medications were in reality only saline
solution.

At a five-day hearing in January 1980, the Tennessee
state board convened to hear the case against Dr. Nick.
Under questioning, the doctor admitted that Elvis had
indeed been addicted to sleeping medications and pain-
killers. But Dr. Nick said that even though he often tried to
get Elvis to quit, the drugs continued to come to Elvis
from other sources. There was great prestige in being
able to say, "I'm Elvis Presley's doctor." There was also a
fortune in cash to be made: The sheer volume of prescriptions involved ran to more than a million dollars.

The result of the hearing by the board was a suspen-
sion of Dr. Nichopoulos' license to practice medicine for
three months and a three-year probation. The doctor was
acquitted of the more serious charges of malpractice

"I Was the One" and "Paralyzed" singles

*In an attempt to break into the
market opened by such rockabilly
groups as the Stray Cats and the
Blasters, RCA Victor repackaged
10 of Elvis' early rock 'n' roll
songs and titled it after the lone
ballad, "I Was the One." Two
singles were issued from the
album, the first being the title
song. This single came with either
a light yellow label on black vinyl
or a bright yellow label on
gold/yellow wax. In addition, two
songs, "Little Sister" and "Rip It
Up," were sent to radio stations on
a special 12" 33⅓ rpm single.*

*Value of "I Was the One" and
   "Paralyzed" singles with picture
   sleeves: $12 each*
*Value of "I Was the One" promo
   single, black wax: $10*
Value, gold wax: $100
*Value of "Little Sister" 12" promo
   single: $100*

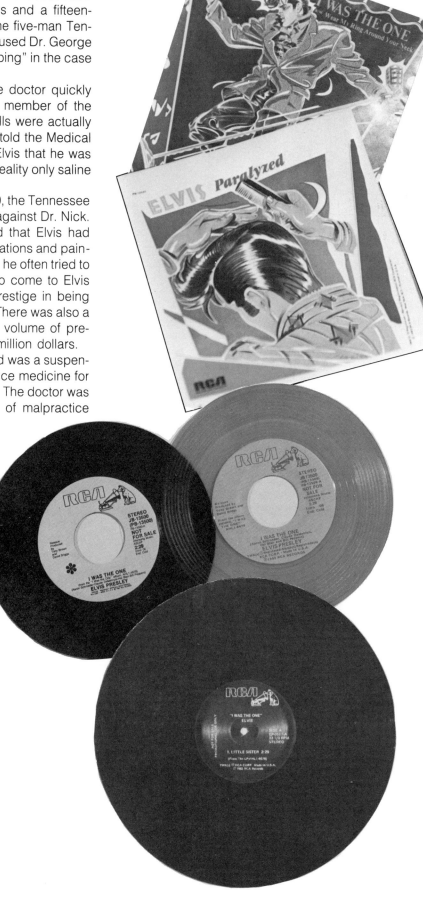

Cadillac Elvis bootleg album

This concept album presents a radio show format, with Elvis singing rare items snitched from previous bootlegs, sandwiched between tributes from several stars who knew Elvis whose comments were made available on the evening news after Elvis died. It's a nice idea, brought off in a pleasing manner. The fact that some of the songs and interviews are available only on this bootleg makes it also very collectible. The record is pressed on shocking pink vinyl.

Value: $75

Music box

"J.S.N.Y." is the only marking on this music box featuring a ceramic semilikeness of Elvis atop what appears to be an aquamarine cake. Unlicensed merchandise such as this was the reason critics were so appalled at the merchandising of Elvis.

Original price: $10

This familiar image of Elvis was used in the diecut cardboard piece promoting Elvis: The Paperdoll Book by Jim Fitzgerald. Only a few hundred of the promotional pieces were produced in 1983 by the publisher, St. Martin's Press.

Cardboard cutout, value: $100

Memories of Christmas album and calendar

Memories of Christmas *offers fans outtakes and longer versions of several familiar Christmas songs previously released by RCA Victor. The album came with a limited edition 7″ × 9″ calendar.*

Album value: $10
Calendar value: $10

Elvis—A Legendary Performer, Volume 3 picture disk

The first official Elvis picture disk was the third album in the highly acclaimed series, Elvis—A Legendary Performer. The album was also available on black vinyl. Also pictured is the standup display for the album.

Value of picture disk: $15
Value of regular disk: $10
Value of album display: $25

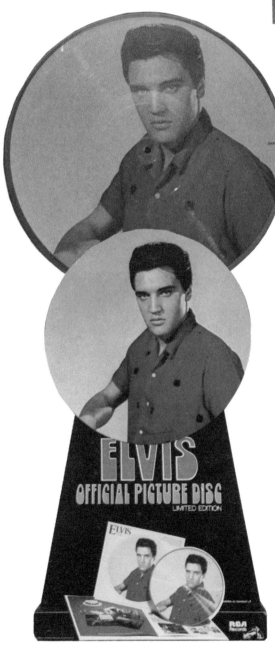

Auto Shade

Stay cool with the Elvis Presley Auto Shade, manufactured by Celebrity Shade. The four-color, fold-up shade features two 16″ photos of Elvis and is made of corrugated board. It is designed to fit inside a car windshield in order to keep the interior cool when parked in the sun. The Auto Shade is available directly from the manufacturer for $5.99 or at retail outlets.

Collector's plates and figurines

Each piece in the Royal Orleans series of collectibles depicts Elvis at one of his best-known concerts. The collector's plate is 8½" in diameter and is made of porcelain with an 18-karat gold trim. The retail price is about $35. The 10" figurine is bisque and sells for about $125. Each piece is limited to an edition of 20,000. Concerts featured in the series are "Live in Las Vegas," "Aloha from Hawaii," and "The Mississippi Benefit Concert."

Richards & Southern

Richards & Southern manufactures a large line of Elvis products ranging from bumper stickers to baseball caps. Individual orders are not accepted, but customers may be able to get merchandise, price, and dealer lists by writing to the company.

"King of Rock Game"

*"Big excitement" . . . "fun galore."
Travel the same road Elvis took to
fame and glory. In this game
players move around the board by
accumulating points based on
Elvis' life and career. The game
was copyrighted in 1979, but not
licensed.*

Original price: $14

"Always Elvis" wine

*"Elvis never drank wine," said
Colonel Parker, "but if he did, this
is the wine he would have
ordered." In 1979, Boxcar
Enterprises authorized 100,000
cases of "Always Elvis" Blanc
D'Oro to be imported from Italy by
Frontenac Vineyards. This "spritzy,
light" white wine had a lower than
normal (7 percent) alcohol content.
A second bottle was planned in
the series with a "Portrait of Elvis"
neck band replacing the "Always
Elvis" band.*

Original price: $4 per bottle

Foil poster

*This 16" × 20" poster is produced
on foil by a specialized printing
and embossing technique. It is
manufactured by F. J. Warren
Limited in England, but is no
longer in stock. The original retail
price was approximately $24.*

Sepia prints

Sepia prints of the king are part of the product line of Ludlow Sales, Inc. Flat prints retail for about $3, framed for about $15. Customers may call or write Ludlow for the name of their nearest dealer.

and unethical conduct, but he was criticized for poor record keeping. Many of the drugs prescribed in Elvis' name, it was learned, had actually been taken by the 70 to 100 members of the traveling entourage, but Dr. Nichopoulos kept no specific records when dispensing them. At the end of each tour, unused pills were often flushed down a toilet, again with no record being kept. In addition, prescriptions specifically meant for others were routinely written in Elvis' name, with the resulting bill sent to him. In the end, the board actually praised Dr. Nick for what one member termed his "considerable restraint" in handling what was an "extraordinary" situation.

But the doctor's problems were not yet over.

The Shelby County District Attorney brought charges against the doctor including fourteen counts of "feloniously dispensing" prescription drugs to Elvis and a number of other people including singer Jerry Lee Lewis. The jury trial covered the same ground covered in the medical board hearings, and in October 1981, Dr. Nick was acquitted by the Shelby County grand jury after he and the other witnesses convinced the jurors that Dr. Nichopoulos had acted in an ethical manner in treating Elvis in the hopes of eventually curing him.

The year 1980 ushered in another legal case. During the long ups and downs of Elvis' career, there was never any doubt that Colonel Tom Parker was the mastermind in showcasing Elvis' phenomenal talent. Even after Elvis' passing, it was the Colonel who made certain that everyone was "taking care of business." By late 1980, the honeymoon was finally over. With Vernon's death a year earlier, Priscilla and her co-executors and lawyers had taken over management of the estate. Whereas Vernon had been agreeable to every move made by the Colonel, Priscilla and her co-executors were more apt to question everything.

On May 5, 1980, Memphis lawyer Blanchard E. Tual was appointed by the court to make certain that the interests of Lisa Marie were protected. After much research, Tual filed several reports with the probate court in Memphis during 1980 and 1981 that convinced the court to order the executors to sue Colonel Parker for having "violated his duty both to Elvis and the estate" since August 1977. The executors also sued RCA for acting as Parker's accomplice.

Specifically, Parker's continuing commission of 50 percent of all Elvis' posthumous earnings was seen as being "excessive, impudent . . . and beyond all reasonable bounds of industry standards." According to the report prepared for the hearing, "Elvis was naive, shy, and unassertive. Parker was aggressive, shrewd, and tough. His strong personality dominated Elvis, his father, and all others in Elvis' entourage."

The case went back and forth through the court system for two years. At one point, the Internal Revenue Service (IRS), acting on information from the various proceedings, charged that taxes of $16.6 million were owed on an estate valued at close to $30 million, most of which existed in unpaid royalties. It looked as though, after twenty-one years as one of America's greatest entertainment phenomenons, Elvis' estate would be bankrupt.

On June 16, 1983, all parties involved issued a statement that they had "amicably resolved the various matters of controversy among them." The estate went so far as to acknowledge "the significant contribution of Colonel Parker and RCA Records in the unparalleled career of Elvis Presley." Parker, it was learned, had chosen to discontinue his association with the estate and had agreed to furnish the estate a sampling of his collection of Elvis Presley memorabilia that he had stored in his warehouse in Madison, Tennessee.

Negotiations with the IRS proved even more complex than those with the Colonel. By 1985, the IRS had agreed to reduce its assessment of the estate from $30 million to $12 million, which was more in line with what the trustees had claimed in the first place. Of this amount, all that was owed was $3.5 million in taxes instead of the original $16.6 million claimed.

In April 1981, in the middle of litigation involving the estate, RCA, and the Colonel, the "official" documentary film covering Elvis' career premiered in Memphis. *This Is Elvis,* released by Warner Brothers, one film company for which Elvis never worked, was a mixture of actual footage of Elvis, a large percentage of which had never been seen publically before, and "docudrama" scenes using actors that covered portions of his life for which there was no existing film (his early years, for example). The film was eerily narrated in the first person by Elvis sound-alike Ral Donner as well as by actors playing Gladys, Vernon, and Priscilla. Linda Thompson and Joe Esposito appeared as themselves, and Colonel Parker was the technical advisor, a job for which he was paid $5,000 a week during production.

As early as February 1981, it was obvious that something had to be done with Graceland. Upkeep of the mansion and repair of the grounds was running $100,000 a year, with another $400,000 going to salaries for the full-time staff and security. Conversely, the amount of money coming into the estate had dwindled yearly as the public moved on to other matters, with the net result that the estate's assets were being whittled away at the rate of $500,000 a year. The city of Memphis had first expressed a desire to purchase the mansion and turn it into a museum in 1978. Now, however, with Elvis, Gladys, Vernon, and Grandma Minnie (she died in 1980) buried there, "the estate couldn't put up a For Sale sign in the front yard," explained Jack Soden, current executive director of Graceland.

One of the problems that befell Graceland during the first years after Elvis' death was a local law that prohibited charging a fee to visit a private home. Con-

Collector's dolls

The Elvis Presley Limited Doll Series is issued by World Doll. Each is a limited edition and is sculpted by Joyce Christopher, a noted doll portraitess. Pictured from left are the 21" vinyl "All American Elvis," $125; the 21" vinyl "Flame," $100; the 21" vinyl "Phoenix," $100; the 21" vinyl "Supergold," $100; and the 19" porcelain "Gold and Platinum," $285.

Sally Evans prints

FACES, Inc. sells exact reproductions of a painting by Sally Evans. They are available as 5" × 7" postcards or as 18" × 24" prints. Postcards retail for approximately $.80; prices for prints range from about $12 unframed to $40 framed.

Elvis radio

Cheap and gaudy, this 1977 radio from Hong Kong is just the type of knock-off that those in charge of licensing Elvis merchandise hope to stop.

Original price: $20

sequently, visitors to Elvis' gravesite were still being admitted free of charge. Late in 1981, the estate applied for, and soon received, a variance in the zoning ordinance so that portions of the mansion could be opened for escorted tours. At first it was planned to open only the trophy room and the raquetball court; but by the time the first tours started, on June 7, 1982, most of the first floor and basement of the mansion had been included as well, even though Priscilla at first objected. Plans to open a souvenir stand at Graceland were briefly considered, but it was decided that no money should change hands on the grounds. All business transactions, including ticket sales, are conducted across the street.

Within just a few weeks of the opening, it was obvious that Graceland was going to be *the* major tourist stop in Memphis. The lure of being able to actually walk inside Elvis' home brings fans to Memphis from all over the world throughout the year. The numbers are staggering: The first full year of operation 500,000 visited the mansion (more than visit Thomas Jefferson's Monticello), and Graceland brought the estate $4.5 million in revenues. The U.S. Travel Data Center estimates that tourists visiting Graceland spend $50 million each year for airline tickets, hotel rooms, car rentals, and food, as well as an average of $10 per person for souvenirs. And all these people aren't "died-in-the-wool" Elvis fans, at least not when they first stop at Graceland. Over 80 percent are just tourists who are in the vicinity of Memphis.

The opening of Graceland created a new wave of optimistic enthusiasm on the part of thousands of fans who had continued to stick by their idol. They turned away from the bad news, concentrating on the good that Elvis accomplished during his career.

The annual August gathering in Memphis of Elvis' fans began to take on a cohesive format. Now officially known as "The Elvis International Tribute Week," this celebration is a logical continuation of the August conventions in Memphis begun in the 1970s. This week-long celebration of Elvis' life offers fans a wide variety of events including a nostalgia concert featuring a reunion of Elvis' musicians and friends, a trivia contest, and the annual memorial service at Memphis State University. There are also twenty or so other activities during the week including the popular Elvis Presley Memorial Run, which raises money for cerebral palsy research; the fantastic "Elvis: Legacy in Light" laser show at the Pink Palace Planetarium; the memorabilia "fanfest"; either a ballet or symphony tribute to Memphis music; several art exhibitions, including one open to artwork by the general public; a couple of auctions; a sock hop; and a "social" where fans can greet each other and the Graceland staff. Libertyland, the amusement park often rented by Elvis for his midnight pleasure, offers a Las Vegas-styled production dedicated to Elvis. A number of locations in Memphis are open for tours during the week, including the American Sound Studios where Elvis worked tirelessly and successfully to revive his sagging recording career in 1969 and 1970, Kang Rhee's Karate Studio where Elvis trained, Elvis' high school (now Humes Junior High), and Lansky Brothers Emporium that bills itself as "clothier to the king." The emotional candlelight ceremony has become an annual tradition attended by thousands. Starting at 11 P.M. each August 15, fans begin their silent trek up Graceland's gently winding drive to the Meditation Garden. For most, this one event completely transcends the more commercial exhibits and tribute shows.

Many of the active Elvis fan clubs hold annual conventions to raise funds that are then donated to various institutions and charities in Elvis' name. In the beginning, the most common recipient of these funds was the Elvis Memorial Chapel in Tupelo. After that project was completed, clubs often looked closer to home for needs to be filled. In Atlanta, the Happiness Is Elvis Fan Club raised enough money to donate a kidney dialysis machine to a hospital; in Seattle, money was raised by Elvis fans to supply a children's ward with books and toys; and The Elvis Now Fan Club of San Jose donates money from its yearly get-together to a children's shelter. Many fan clubs around the country have chosen to raise money for the American Heart Association, Muscular Dystrophy, or other national foundations. But the biggest goal of all was the $10 million needed to build the Elvis Presley Memorial Trauma Center at the City of Memphis Hospital Complex. The dedication of this much-needed facility took place August 15, 1983.

Collector's mugs

Collector's mugs are rimmed in 24-carat gold and are sold individually for $4.50 or in a set of four for $18. Mugs are titled "Hound Dog," "Lonesome Tonight," "Teddy Bear," and "Don't Be Cruel." Write to Nostalgia Collectibles for availability information.

1978 Elvis bubble gum cards

In 1956, Elvis Presley Enterprises authorized the largest distributor of bubble gum cards, the Topps Gum Company, to issue a set of 66 Elvis cards. In 1978, the license went to the fledgling Donruss Company of Memphis for another set of 66 cards. Unlike the 1956 set in which each photo was hand colored, the Donruss set uses color only if the original photo was in color.

Original price: 15¢ per pack

Concert photo album

This 1977 tour photo album was reportedly made for Elvis' last tour. After his death, it was supplied with a "Certificate of Authenticity" from Vernon Presley, an application for the Elvis Presley Fan Club of Great Britain, and several flyers listing goods available from Factors. It was packaged in a gold box.

Original price of tour book package: $10

Commemorative plate

The Nostalgia Collectibles Commemorative Issue plate was designed by award-winning artist Bill Jacobson. The china plate is rimmed with 24-carat gold and is limited to an edition of 25,000. It retails for about $45.

Elvis playing cards

This is just one of about a dozen different packs of playing cards issued by various manufacturers after Elvis' death.

Original price: $3 to $5 each pack

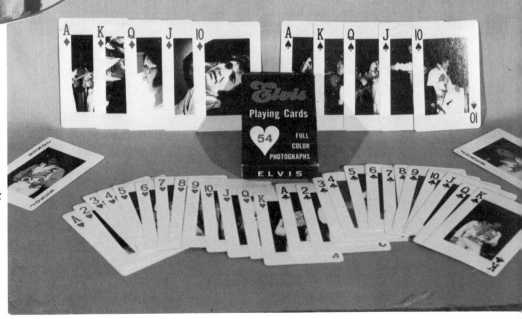

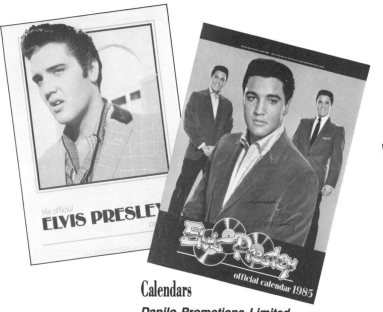

Calendars

Danilo Promotions Limited produces and markets Elvis calendars in England where they sell for about 3 pounds.

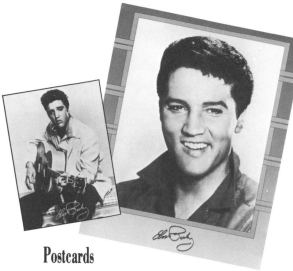

Postcards

Reflex Marketing Limited is a British company whose products are available only in Europe. Postcard prices are approximately 30 pence.

Clocks and watches

Bradley Time manufactures a line of Elvis Presley time pieces, including a wrist watch, travel alarm clock, pocket watch, and two wall clocks. Prices start at about $25.

Decanters

"Elvis & Hound Dog" is the second in McCormick Distilling Company's series of decanters "Elvis' Musical Pets." Elvis' jacket is decorated in 22-carat gold overlay and the music box actually plays "Hound Dog." The suggested retail price is $199.95. Decanters can be purchased through liquor stores or by contacting McCormick Distilling Company.

Wood plaques and clocks

Handworked wooden plaques and clocks are manufactured by Venson & Co. Sizes range from 10″ × 12″ to 19″ × 40″ and prices from $10.95 to $64.95. A complete catalog and price list is available from the company for $2 and individual orders are accepted.

Blanket

This blanket features one of Elvis' favorite portraits, one that he commissioned in 1969. It is available in two sizes, 50″ × 60″ and 60″ × 80″ and is 100 percent acrylic. The throw retails for about $30, the larger blanket for about $40, and both are available directly from TAC Industries.

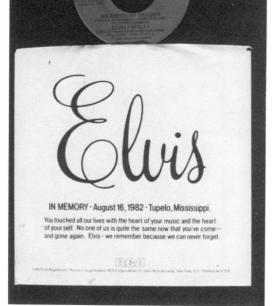

1982 Tupelo free single

To commemorate the fifth anniversary of Elvis' death, RCA Victor issued a limited pressing of a special 45 rpm single coupling "The Impossible Dream" with "The American Trilogy." These singles were handed out free to fans at Elvis' birthplace in Tupelo.

Value of record: $100
Value of sleeve: $100

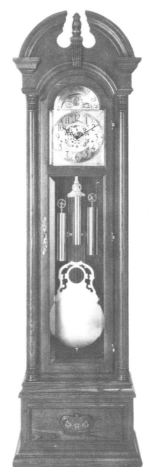

Graceland Grandfather Clock

The Pearl Grandfather Clock Company produced this limited edition Graceland Grandfather Clock in 1985. Only 6,000 were manufactured. Each clock is handcarved from solid oak and ornamented with beveled glass and solid brass. The moon dial features a lunar calendar and an etched engraving of Graceland itself, and in the base panel is a crown, handcarved from an oak tree that once stood on the grounds of Graceland. The clock sells for $3,000.

The anniversary of Elvis' 50th birthday in 1985 was a time for an outpouring of commercial tributes, as well as a time for fans to reflect on Elvis' place in history. RCA announced that they were scheduling an average of one special Elvis album per month for the entire year, starting with *Elvis-A Golden Celebration,* a six-record set packaged in a gold box. On the night of January 8, 1985, the Home Box Office cable TV channel premiered a one-hour, unedited concert taped in June 1968 for the TV special, *Elvis.* Later that same evening, Priscilla took a Showtime cable TV audience for an exclusive tour of Graceland. It was even announced that plans were afoot for a Saturday morning cartoon show to feature Elvis.

Today, as we approach the tenth anniversary of Elvis' death, the legacy of Elvis Presley is healthy and growing, largely because of the efforts of the people in charge of Elvis Presley Enterprises and the Elvis Presley Estate.

Who are these new players in the Elvis money game? In charge of the estate left by Elvis is the triumverate of executors: Priscilla Presley (executor), Joseph A. Hanks (Elvis' CPA), and the National Bank of Commerce of Memphis. These three (and court-appointed attorney Blanchard Tual until Lisa Marie's eighteenth birthday in 1986) control the Elvis Presley Residuary Trust (which incorporates the estate). They are also officers of Elvis Presley Enterprises, Inc., a reincarnation of Colonel Parker's money-making arm from 1956, now a corporation charged with the merchandising of Elvis' good name.

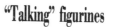

"Talking" figurines

Nostalgia Collectibles also produces the Elvis Presley "talkie." Each hand-painted, porcelain figurine contains a cassette player with recordings of five Elvis hits. Limited to an edition of 25,000, the retail price is about $99.

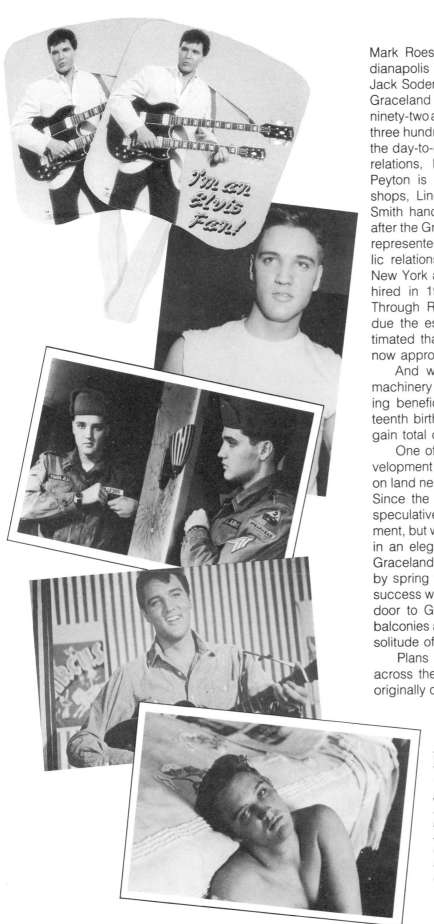

Mark Roesler of the Curtis Licensing Company in Indianapolis is the licensing agent for Elvis merchandise. Jack Soden of Memphis is the executive director of the Graceland Division of EPE, overseeing a full-time staff of ninety-two and a part time seasonal staff of approximately three hundred. On Soden's staff, Debbie Jarvis oversees the day-to-day operations, Todd Morgan handles public relations, Monnie Speed manages the tours, Carla Peyton is in charge of operating the eight retail gift shops, Linda Floied supervises bookkeeping, Carolyn Smith handles group tours, and Ron McElhaney looks after the Graceland distribution center. Graceland is also represented by David Beckwith of the Los Angeles public relations firm Rogers & Cowan. Joseph Rascoff, a New York accountant and entertainment producer, was hired in 1983 to be the business manager for EPE. Through Rascoff's dogged pressure, annual royalties due the estate jumped 200 percent in 1984. It is estimated that the gross revenues from the entire estate now approach $10 million a year.

And who gets all the money that this new Elvis machinery is generating? Lisa Marie is the sole remaining beneficiary of Elvis' will. She celebrated her nineteenth birthday in 1987, and in six more years she will gain total control of the trust.

One of the most exciting steps currently under development by the Elvis estate is a hotel that is being built on land next door to, but not on, the Graceland property. Since the Elvis trust is forbidden by law from making speculative investments, the estate has no direct investment, but will receive a percentage. The hotel will be built in an elegant ante-bellum style and will be called The Graceland Hotel. Initial plans call for 205 rooms opening by spring 1988, which can be expanded to 400 rooms if success warrants. Guests, while they will be staying next door to Graceland, will not be able to stand on their balconies and look into Elvis' backyard. The isolation and solitude of Graceland will be maintained.

Plans are also under way to redevelop the land across the street from Graceland, some of which was originally owned by Elvis. The plaza directly across from

Fans and postcards

These Elvis "fans" and postcards are copyrighted by the American Postcard Company, Inc. The fans retail for $2 and the postcards for $.50. Customers may write to the company for the nearest dealer, but orders for individual items are not accepted.

Athena International

Athena International markets posters, postcards, and greeting cards worldwide. Customers may write to the company for dealers and prices.

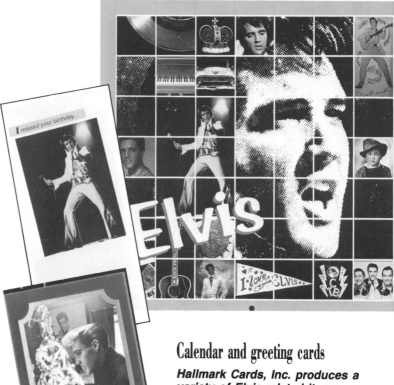

Movie Ad Corporation

Movie Ad Corporation markets a number of different Elvis-related items ranging from buttons to posters to stationery. Individual orders are not accepted, but customers may get dealer and price information from the company.

Calendar and greeting cards

Hallmark Cards, Inc. produces a variety of Elvis-related items including the calendar and greeting cards. Individual Hallmark stores are the best source of information regarding pricing and availability.

Gold-plated records

California Gold Record Co. offers a limited edition gold-plated record collector series. Each record is plated with pure 24-carat gold and is framed in solid oak. Two LP/Single Combos are available for $169 each: "Elvis Golden Records" and "50,000,000 Fans Can't Be Wrong." Singles include "That's All Right," "Blue Suede Shoes," "Love Me Tender," "Heart Break Hotel," "Hound Dog," and "All Shook Up." Singles sell for $89. Orders may be placed directly to California Gold Record Co.

Wall paneling

Wall paneling featuring scenes from Elvis' life is available from Welsh Forest Products. Designs are in shades of brown on a pecan background. Individual panels are 4' × 8' and sell for about $18. A smaller souvenir panel, 16" × 24", is available directly from Welsh Forest Products for $9.95.

Pins and key chains

Gift Creations produces eight styles of pins and six styles of key chains. Each is handpainted in enamel, and all are sold only through retail outlets for $3 to $4.

Graceland where a number of souvenir shops sprang up immediately after his death has been obtained for use by the estate through a consortium of Kansas City developers. In the spring of 1987, the present site of the banquet hall will become a permanent visitors' facility replacing temporary housing used since 1982. There are also plans to renovate the airplane area that displays the pride of Elvis Presley Airways, the *Lisa Marie* jetliner and the *Hound Dog I* jetstar. When the old visitor's building is torn down, the space will be used for additional parking. It will be connected by a new bridge crossing the creek to a picnic and recreational area along the back part of the property. The fronts of the gift shops and the adjacent parking area will be attractively landscaped and will include a fountain built with fan's donations. Long-term plans call for the estate to erect a music museum dedicated to the early roots of rock 'n' roll; later a performing arts center with a modern theater will be added.

A very popular exhibit opened at Graceland on May 24, 1986. It features some of Elvis' personal memorabilia and artifacts from Graceland and is appropriately titled "Elvis-Up Close." According to Todd Morgan, "There's not a guitar in the whole exhibit . . . it's not the career of Elvis, it's the person of Elvis. It's photographs . . . the at-home Elvis . . . the family Elvis with his horses and his motorcycles. It's Elvis just being Elvis."

Morgan also edits *Graceland Express,* a quarterly newspaper devoted to keeping fans up to date on the happenings in the continuing world of Elvis Presley. The Graceland Division began publishing the paper in 1986; it replaced the "church bulletin"-sized *Graceland Insider.*

So Elvis can finally rest, confident that the keepers of the flame have a careful watch on his memory. The movies, the records, Graceland, and the merchandise are in competent hands. The image remains alive.

But the worldwide legion of fans are not attracted to Elvis' image alone. They also see the tenderness in his eyes and the warmth in his smile. They cherish Elvis' devotion to his mother, his Southern manners, and his glittering life style. They remember his rebelliousness as well as his instant generosity. Most of all, they still hear his remarkable singing voice, reaching deep inside the lyrics of a song to bring out the poet's most touching message and give it life. The man may have passed from our midst, but the legend still lives on.

Stationery

The poses on these hand-tinted notecards were selected by the president of the Elvis Presley Fan Club. They retail for about 95 cents and are produced by Portal Publications. Individual orders are not accepted.

ELVIS PRESLEY ENTERPRISES, INC.

Licensed Manufacturers

Advanced Graphics
99 S. Buchanan Circle
Pacheco, CA 94553
(415) 827-4600
Poster

S. Alden, Inc.
2401 Martha Truman Rd.
Kansas City, MO 64131
(816) 941-3647
Board/Trivia game

**Americana Art China
Company**
356 East Marland Ave.
Sebring, OH 44672
(216) 823-9142
Stein

American M.W., Inc.
5333 West 146th St.
Lawndale, CA 90260
(213) 643-6666
*Greeting card with musical tee
shirt*

American Postcard Company
285 Lafayette St.
New York, NY 10012
(212) 966-3673
Postcards, paper fans

Angel Gifts
1900 W. Stone
Fairfield, IA 52556
Poster

Antique Company
3186 Thousand Oaks Blvd.
Thousand Oaks, CA 91362
(805) 497-7793
Prints

Art One Images
751 Monterey Pass Rd.
Monterey Park, CA 91754
(213) 269-4733
Posters

Athena International
POB 13
Bishops Stortford
Hertfordshire
England CM23 5PQ
(02) 795-6627
*Posters, postcards, greeting
cards*

Avon Products, Inc.
9 West 57th St.
New York, NY 10019
(212) 546-8336
Porcelain figurine

Award Design Metals
P.O. Box 1180
1002 Hamilton Dr.
Noble, OK 73068
(800) 654-3800
Belt buckle

Azhari Trading Company
1225 Broadway
New York, NY 10001
(212) 683-8080
Tapestry

Bradley Time
1115 Broadway
New York, NY 10010
(212) 243-2424
*50th anniversary wrist watch,
alarm clock, wall clock, clock
radio with cassette*

Button Up Company
2011 Austin
Troy, MI 48084
(313) 528-1961
Buttons

California Gold Record Co.
2670 #1 Walnut Ave.
Tustin, CA 92680
(714) 730-7771
Gold-plated record

Celebrity Shade
49 Corona Ave.
Long Beach, CA 90803
(213) 596-1058
Automobile sun shades

Clay Art
380 Bayshore Blvd.
San Francisco, CA 94124
(415) 285-1411
Ceramic masks

Collegeville Flag
4th Ave. & Walnut St.
Collegeville, PA 19426
(215) 489-4131
Halloween costumes

Comptoir Murino
2 rue des Tournelles
77170 Brie Comte Robert
France
Umbrellas

Container Tech. Inc.
22160 N. Pepper Rd.
Barrington, IL 60010
(312) 382-1000
*Life-size posters, latex balloons,
mylar balloons*

CONTINUED

Licensed Manufacturers

CONTINUED •

Creative Accessories Ltd.
1536 Broad St.
Bellmore, NY 11710
(516) 221-4438
Mirrored acrylic

Custom Images, Inc.
3N 545 N. 17th St.
St. Charles, IL 60174
(800) 334-6499
Silk-screened mirror & glass

D & G Philatelic, Inc.
Box 237
West Hempstead, NY 11552
(516) 486-6511
Commemorative stamp

DRG Stationery
Apsley, Hemel Hempstead
Herts, HP3 9SS
England
(04) 424-2124
Stationery

Danbury Mint
47 Richards Ave.
Norwalk, CT 06857
(203) 853-2000
Porcelain doll

Danilo Promotions
3947 East Rd.
London N16AH
England
(01) 253-4303
Calendar

Dixie Seal & Stamp Co.
755 North Ave, NE
Atlanta, GA 30306
(404) 875-8883
License plate, small signs

Duncan, W.J. Ltd.
P.O. Box 150
Warragul, 3820
Victoria, Australia
056-231815
Miscellaneous

Elvis Presley Museum
110 Poplar St.
Franklin, TN 37064
(615) 790-7009
Museum, traveling exhibit

Ernst
148 S. Vinewood
Escondido, CA 92025
(619) 745-5556
Collector plates

Eugene Doll & Novelty
4012 Second Ave.
Brooklyn, NY 11232
(212) 788-1313
Porcelain doll, vinyl doll, plastic doll

Evans, Sally Collection
P.O. Box 726
Crown Point, IN 46307
(317) 663-5375
Prints painted by Sally Evans

G & E Distributing, Inc.
dba Elvis Gold Limited
109 Northshore Dr.
Suite 400
Knoxville, TN 37919
Framed 45 rpm gold record

Gift Creations
7633 Varna Ave.
N. Hollywood, CA 91605
(800) 468-0773
Pins, keychains

Glen Gary Associates
3060 Ellen Ct.
Newbury Park, CA 91320
(805) 498-4062
Postcards, photographs, posters

Great American Gift Co.
33 Portman Rd.
New Rochelle, NY 10801
(914) 576-7660
Glassware, belt buckle, money clip, weather thermometer

Hallmark Cards, Inc.
2440 Pershing Rd.
Kansas City, MO 64108
(816) 274-5737
Posters, satin pillows, puzzle, "campaign" buttons, greeting cards, calendars, postcards

Husta, Shelley
608 Sheridan Rd.
Evanston, IL 60202
(312) 491-6818
Museum of original artifacts

Ideal Decor
Wizard & Genius
Seefeldstr 88
8008 Zurich, Switzerland
Poster

International Custom Design
4809 Colorado Blvd.
Denver, CO 80216
(303) 355-0771
Tee shirts

JKA Specialties
RD 4, Eayerstown-Red Lion Rd.
Vincetown, NJ 08088
(609) 859-2090
Celluloid picture buttons

K & M Inc.
6528 Saginaw Rd.
Memphis, TN 38134
(901) 382-1398
Souvenir items

Landmark General
51 Digital Dr.
Novato, CA 94947
(415) 883-1600
calendar

Lapin Products
1501 Allen St.
P.O. Box 2227
Asbury Park, NJ 07712
(201) 774-3322
Toy 1950 pink Cadillac, toy touring van, toy guitars (3 versions)

Legends In Concert
John Stuart Productions
Imperial Palace
3535 S. Las Vegas Blvd.
Las Vegas, NV 89109
(702) 731-3311
Concert recreation

Lenan Company
c/o Silve Enterprises
5776 Rodman St.
Hollywood, FL 33023
(305) 961-0000
Tribute in Blue program: Suede ribbons, tee-shirts, posters

Ludlow Sales
Box 554
Chelsea Station
New York, NY 10011
(800) 221-4130
Postcards, sepia framed prints

Marketcom, Inc.
3101 South Hanley Rd. #200
St. Louis, MO 63143
(314) 781-6600
Posters

McCormick Distilling Co.
Weston, MO 64098
(816) 386-2276
Ceramic spirit decanters

Mobile Merchandising Ltd.
12 Ossory Road
London SE1 5AN
England
(01) 231-1191
Tee shirts

Modern Crafts Marketing
103 Prospectus
Ogallala, NE 69153
(308) 284-6065
Latch hook wall covering, latch hook pillow

Movie Ad Corp.
3111 University Dr.
Suite 320
Coral Springs, FL 33065
(800) 327-4989
Stationery, envelopes, memo sheets, sepia art prints, note cards, stick-on seals, greeting cards

Nardico Western Sculptures
2721 Teakwood Dr.
Garland, TX 75042
(214) 530-4785
Carved Italian terra stone

Nathan
c/o Art Taylor & Assoc.
200 Fifth Ave.
Suite 404
New York, NY 10010
(212) 243-8728
Character puzzle

National Historic Mint
1200 Shames Dr.
Westbury, NY 11565
(516) 997-8881
Commemorative medallion, belt buckle

Natural Choice Industries
31220 La Bakya Dr.
Suite 110
Westlake Village, CA 91362
(818) 706-0219
Hair care products, body care products

New Lugene's Inc.
P.O. Box 310
West Highway 76
Branson, MS 65616
(800) 641-4514

*Shot glasses, beer mugs, old-
fashioned glasses*

Nexus
570 S. Miami St.
Wabash, IN 46992
(219) 563-8302

Tee shirts, sweatshirts

Nostalgia Collectibles
2840 Maria Ave.
Northbrook, IL 60062
(312) 480-1100

*Electronic "talkie," commem-
orative plates, 3 smaller
versions, of collector plate,
mugs*

Nugeron
16 rue Cave
92300 Levallois
Perret, France

*Postcards, novelty boxes,
miniposters*

Omni Group Cruises
6513 Hollywood Blvd. #205
Hollywood, CA 90028
(213) 467-9292

Cruise ship package

On-The-Road
18653 Ventura Blvd.
Suite 534
Tarzana, CA 91356
(818) 981-7623

Replica street sign

Orbis
Greater London House
3rd Floor
Hampstead Rd.
London NW1 7QX
England
01) 377-4600

Musical pop-up book

Orion Press
5 1-Chome
Kanda Jimbocho, Chiyoda-ku
Tokyo, Japan
03) 295-1400

Cardboard prints

Paul Miller Commemoratives
710 Cumberland Point Dr.
Suite 21
Marietta, GA 30067
(404) 952-0334

Prints

Pearl Enterprises
3790 Knight Rd.
Memphis, TN 38118
(901) 365-4000

*Two versions of 50th anniver-
sary grandfather clocks
(retail & mail order)*

D & G Philatelic Inc.
Box 237
West Hempstead, NY 11552
(516) 486-6511

Commemorative stamp

PM & Company
206 South D. St.
San Bernardino, CA 92410
(714) 381-1614

Art enamel pins

Portal Publications
21 Tamal Vista Blvd.
Corte Madera, CA 94925
(415) 924-5652

Notecards, posters

Rains, Bill Productions
322 Glenhaven Pl.
Billings, MT 59107
(406) 248-2556

*Bronze statue, porcelain statue,
posters, postcards*

Ramallah Wholesale
340 Valley Dr.
Brisbane, CA 94005
(415) 468-0900

*Towels, shower curtain, bed
spread, panel, and pillow*

Rauch Industries, Inc.
P.O. Box 609
Gatonia, NC 28053
(704) 867-5333

Christmas ornament

R.B.S.
c/o R.K. Metals
1510 Jersey Ave.
N. Brunswick, NJ
(201) 247-7614

*Sublimatic framed prints, satin
jackets*

Reed Productions
1102 Church
San Francisco, CA 94114
(415) 282-8752

*Spiral pads, postcards, pocket
covers*

Reflex Marketing
33A Church Rd.
Watford
Herts WD1 3PY
England
(09) 235-2989

Laminated prints

Richards & Southern
503 N. Main St.
Goodlettsville, TN 37072
(615) 859-4121

*Postcards, baseball cap,
bumper sticker, pens &
pencils, photo book,
placemat, datebook*

Ricordi
Via Cortina d'Ampezzo
10 20139 Milano
Italy

Postcards, notecards, posters

Royal Orleans
4500 Tchoupitoulas
New Orleans, LA 70015-1598
(800) 228-3739

*Porcelain plate, porcelain
figurines, limited edition
lithograph, Christmas
ornaments*

Scandecor Int.
Box 656 S-751 27 Uppala
Sweden

Posters

Starr Associates
444 Madison Ave.
New York, NY 10022
(212) 421-5800

Doll

TAC Industries
295 Fifth Ave.
Suite 504
New York, NY 10016
(212) 689-2314

Blankets

Tomy Corporation
P.O. Box 6572
Carson, CA 90749
(213) 549-2721

Figural mugs

Unique Plastics Co.
1325 S.E. 9th Ave.
Portland, OR 97214
(503) 231-9697

*Decoupage plaques,
decoupage clocks*

USA Corporation
Doug Pittman
4888 Matterhorn Dr.
Old Hickory, TN 37138
(615) 758-2103

Plastic jet

Venson & Company
1115 Thompson Ave. #3
Santa Cruz, CA 95062
(408) 462-3478

*Decoupage plaques,
decoupage clocks*

Verkerke
CH-6403 Kussnacht
am Rigi, Switzerland
Tel: (41) 041-81 5252
Telex: (045) 868805

Posters, pennant posters

Walker-McNeil
409 Jones Hollow Rd.
Marlborough, CT 06447
(203) 295-0848

Music box

Warren, F. J.
63 Walsworth Rd.
Hertsforshire SG4 9SX
England
Telex: 825865 (DUFEX G)

Art print, postcards

Wendell, John
1020 Ridgecrest Dr.
Clarksville, TN 37040
(615) 647-4311

Gold record

Welsh Forest Products
P.O. Box 17785
Memphis, TN 38187-0785
(901) 372-7070

Wood paneling

Yorkshire Company
650 Roosevelt Rd.
P.O. Box 2932
Glen Ellyn, IL 60138
(312) 790-0300

Plush hound dog

Zippo Manufacturing Co.
33 Bradford Place
Bradford, PA 16701
(814) 362-4541

Commemorative lighter